D0932596

Digital Privacy and Security Using Windows

A Practical Guide

Nihad A. Hassan
Rami Hijazi

Apress®

AURORA PUBLIC LIBRARY

Digital Privacy and Security Using Windows: A Practical Guide

Nihad A. Hassan
New York

Rami Hijazi
Toronto, Canada

ISBN-13 (pbk): 978-1-4842-2798-5
DOI 10.1007/978-1-4842-2799-2

ISBN-13 (electronic): 978-1-4842-2799-2

Library of Congress Control Number: 2017947159

Copyright © 2017 by Nihad A. Hassan and Rami Hijazi

This work is subject to copyright. All rights are reserved by the Publisher, whether the whole or part of the material is concerned, specifically the rights of translation, reprinting, reuse of illustrations, recitation, broadcasting, reproduction on microfilms or in any other physical way, and transmission or information storage and retrieval, electronic adaptation, computer software, or by similar or dissimilar methodology now known or hereafter developed.

Trademarked names, logos, and images may appear in this book. Rather than use a trademark symbol with every occurrence of a trademarked name, logo, or image we use the names, logos, and images only in an editorial fashion and to the benefit of the trademark owner, with no intention of infringement of the trademark.

The use in this publication of trade names, trademarks, service marks, and similar terms, even if they are not identified as such, is not to be taken as an expression of opinion as to whether or not they are subject to proprietary rights.

While the advice and information in this book are believed to be true and accurate at the date of publication, neither the authors nor the editors nor the publisher can accept any legal responsibility for any errors or omissions that may be made. The publisher makes no warranty, express or implied, with respect to the material contained herein.

Cover image by Freepik (`www.freepik.com`)

Managing Director: Welmoed Spahr
Editorial Director: Todd Green
Acquisitions Editor: Susan McDermott
Development Editor: Laura Berendson
Technical Reviewer: John Walker
Coordinating Editor: Rita Fernando
Copy Editor: Kim Wimpsett

Distributed to the book trade worldwide by Springer Science+Business Media New York, 233 Spring Street, 6th Floor, New York, NY 10013. Phone 1-800-SPRINGER, fax (201) 348-4505, e-mail `orders-ny@springer-sbm.com`, or visit `www.springeronline.com`. Apress Media, LLC is a California LLC and the sole member (owner) is Springer Science + Business Media Finance Inc (SSBM Finance Inc). SSBM Finance Inc is a **Delaware** corporation.

For information on translations, please e-mail `rights@apress.com`, or visit `www.apress.com/rights-permissions`.

Apress titles may be purchased in bulk for academic, corporate, or promotional use. eBook versions and licenses are also available for most titles. For more information, reference our Print and eBook Bulk Sales web page at `www.apress.com/bulk-sales`.

Any source code or other supplementary material referenced by the author in this book is available to readers on GitHub via the book's product page, located at `www.apress.com/9781484227985`. For more detailed information, please visit `www.apress.com/source-code`.

Printed on acid-free paper

To my mom, Samiha, thank you for everything. Without you, I'm nothing.

—Nihad A. Hassan

Contents at a Glance

Contents

About the Authors

Nihad A. Hassan is an independent information security consultant, digital forensics and cybersecurity expert, online blogger, and book author. He has been actively conducting research on different areas of information security for more than a decade and has developed numerous cybersecurity education courses and technical guides.

Nihad focuses on computer forensics and anti-forensics techniques on the Windows OS. He has completed numerous technical security consulting engagements involving security architectures, penetration testing, computer crime investigation, and anti-forensics techniques. Recently, he has shifted his focus toward digital privacy and security.

Nihad has authored two books and scores of information security articles in various global publications. He also enjoys being involved in security training, education, and motivation. His current work focuses on digital forensics, anti-forensics techniques, digital privacy, and web security assessment. He covers different information security topics and related matters on his blog at www.DarknessGate.com. Nihad has a BSc honors degree in computer science from the University of Greenwich in the United Kingdom.

Nihad can be reached through his web site, www.ThunderWeaver.com, and you can connect to him via LinkedIn at https://www.linkedin.com/in/darknessgate/.

Rami Hijazi is the general manager of MERICLER Inc., an education and corporate training firm in Toronto, Canada. He is an experienced IT professional who lectures on a wide array of topics, including object-oriented programming, Java, e-commerce, agile development, database design, and data handling analysis. Rami also works as a consultant to Cyber Boundaries Inc., where he is involved in the design of encryption systems and wireless networks, intrusion detection and data breach tracking, and planning and development advice for IT departments concerning contingency planning.

About the Technical Reviewer

John Walker, CFIP, FRSA, served 22 years in the Royal Air Force in security, investigations, and counterintelligence operations (both overt and covert), working with Government Communications Headquarters (GCHQ), Communications-Electronics Security Group (CESG), and other British intelligence agencies, as well as U.S. agencies. He is a visiting professor at the School of Science and Technology at Nottingham Trent University and has been a visiting professor/lecturer at the University of Slavonia, a visiting lecturer at Warwick University, and a visiting lecturer of digital forensics at the National Defence University of Malaysia. John is a registered expert witness, certified forensics investigator practitioner, editorial member at MedCrave Research for forensics and criminology, ENISA CEI expert, editorial member of the Cyber Security Research Institute, digital forensics/cybersecurity trainer at Meirc in Dubai, and fellow of the Royal Society of Arts.

Acknowledgments

I start by thanking God for giving me the gift to write and convert my ideas into something useful. Without God's blessing, I would not be able to achieve anything.

I want to thank Rami Hijazi for always being there; his precious feedback has always enlightened my road. Even after years of working together, I am constantly surprised by his amazing intelligence, innate humility, and genuine friendship.

I'd also like to thank John Walker, the book's technical editor. It was a great honor to work with such an experienced cybersecurity mind. John is an encyclopedia of cybersecurity; he put decades of pure cybersecurity experience in our hands while authoring this book. I consider him the best man in the field. His valuable feedback, fast response, and dedicated work helped us to shape this book. Thank you, John, you are simply the best.

Now, I want to thank the ladies at Apress: Susan, Rita, and Laura. I was pleased to work with you and very much appreciate your valuable feedback and suggestions. I hope I have the chance to work with you again.

Specifically, to book acquisitions editor Susan McDermott, thank you for believing in my book's idea and for your honest encouragement before and during the writing process. I hope I have the chance to work with you again. To book project editor Rita Fernando, you've been very supportive during the writing process. You made authoring this book a joyful journey. To book development editor Laura Berendson, thank you very much for your diligent and professional work in producing this book.

I also want to thank all the Apress staff who worked behind the scenes to make this book possible and ready for launch. I hope you will continue your excellent work in creating highly valued computing books. Your work is greatly appreciated.

Finally, I want to thank Jodi L. Colburn for her help at the start of my career as an information security professional. I will always remember your encouragement and faithful advice.

—Nihad A. Hassan

Introduction

Digital Privacy and Security Using Windows is about the skills you need to survive in today's digital age. This book presents you with a wide array of methods and techniques to fight digital crime, protect your privacy, and prevent others from tracking you when you are online.

The Internet is full of risks! Cybersecurity threats and incidents have increased lately, leading to significant economic and social consequences for business organizations and individuals. We know that global mass surveillance is now a reality after the continued revelations of secret documents via WikiLeaks. We live in the golden age of government and corporate surveillance, where everyone spies on everyone else. As our society moves to become more digitally dependent and devices get increasingly connected, we are being exposed to greater cybersecurity threats, which are expected to intensify in the future.

Digital Privacy and Security Using Windows is an important tool in the arsenal of any computer user who values privacy. This book provides useful information for people who know a little about cybersecurity risks but want to know more; it teaches them in a practical way how to secure their communications and data in the virtual world through a plethora of security tools and protective measures. Professional users will also find this book useful because it will draw their attention to current and future cyber-threats and how to mitigate them properly.

This unique book will teach you in a practical step-by-step manner how to become digitally invisible. You will learn how to secure your online communications and become anonymous online. You will learn how to secure your online identity, encrypt your digital data at rest and in transit, secure personal devices, secure your online presence, secure cloud data and the Internet of Things (IoT), mitigate social engineering attacks, keep your purchases secret, and conceal your digital footprint. You also will learn best practices to harden your operating system and delete digital traces using the most widely used operating system, Windows.

In the ever-changing online world, acquiring cybersecurity knowledge is a must for any computer user, and this book will teach you everything you need to know to feel confident when going online.

Target Audience

The following people will benefit from this book:

- End users

- Journalists and human rights activists

- Management staff in different industries

- Information security professionals

- Information security students

- Any user seeking privacy

Summary of Contents

Here is a brief description of each chapter's contents:

- *Chapter 1, "Introduction to the Current Status of Online Privacy"*: This chapter discusses the status of online privacy in today's world; it talks about different parties that are interested in having your personal data and the motivation behind that. It also differentiates between the two types of private information available online and how each one can be exploited to track users' online activities. This chapter also explains how web tracking technologies work to connect users' web browsing behavior to their real identity and finally concludes with talking about the different regulations that exist worldwide for dealing with digital privacy and handling users' personal data across national borders.

- *Chapter 2, "Essential Privacy Tips"*: This chapter gives you important advice to assure your privacy when going online. It begins by talking about cybersecurity risks and then moves on to give suggestions to mitigate those risks. Protecting kids' privacy and handling data in the cloud are also covered within this chapter.

- *Chapter 3, "Windows Security"*: In this chapter, we present ways to harden the Windows OS so it becomes more privacy friendly. Data destruction techniques and Windows 10 privacy settings are also covered in detail.

- *Chapter 4, "Online Anonymity"*: This chapter teaches you everything you need to know to become invisible online, including web browsing using TOR, using virtual private networks and proxies, configuring web browsers to cover your digital footprint, and using anonymous payments via bitcoins. This chapter is your ultimate guide for disappearing online.

- *Chapter 5, "Cryptography and Secure Communication"*: This chapter teaches you how to protect your private data using cryptography, which includes two major subcategories: encryption and steganography. In the encryption section, we discuss how to obscure your data at rest and in transit by scrambling it; in the second section, we briefly cover steganography and give examples on how to use some of its techniques to hide your private data in plain sight.

- *Chapter 6, "What's Next?"*: This is the final chapter, where we talk about future trends and advancements in computing technology and how they will affect your privacy.

Comments and Questions

To comment or ask technical questions about this book, send an e-mail to nihad@protonmail.com.

For additional references about the subject, computer security tools, tutorials, and other related matters, check out www.DarknessGate.com.

CHAPTER 1

Introduction to the Current Status of Online Privacy

Who Is Watching You Right Now?

In today's digital era, the use of computerized systems to provide services and store information is prevalent in both the public and private sectors. The public sector uses computers to better serve the public, while private companies use them to improve business agility through better management of available resources. In addition, individuals use computing devices heavily in their daily lives; it is seldom to see a person who is not dependent on some form of computing device to organize his or her digital data or to communicate with others.

Cybersecurity threats and incidents have increased lately, leading to significant economic and social consequences for business organizations and individuals. Nowadays, cybersecurity and digital privacy are high priorities in all developing countries. Our society is being exposed to greater security threats as devices get increasingly connected. Developing skills around Internet privacy and safety is crucial to protect our nation and welfare.

Most computer users—and even some businesses—will not think about computer security until a problem arises. At this point, a breach in security can cause huge and potentially harmful problems to your business and/or your customers. For individuals, the risk of breach can cause serious damage to personal reputations (you may remember the iCloud leaks of celebrity photos in 2014) and even to lives. To survive in today's digital world, it is essential to make sure that the information held in your computers and that travels the Internet is safe and secure. Please note that the information stored in your computing device can be either persistent data or fragments (remnants of data left after processing it). Destroying remnant data is equally important as protecting the primary data storage units; such data may contain confidential data and can be recovered using a variety of techniques without your consent.

Recent events have focused an intense spotlight on online privacy and security. Yahoo announced that more than 1 billion user accounts were hacked in August 2013. The data stolen included the username, e-mail, password, phone number, and date of birth for each hacked account. This is considered the largest cyber-attack ever recorded.[1] Yahoo is not the only one that has faced such a breach; the international press announces such news almost daily.

As we become more dependent on the Internet, the threat of cyber-criminals and other intruders increases rapidly. In contrast, most people still have a limited understanding of the security and privacy implications when using the Internet in their daily lives. To understand Internet risks, you need first to categorize them according from where they first emerged.

© Nihad A. Hassan and Rami Hijazi 2017
N. A. Hassan and R. Hijazi, *Digital Privacy and Security Using Windows*, DOI 10.1007/978-1-4842-2799-2_1

You should work on two levels to increase your computer system's resistance against cyber-attacks.

- The first level is to fight against outside attackers such as cyber-criminals, black hat hackers, identity thieves, mass surveillance programs, and any outside party trying to invade your personal data. This type of attack presents the greatest risk that any computer user or business faces when going online.

- The second level is related to inner attacks. This level is mostly concerned with attacks that come from within a business organization, such as from an employee. Protecting sensitive business data by setting different security access permissions for each user group and updating them continually is the first defense against such risks. Individuals also can become targets of internal attacks. For example, using the same PC at home or work by more than one user can lead to inner privacy violations.

Types of Attacks

Cyber-attacks come in two main forms: passive attacks and active attacks.

Passive Attack

In a *passive attack*, an intruder monitors a system and network communications and scans for open ports and other vulnerabilities (for example, an unpatched system). The intruder will try to collect as much information as he or she can to use it later to attack the system or network; this type of attack is also known as *footprinting* and is used to gather intelligence about the target system to attack it in a later step. An example is when an intruder records network traffic using a packet analyzer tool (such as Wireshark) for later analysis. Installing a keylogger is also a kind of passive attack where an intruder waits for the user to enter his or her username and password and records them for later use.

Active Attack

An *active attack* involves using information gathered during a passive attack to attack a user or network. There are many types of active attacks. In a masquerade attack, an intruder will pretend to be another user to gain access to the restricted area in the system. In a reply attack, the intruder steals a packet from the network and forwards that packet to a service or application as if the intruder were the user who originally sent the packet. Other kinds of active attacks are denial-of-service (DoS) and distributed denial-of-service (DDoS) attacks, which work by preventing authorized users from accessing a specific resource on a network or the Internet (for example, flooding a web server with more traffic than it can handle).

To counter these Internet attacks, individuals and companies deploy a set of defenses to protect their digital assets; however, despite your precautions, it is always possible that your system will get breached. This book will present you with a wide array of techniques and tools that teach you in detail how you can assure your privacy and security are at the highest level. Following the steps in this guide, not only will you learn how to protect your private data, but you will also become computer security literate, meaning you will be able to understand what current and future risks you are facing online and how to counter them. You will also learn how an intruder, whether a person or an entity, can invade your PC and what best practices should be implemented when using the Internet in your daily communications.

The majority of Internet users, especially nonprofessionals, do not consider Internet privacy an issue! For this reason, we will start by talking about who wants your private data when you are surfing online. Later, we will show how outside observers can benefit from the accumulated information by exploiting it to draw a complete picture about all your life's aspects.

We Live in a Dangerous World

Technological developments since the Cold War, during which espionage and the monitoring of civilians were widespread, have increased the intrusiveness and the power of surveillance. The ability to monitor the communications of entire groups and nations on a mass scale is now a technical reality. This poses great concerns about abusing such techniques and violating human rights.

Effectively, anything you do online is monitored and recorded! This sentence may not seem realistic at first, but, unfortunately, this is the truth.

In this section, we will briefly introduce you to the topic of global surveillance. Knowing who is involved in monitoring people's activities online is essential to being careful when using many services, applications, and other digital products.

Historical Background

Global surveillance is defined as conducting a mass surveillance of the entire population across national boundaries. The modern term comes from the 1950s, when the United States and United Kingdom collaborated to exchange the information collected from their spying activities. Later, many countries joined this collective, forming what is known as the Five Eyes.

The Five Eyes began making cooperation agreements with other nations, eventually forming a huge spying network that has the codename Echelon according to many sources from both the European Union and United States.

Echelon is a global network of spy stations and spying satellites that can eavesdrop on telephones, faxes, and all digital communications and satellite transmissions. Echelon has the ability to sniff Internet traffic on a global level. In addition to this, many sources have accused it of planting underwater devices to monitor transcontinental fiber-optic phone cables, giving its operators a greater ability to record all online communication and then filter the data using advanced artificial intelligence technology in voice recognition and keyword matching to extract useful information.

Echelon is not the only global surveillance system; there are many domestic and even continental networks. However, Echelon is the most famous because of resources and global coverage.

Five Eyes' Global Surveillance

The Five Eyes (FVEY) alliance is a secretive, global surveillance arrangement of countries comprised of the United States, United Kingdom, Canada, Australia, and New Zealand, originally gathered to monitor the communications of the socialistic mass. Nowadays, its main focus is on monitoring digital communications across the globe.

After the September 11, 2001, attacks on the United States and the ongoing war on terror since 2001, FVEY further expanded its surveillance capabilities, with much emphasis placed on monitoring the Internet. In an interview, former National Security Agency (NSA) contractor Edward Snowden once described Five Eyes as a "supranational intelligence organization that doesn't answer to the known laws of its own countries." Documents leaked by Snowden in 2013 revealed that FVEY have been spying on one another's citizens and sharing the collected information with each other to circumvent the restrictive domestic regulations on the surveillance of citizens.

FVEY has made partnership agreements with many countries (termed *third-party partners*) to share intelligence information.

- *9 Eyes*: This includes the countries in FVEY plus Denmark, France, the Netherlands, and Norway.

- *14 Eyes*: This includes the countries in 9 Eyes, with the addition of Germany, Belgium, Italy, Spain, and Sweden.

- *41 Eyes*: This includes all of the above, with the addition of the allied coalition in Afghanistan.

The majority of information about mass surveillance programs remains top secret; however, the recent revelation of the Snowden documents cast light on the underground world of mass surveillance programs and their huge impact on each citizen's privacy.

Most Recent Surveillance Laws

Despite the existence of many domestic and international surveillance programs controlled by both superpowers and national intelligence agencies, the government surprises us continually with new bills (mainly issued in western democratic countries) regarding the monitoring of online communications. We cannot understand why democratic nations try to issue such restrictive bills while they already have their own shadow surveillance programs that do not adhere to the law. We think the driving force beyond such bills is that these countries are afraid of disclosing information about their illegal monitoring activities on their own citizens and others, so they work to govern their surveillance activities with laws.

In this section, we will talk about the most recent bills and other actions concerning user privacy.

UK Investigatory Powers Act 2016

This bill will become a law after receiving the royal assent in November 2016. This law will legalize the UK's global surveillance program, which intercepts communications from around the world. It will also introduce new domestic terms to access any citizen's Internet connection records without a warrant or judicial oversight. UK security services will be empowered to hack individuals, Internet infrastructure, and even whole cities—if the government deems it necessary.

As the United Kingdom has legalized the most extreme surveillance in the history of western democracy, we can expect to see similar bills in the future in different countries around the world.

U.S. Government Starts Asking Foreign Travelers to Disclose Their Social Media Accounts

The U.S. Customs and Border Protection has started demanding that foreign travelers hand over social media information upon entering the country. U.S. officials say this policy will help them to counter future terrorist threats by denying entrance to any foreigner who is involved in, or supports in any means, foreign terrorist groups.

This act is still voluntary, and it targets only those travelers who come through the visa-waiver program; nevertheless, it soon may become a law that would be enforced on all travelers.

With the rise of terrorism threat, you can expect that the United States and other countries may enforce this policy on all travelers reaching their borders. This raises serious privacy concerns for people traveling to such countries. The amount of information that can be collected is tremendous and will certainly contain highly sensitive information about each traveler's opinions, beliefs, identity, and community.

Internet of Things Security

Mass surveillance goes beyond communications surveillance. As we move toward "smart" devices and cities, more and more of our activities will be collected and analyzed. Smart cities track individuals and vehicles using cameras and sensors; effectively enables authorities to draw a diagram of the entire population's movements daily. Many cities are expanding the network of free Wi-Fi in public spaces, allowing government to collect a wealth of information from the connected devices including their geolocation.

The term *Internet of Things* (IoT) is used to describe any device that can connect to the Internet and that has the ability to collect and exchange data. The list of devices includes cell phones, coffee makers, washing machines, headphones, lamps, wearable devices such as watches, security systems including alarms, Wi-Fi cameras, baby monitors, smart refrigerators, smart TV sets, smart air-conditioning systems that can adjust the heat remotely, and almost anything else you can imagine and can be connected to the Internet and controlled remotely.

The analyst firm Gartner forecasts that 8.4 billion connected "things" will be in use in 2017, which is up 31 percent from 2016.[2] Gartner also estimates that by 2020 more than half of major new business processes and systems will incorporate some element of the Internet of Things.[3]

In addition to Internetworking devices, the IoT includes human. This makes the relationships in the IoT network become human-to-human, human-to-things, and things-to-things.

Apparently, the IoT offers wide possibilities for improving our future lives, but this comes with a price. The biggest risk is the danger of abusing IoT devices or an intruder hacking IoT devices.

■ **Warning**   Talking toys can spy on your family. The IoT includes vast categories of Internet-enabled devices, and talking toy are among them.

Many toy firms manufacture specific types of toys that can understand and respond to your children in real time about almost anything. A baby can ask this toy about herself, people, places, and other things, and it will respond instantly. This is an impressive invention, but what is the privacy implication of it?

Most of these toys are connected to smartphone apps using Bluetooth or have a Wi-Fi connection that links it to a router directly and hence to the Internet. To understand the things your child is saying, this toy needs to record his or her voice and send the recording to company servers in order to interpret it and respond. Apparently, this toy will record not only your kid's voice but also everything around it; in addition, the server where the recording is sent for interpretation could belong to a third-party company that is responsible for voice recognition. This means your sensitive information could be spreading all over the world without your consent or even knowledge!

On October 21, 2016, a series of distributed denial-of-service (DDoS) attacks caused widespread disruption of legitimate Internet activity in the United States. This type of attack targets the Domain Name System (DNS), which is used to route Internet users to the right address. The attack lasted for several hours and caused major web sites like Twitter and PayPal to stop working.

This attack was mainly caused by exploiting a weakness in a large number of unsecured Internet-connected digital devices, such as home routers and surveillance cameras. The attacker performed a global scan to find unsecured devices (for example, devices with the default password and username); then the attacker targeted these unsecure devices with malware, making the device act as a botnet. Botnets are collections of millions of infected computers (or any IoT device) that are used maliciously for attacks. Any unprotected Internet-enabled device can be used to create a botnet by an intruder.

This massive DDoS attack shows clearly the risks of exploiting unsecured IoT devices to conduct cyber-attacks on an international level.

The attacks on privacy stemming from the IoT can be serious. The following are some examples:

- *Exchanging private data between IoT devices and unsecured servers*: Imagine a case where a health-related IoT device is exchanging your health information with an unsecure server that gets breached by outside attackers.

- *Hacking webcams to spy on people inside their homes*: The next step could be conducting a crime or a robbery.

- *Hijacking IoT devices to plant and spread malware or to conduct a DDoS*: The previous example from 2016 is this type of attack.

- *Taking control of some connected devices to gain access to property for a robbery*: For example, an attack could hack an IoT door to gain physical access or switch alarm devices off remotely.

- *Hacking and stealing vehicles*: For example, an attacker could break in and steal a car that has an IoT-enabled key system.

This list of examples is not exclusive because more are emerging continually, according to the pace of technological development. In the next chapter, we will talk about how you can mitigate the IoT risks on your privacy and security.

■ **Note**   Shodan, a search engine for the IoT, crawls the Internet at random looking for unprotected IoT devices to add to its list. Shodan can be abused to exploit unsecure IoT devices easily; however, the main purpose of creating it was to shed light on the unsecure nature of such devices if left without proper security configuration.

Printers, webcams, power plants, and more, many of them unprotected or minimally protected, have been found over time, and the revelations have changed the way security and privacy on the Internet is perceived. Shodan has already seen TVs, cell phones, traffic lights, industrial controls, infrastructure plants, and various home appliances pop up in the search results, and more of these IoT devices are added each day as the world is becoming more connected.

You can find Shodan at `https://www.shodan.io`.

What Is Digital Privacy?

In a nutshell, *digital privacy* is the protection of personal data when using the Internet.

As a broad term, digital privacy is concerned with any identifying information furnished online when conducting personal or business communications over public networks. Historically, the debate about digital privacy was concentrated on privacy concerns with social networking services, as viewed from within these services. The revelation of the Edward Snowden documents about mass surveillance programs fueled the public debates about the importance of legalizing surveillance activities and raised the public awareness about the importance of protecting their personal data when working online.

For example, when you conduct a search using Google, your search keyword, date/time of search, and your Internet Protocol (IP) address can be tracked back to you. The majority of Internet users do not know that their browsing activities and online habits are logged to formulate a complete profile about their online activities. Such precious information can be later sold to third parties for different purposes.

To better understand the term *digital privacy*, you need to know the types of information that distinguish each person online. Later we will talk about information types and the different parties interested in acquiring it.

Classification of Personal Information

When working online, there are two types of information can be collected from your activities.

- Personally identifiable information (PII) or sensitive personal information (SPI)

- Anonymous information

PII is any information that can be used on its own or with other information to identify or locate a single person. It includes name, Social Security number, passport number, date/time, place of birth, gender, father and mother names, biometric records, or any other detail that uniquely belongs to you and is personally identifiable.

The advance of computing technology and the popularity of social sites make it easy to harvest a large volume of PII about any Internet user. In fact, open source intelligence techniques (OSINT) tools and methods have matured and become widely available for free. A normal computer user can use OSINT tools to gain access to any published data about any connected user. Non-Internet (offline) users can also suffer from problems when their PII gets breached by black hat hackers invading private and public service organizations. Advertisement companies and giant corporations are thirsty to own more PII about their customers to better target them with customizable products and services. Black hat hackers, on the other hand, want to get PII about specific people to steal their identity or to aid them in the planning of future criminal acts.

As a response to these threats, the majority of countries worldwide regulate the gathering of PII about their citizens. Currently, all reputable web sites mention clearly in their "privacy policy" agreement what PII is collected, how it is saved/processed, and the duration it will remain stored. Lawmakers have also enacted legislation to govern the gathering and distribution of PII.

On the other hand, there is a type of information that cannot be related to your personality. For example, your browser type and version, operating system types and version, connected device type, area code, city, country, school or university name, current location, and anything else shared among more than one person cannot be considered personally identifiable. Maybe you think this type of anonymous information is trivial and not worth protecting. We're afraid you are wrong. Such anonymous information when combined with other information can create a unique digital fingerprint of your connected device that can distinguish you among millions of connected users online. This information can be combined with other details related to you, making it personally identifiable information, as you are going to see later.

Things You Want to Keep Private

When working online, you should keep many types of information private to protect your digital privacy and prevent identity theft. Here is a list of information that you may want to keep private:

- *Contact information*: This includes your full name, phone number, e-mail address, and work and home addresses. Some may argue that such information is already available on the majority of business cards, but did you ask yourself the following question: do you hand your contact business card to anyone?

- *Private and family information*: This includes your marital status, your wife's name, your parents' names, your age, children's names, children's age, children's school/university, and anything that is privately related to you and your close family. Unfortunately, the majority of Internet users already have such information published online (for example, on Facebook). This kind of information is dangerous to reveal as it may help outside observers hack into your online accounts, kidnap your children, and even impersonate you (identity theft).

- *Location information*: As computing technology advances, the majority of smartphones (and many IoT devices) have location sensors connected to different satellite services such as GPS or Glonass; others devices can determine location based on the cell tower network. (Giant companies such as Google and Apple already have large databases of cell towers and Wi-Fi access points that can identify and track a user's current location.) When enabled in smartphones and computers, location services can record your current location and all the places you were in, and Google has a facility (named Google Maps) that can draw a complete map of the places you've been and the routes you've traveled. Although this feature is private by default, we cannot guarantee that it really is. Not all users prefer to reveal their location to the public (although many already do in Facebook); however, when using some apps (for example, using an app to find the nearest restaurant or gas station nearest your current location) that need location services to be turned on to work, they can record your physical location and use it later for different purposes without your explicit consent.

- *Healthcare records information*: This includes your physical characteristics such as your height and weight, eye and skin color, past illness history, medicine taken now and in the past, previous surgery, blood group, and anything that is recorded when you visit your doctor or hospital. Such information is important, and it must be stored on computer records somewhere. Imagine if a security breach occurred and this information gets revealed and viewed by your insurance company or employer. What will be the consequences?

- *Criminal records*: If you have a past criminal record, what will be the consequence if it gets revealed to the public?

- *Financial information*: This includes your bank account details, bank transactions, financial partners, how much money you earn, tax statements, and anything else related to your financial condition.

- *Purchase information*: When you make an online purchase, you are using your credit card to pay for it. Both credit card companies and banks will see your previous purchase history. This is something you cannot hide, and it is attached to your identity (you cannot open a bank account without showing them a valid government ID). If a security breach occurs and your purchase history is revealed, do you have any concerns about what you have already bought in the past from being publicly discovered?

- *Web surfing history and communications log*: When you visit a web site, the pages you visit, the amount of time you view each page, the links you click, the searches you make, every video you watch, every file you download, and the things that you interact with will be collected and recorded by this web site to create a "profile" that links to your web browser. This data is stored somewhere on your computer or mobile phone (using cookies or caches) or somewhere on outside servers like the visited web site server or other third-party server. Once you visit a web site, it is nearly impossible to avoid leaving a digital footprint. Nevertheless, during this book you will learn how to minimize and anonymize your digital fingerprint to avoid being tracked online.

- *Communication logs*: Communication logs are also important; they include all your e-mail messages, Facebook and Twitter private messages, and any other activity conducted on a similar social networking web site. Even after you delete your previous messages, you cannot guarantee that they have been completely deleted from all locations. The main principle here is that what goes online never dies. Although this may be an overstatement in some cases, you should avoid posting or sending anything online that may lead to personal or legal problems if discovered someday.

Maybe after reading the list of information types that you should keep private, you are wondering what you can publish online about yourself! Actually, this question is dependent on each user case; some people may not have a problem revealing a lot of information about their private lives. However, the majority of people care about protecting their private data. The many global surveys already done about the digital privacy issue conclude that the majority of Internet users care about their privacy and are willing to have laws that protect their private data and prevent privacy invasion when going online.

Who Needs Your Personal Information?

Exchanging PII data online is not a problem on its own. We all need to send private e-mails to our friends and family. Many of us send personal pictures using e-mails or cloud storage services when they are on a vacation. We may want to send medical information about our health status to our doctor or hospital (some IoT medical devices do this automatically). We are also used to checking our bank transactions online in addition to making online purchases. All these actions will not impose any problem for our personal data. The problem occurs when such information gets revealed publicly without our consent or simply gets hacked or intercepted by outside parties for different purposes.

There are many people and entities that want private information about you. In this section, we will list them and explain what motivates them to perform such actions.

Online Advertising Companies

Almost all free online services contain ads. You cannot read the news, watch YouTube movies, use Facebook, or conduct Google searches without seeing advertisements.

Web sites need advertisements to fund themselves, so when using a free e-mail service, it is ordinary to see ads. Some e-mail providers even send promotional ads with every sent e-mail to generate some profits. The ads constitute the main stream of money that the web site can exploit to stay in business.

A report conducted by PwC Advisory Services (PwC) shows that Internet advertising revenues in the United States totaled $59.6 billion for the full year of 2015, with Q4 2015 accounting for approximately $17.4 billion and Q3 2015 accounting for approximately $14.7 billion. Revenues for the full year of 2015 increased 20.4 percent over 2014.[4]

Online advertising is a broad term used to describe the paid advertising that publishers put on their web sites or apps to enable them to provide you with content and services for free. But what most people see is a specific type of online advertising that is tailored to your likely interests by companies promoting their products or services. This is known as *Interest-based advertising* (IBA).[5]

To distinguish between the two entities, please note that the *advertiser* is the one who pays the money to get advertisements shown, while the *publisher* is the one who gets the money for showing the ads. The publisher could be a web site or application owner or anyone who has a digital channel to put ads on.

Advertisers are interested in profiling and tracking online users to target them with customized ads. We will cover online tracking and behavioral profiling in the next section.

Intelligence Agencies

Security services are interested to know anything about you and your habits, previous purchases, political opinion, location, and even health status. One of the major works of any intelligence agency is to gather as much information about its citizens, but the problem arises when a nonauthorized person or entity views this information or when it gets hacked by an outside party.

We already talked about the recent act imposed by the United States that certain travelers must reveal their social networking accounts. If, for example, you made a joke about something (political, economic, or military news) and post it to your Facebook account, this joke may be interpreted differently (understand it with a different meaning) by the security officer who is investigating your account before granting you access to cross the border. They can effectively deny your visa and maybe offer you a place in jail!

As we mentioned, the revelation of the mass surveillance programs of the NSA and its global allies beginning in 2013 showed clearly that the intelligence services were collecting data on a global scale to monitor their citizens and also other nations' citizens. This was going on for a long time without following a legal framework that governs access to such data, and such activity will continue in the future, maybe even increasing to counter emerging terror threats spreading all over the world.

Big Data

As the world becomes more technology dependent, the volume of digital data produced globally is expected to have explosive growth. Digital information from cell phones, Internet communications, IoT devices, cloud storage, satellite sensors, social networking, and other countless digital sources, which produce both structured and unstructured data, are forming what is known today as *big data*.

Intelligence services around the globe are eager to develop new capabilities to manage and exploit big data. CIA chief technology officer Ira "Gus" Hunt appreciates the importance of big data gathering for his agency by saying, "It's the CIA's job to leverage the world of big data, find out what actually matters, connect the dots, and figure out what our adversaries are intending to do."

Big data can be analyzed for different purposes. For example, advertisers can use such data to profile and target users with customized ads, and security services can use it to extract a wealth of economic, security, and political information about any nation to make future predictions.

Black Hat Hackers

Some intruders may want to target you for fun; others may want to steal your data and money (stealing credit card and bank information). These latter intruders are called *black hat hackers*. There are many methods that can be employed to steal your confidential data. You will learn about them during this book and learn some mitigation strategies beginning in Chapter 2.

Black hat hackers usually target people who know a good number of details about them, which is why you should publish only a small amount of private information about you, your family, and work online to avoid becoming an attractive target.

People Who Know You

Your relatives, work colleagues, ex-wife or ex-husband, and any individual you have problems or a legal dispute with can use your personal information against you in some context.

Other Parties

There are additional groups of people who might become interested to know your private information. For example, your future employer may seek to know information about you before signing a contract with you. If you, for example, have pictures of yourself on your Facebook profile that can give a sense about you that you are an unreliable person, this may reduce your chances of landing a new job.

Insurance companies also have great interest in gaining private information about their clients. If you post your picture to your Facebook account while you are in the hospital, this can give a negative sign to your insurance company about your current health condition and may raise your health insurance rate.

Banks also need private information about their clients. If you need a loan, your bank will need to know as much information about you as it can. If, for example, the bank discovers while searching in your social networking activities things that may make it see you as an unreliable or untrusted person, the bank will refuse to give you the loan.

As you can see, different parties are interested in your private information. Even the smallest detail about your life can be exploited and merged with other trivial details to form a picture about your personality and social behavior.

If everything mentioned up to now did not scare you, continue to the next section.

Invading Personal Privacy Through Online Tracking and Behavioral Profiling

Online behavioral advertising (OBA) describes a set of techniques used by advertisement companies to show customized ads to online users based on their browsing activities and online habits. Social networking sites and other online merchants also engage heavily in collecting data about their users to achieve a higher return from the delivery of advertising tailored to their specific needs.

Although the majority of data collected for OBA is considered nonidentifying information, it can be easily combined with other sources to become PII, making it a real invasion of user privacy. For instance, data collected for OBA can include the following:

- Age

- Gender

- Country and city where you live

- Purchase interest (for example, shoes, tea, fiction books, and so on)

Behavioral marketing can be used on its own or in conjunction with other forms of targeting based on factors such as geography, demographics, or contextual web page content. It's worth noting that many practitioners refer to this process as *audience targeting*.[6]

For example, say you are searching the Internet for a cheap flight ticket to Hawaii. After browsing a few web sites to find the cheapest one, you decide to stop and go read your favorite news web site. There you see advertisements about what you were looking at few moments ago. To make things more interesting, you then go to your account on Facebook and see the same advertisements about cheap airplane tickets to Hawaii!

Advertisers need to generate profits from their advertisements, and this can happen only if they target the correct customer. In the previous example, the advertiser knows you were searching for a ticket to Hawaii (using some techniques mentioned next), so the advertiser instantly targets you with similar ads because you are highly likely to buy a ticket, which will result in a sale and, consequently, generate a profit for the publisher and for the web site owner who displays this ad (the advertiser could be the publisher and the web site owner at the same time).

Targeting customers is not limited only to what they search for or watch online; tracking users across many web sites can help advertisers to formulate a profile about each one, thus suggesting products and services that you may not ever think about but may be interested in once you see it in front of you.

A new study in *Psychological Science*, a publication of the Association for Psychological Science, suggests that advertisements can be more effective when they are tailored to the unique personality profiles of potential consumers.[7]

Online tracking is defined as the process of collecting and processing data acquired from Internet users' devices (computers, tablet, and smartphones). There are two kinds of online tracking: direct tracking and third-party tracking. In *direct tracking*, the tracking is conducted by the web site or application the user is accessing. In *third-party tracking*, there is a third party (other than the web site/application the user is accessing) that tracks user-browsing activities over multiple web sites (the user is the *second party*). A tracking log can be stored either on the user computer (for example, using cookies) or on the third-party server.

This kind of tracking is dangerous to privacy because it can link your browsing and searching activities and tie them to your real identity. We'll show an example to demonstrate this idea.

The majority of web sites have Facebook Like and Share buttons among other social networking symbols (like the Tweet button from Twitter). For example, if you are reading an article on my blog at www.DarknessGate.com and you like it, you can click the Like button, which exists on each article page, and this post title will appear on your Facebook news feed. It will also appear in various places on your friends' and followers' newsfeeds and tickers, as the Facebook algorithm sees fit. Up to now everything is normal. The problem of privacy is that whenever you visit a web site that has the Facebook Like or Share button, Facebook will know that you were visiting this web site even if you did not click this button. At the beginning of October 2015, Facebook began to feed users' web browsing habits collected from these Like and Share buttons into the company's ad targeting systems. By doing this, Facebook not only can target its users with customized ads but also can link their browsing habits and search activities to their real identities on their Facebook accounts.

In June 2016, Facebook announced it will be expanding its tracking activities (to target people with better customized ads) to include non-Facebook users. In the past, Facebook collected information about its registered users' tastes and online behaviors and targeted them with customized ads when using its service or visiting any of its third-party-affiliated web sites. But now it is aiming to track all online users, even non-Facebook users, through its Like and Share buttons and then target them with customized ads according to their online preferences.[8]

Andrew Bosworth, vice president of ads and pages at Facebook, said, "Our buttons and plug-ins send over basic information about users' browsing sessions. For non-Facebook members, previously we didn't use it. Now we'll use it to better understand how to target those people."

Personalization technologies offer powerful tools for enhancing the user experience in a wide variety of systems, such as finding the best product/service and price combination, but at the same time personalization technologies raise new privacy concerns if they get revealed publicly or combined with other information about you to formulate a complete profile about your online habits attached to your real identity. The dangers of online tracking and user profiling will be covered thoroughly next.

The Danger of Online Tracking

In this section, we cover the main dangers and examples of the risks associated with online tracking.

Mass Surveillance

We've already talked about how Facebook collects different information about its users (and also non-Facebook users) to target them with customized ads. Let's focus on the user who already has a Facebook account. Facebook has the ability to maintain a complete log of online activities about each user. This log will be connected to a user profile on Facebook (usually his or her real identity). This is a large amount of personal information stored in one place about each user. Let's now consider the consequences on this privacy; what will happen if the Facebook servers get hacked by an outside party (Russia or China, for example)? What if Facebook hands this information to a security service agency?

We are focusing on Facebook because it is a giant among other social networking web sites, but do not forget the rest of the major social networking web sites that definitely suffer from the same privacy and security issues.

▓ **Note**   Remember that the Yahoo hacking case revealed in 2016 that information from 1 billion user accounts had been hacked.

Service/Price Discrimination

Using profiling and tracking techniques, companies can customize service and price discrimination to each individual. In other words, people can be charged different prices based on a certain demographic factor, including location and/or socioeconomic status.

For example, if you seem like a well-educated professional searching for luxury items using the latest iPhone device, this tells the merchant or the advertiser that you might be willing to pay more than average for some items.

The same applies to many services; if you continually search for medicine or natural products, this may indicate that you suffer from a health problem. Such information may disqualify you, if your future employer or insurance company knows about it.

▓ **Note**   If you suspect that you are a victim of price discrimination/differentiation, try this test: set up a proxy server or virtual private network (VPN) to obfuscate your IP address (an IP address is used to determine your current physical location) and visit the same item page of your preferred merchant. Check the item price before and after obscuring your IP address to see whether the price changes. In the coming chapters, we will teach you how to anonymize everything you do online.

Content Personalization Risks

As we already talked about, user profiling helps a service provider (whether it is a merchant or a free online service) personalize its content to users.

Content personalization can be embraced in many ways. For example, when searching for sexual items, Facebook will show related ads on your Facebook profile, and the same will appear on search engine result pages.

Search engines also track and profile users according to their previous searches. This is not always good because it will return homogeneous results and even discard some. Such results can also be biased in some way.

When you search an online merchant for some products, it will continually display ads that are related to your previous searches or saved profile, thus eliminating many results that may be of interest to you.

The examples of the danger of content personalization are endless, but the greatest danger is related to ordinary individuals who are unaware of personalization's risks; the majority of people do not understand the context within which data collection and algorithms operate.

Slowing Page Load Time

This is not a privacy risk. Instead, it is a technical issue but is worth mentioning. A web site that utilizes social sharing tools like AddThis or ShareThis and other social networking widgets can load slower than the web sites that do not utilize such tools. This because upon loading the page with social networking tools, it will wait for responses from the third-party web sites (like Facebook and Twitter) affiliated with it. This will effectively increase the loading time.

Benefits of Online Tracking

Actually, we do not consider user tracking to be a completely bad practice. For instance, direct tracking conducted by web site owners is beneficial to customize the user experience across sessions (for example, saving user theme customizations and preferences). Besides, many e-commerce web sites need to track users to keep their shopping cart contents while they browse different pages/web sites.

Online tracking is also used to fight against online fraud. It is used to detect online payment fraud by looking at some technical indicators that may raise suspicion.

- When the billing country and the IP country (IP determines physical location) do not match

- When a proxy server is used to change the user's real IP address

- If your connection originates from a high-risk country

Personalizing content is beneficial in many cases, especially for ordinary Internet users, as people with average Internet literacy may not be able to find content easily online, and this selective content is more likely to be of relevance to them.

Online tracking is used extensively in web analytics and measurement techniques. Such techniques are used for analyzing web site data such as number of visitors, their origin country, which pages they visit, and how long they stay on each page. The compilation of this data helps web site owners to better develop relevant and effective ad campaigns in addition to identifying key performance to achieve the highest return possible.

Web site owners (first-party trackers) can develop their own analytical techniques. However, the majority prefers to use third-party services like Google Analytics, Alexa, and Bing Webmaster Tools, to name a few. Web analytics track users online using different techniques (described next) and store their browsing activity across many web sites. This information helps them to create aggregated statistics to measure the effectiveness of their advertisements and to optimize web site contents accordingly.

Finally, web tracking is also beneficial to stop certain kinds of attacks against web sites, for example, to stop a particular machine (or machines) from launching continual brute-force attacks or to recognize attackers when they return.

How Online Tracking Works Technically

In this section, we will delve into the technical side of online tracking and behavioral profiling to describe how outside observers can track your online activities and what techniques they deploy to profile and predict your future activities.

The Concept of an IP Address and Its Role in Tracking Users Online

You cannot consider an IP address as PII, but if combined with other information or used to build a profile about a specific person, it will become PII regardless of whether the individual's name is known. It is essential to understand the concept of an IP address and how devices are connected to the Internet because the majority of anonymizing techniques work by obscuring your real IP address to avoid tracking. Besides, you cannot protect your digital privacy without knowing how Internet devices are connected in today's digital world. For this reason and more, we will dedicate this section to describing the IP addressing scheme and how different laws perceive it in relation to user privacy.

What Is an IP Address?

An Internet Protocol address is a unique address that computing devices such as PCs, tablets, smartphones, or anything that can connect to the Internet use to identify themselves and communicate with other devices in the IP network. No two devices can have the same IP address on the same IP network. You can describe the IP address as like your telephone number (including its international code) in that it is used to uniquely identify you globally.

There are two standards of IP addressing already in use. The IPv4 standard, which is the most used one, is already supported everywhere on the Internet and can accommodate a maximum of 4.3 billion addresses. Apparently, this number of addresses is not enough in today's digital world, especially after the explosive growth of IoT devices. This resulted in another standard being developed named IPv6, which can accommodate more than 7.9×1028 times as many as IPv4.

IPv4 addresses consist of 4 bytes (32 bits), while IPv6 addresses are 16 bytes (128 bits) long. Up to now, the majority of online services are still using IPv4, and the adoption of IPv6 is still moving slowly.

When connecting to the Internet, you either use the same IP address each time (*static IP*) or use a different number each time (known as *dynamic IP*).

A static IP address is an address assigned by your Internet service provider (ISP) and does not change over time; you can consider it like your phone number, which remains fixed (until the provider withdraws it from you). Static addresses are usually used by businesses, public organizations, and IT companies that offer IT services to individuals and the private sector. For example, a server hosting web sites or providing e-mail services needs a static IP address. To use a static IP address, you need to manually configure your router or server to use it.[9]

By contrast, a dynamic IP address is assigned dynamically by your ISP whenever you connect to the Internet. It uses a protocol called Dynamic Host Configuration Protocol (DHCP) to assign you a new IP address every time your computing device or router gets rebooted. Some ISPs may allocate the same IP number previously assigned to you many times, but this is not a rule of thumb.

To determine whether you are assigned a dynamic or static IP address, disconnect your Internet connection from your computing device (you can also reboot your router), reconnect, and then check your IP address again. Another method is to use the command-line prompt in Windows, as shown in Figure 1-1. Find the line containing DHCP Enabled under your current network connection; if DHCP Enabled is set to Yes, then you most likely have a dynamic internal IP address.

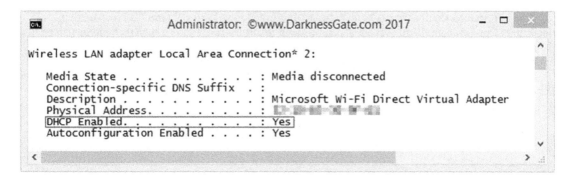

Figure 1-1. *Determine whether your PC is using a dynamic or static IP address. In this case, we're using a dynamic IP address.*

You can also check what your IP address is by going to `https://www.dnsleaktest.com`.

IP addresses come in two types: public and private IP addresses. A public IP address is the one that allows direct access over the Internet. For example, an e-mail server needs to have a public IP address to access it directly. The public IP address is unique globally.

A private IP address is a non-Internet-facing IP address on an internal network and is used to assign a private number to your computing devices in your home or office network to avoid exposing them directly online. For example, you can have one public IP address assigned to your router on your office network, and each of the computers, tablets, and smartphones connected to your router (via wired or Wi-Fi) get a private IP address from your router via DHCP.

▓ **Note**   DHCP is a network protocol used on IP networks. It works by dynamically allocating IP addresses to a set of connected hosts based on a preconfigured pool of addresses.

How an IP Address Is Used to Track You Online?

Whenever you visit a web site, your current connection's IP address will be available to it. Most web sites record all IP addresses visited by default; they also record the date/time of each visit in addition to other information, such as what pages you have been visiting and the time spent on each one.

Your ISP will also record your web browsing activities and will save them in a log attached to your real identity (the majority of ISPs need a valid government ID to give you Internet access). Even if you are using a dynamic IP address or connecting from behind a Network Address Translation (NAT) device, your browsing activities can still be tracked back to you because your ISP knows what IP was allocated to each user and when. Users connected from within local area networks (LANs) and sitting behind a router that offers NAT service can also be tracked back (but this is technically more difficult) because the router tracks basic data about each active connection (particularly the destination address and port). When a reply returns to the router, it uses the connection tracking data it stored during the outbound phase to determine the private address on the internal network to which to forward the reply.

By knowing your IP address, outside trackers can determine your ISP and current location including your country and city. Bear in mind that the location information based on the IP address alone is not always correct. An ISP can own a pool of addresses allocated to different countries around the world; it may assign your computer an IP address that is registered in the United States while your physical location could be in the United Kingdom.[10]

There are different laws globally regarding how to handle users' IP addresses. Currently, there is no clear law that overtly states that an IP address is considered PII. It seems not all countries handle this issue the same; many of them judge it on a case-by-case basis.

The Information Commissioner's Office (ICO), the United Kingdom's data protection watchdog, declared to Out-Law.com, "If an individual can be identified from an IP address, then it would be personal data, but that would not always be the case and 'needs to be judged on a case-by-case basis.' As part of the analysis, organizations need to assess how specific an IP address is to the device or user."[11]

The following is according to the advisory guidelines (revised in December 2016) issued by the Personal Data Protection Commission in Singapore about the issue of whether an IP address is PII:

"An IP address, or any other network identifier such as an IMEI number (used to identify phones), may not be personal data when viewed in isolation, because it simply identifies a networked device."[12]

The United Kingdom and Singapore seem to use the same approach to handle the dilemma of whether an IP address is considered PII; however, after the recent judgment issued by the European Court of Justice (ECJ) on October 19, 2016, that rules IP addresses are PII,[13] this will create problems for a lot of companies that record users' IP addresses for different reasons, as they must treat this information according to privacy rules that govern PII data.

In the future, you can expect EU countries and maybe soon the United States to follow the ECJ rule when considering IP addresses as PII.

Online Tracking Techniques

The IP address is not the only thing used to track your online activities. Actually, most online tracking and behavioral profiling methods work by using other techniques. In this section, we give examples of these techniques.

Cookies

Cookies are small text files usually stored in the client computer's browser. They often come encrypted (only the web site that creates the cookie can read it) and contain information that distinguishes the client computer. The main components of a cookie are the cookie web site name and user ID in addition to the cookie expire date. Cookies are downloaded when you visit a web site for the first time. When you visit the same web site again, your browser will send the cookie information to the web site. This allows web site owners to offer a customized experience, among other things, to their visitors.

In addition to tracking user movements across the web site that planted it (some types of cookies can track you across many domains), cookies are widely used to remember user login credentials, save the user theme (page layout) preferences, maintain your shopping cart while browsing the web site for items, and enable advertising technology.

There are two main types of cookies: session cookies and persistent cookies. A *session cookie* (also called a *transient cookie*) is stored in a temporary location in the client web browser and erased when the user closes the web browser or logs out. This type of cookies does not record information about the user's activities or computer and does not have an expiration date. A famous example of session cookies is shopping cart functionality for e-commerce web sites that allows users to add items to their shopping carts while browsing different item pages.

Persistent cookies (like Flash and evercookie cookies) raise serious privacy concerns. Half of a cookie's contents are first-party and belong to the site you are visiting, and half are third-party and belong to partners, services, or advertisers working with the site. Third-party cookies are used to track activity (across multiple web sites) and recognize frequent and returning visitors, to optimize advertising, or to improve the user experience by tailoring the content or offers based on that cookie's history.

HTTP Cookies

HTTP cookies are what the majority of people mean when talking about web cookies. An HTTP cookie is a simple text file used for tracking user visits to the web site that deployed it. HTTP cookies without an expiration date are automatically deleted when the browser is closed. However, expiration dates can be many years into the future.

Flash Cookies

A *Flash cookie* (also known as a *local share object* [LSO]) is a collection of cookie-like data that a web site running Adobe Flash can place on your hard drive. Like regular cookies, Flash cookies contain information about when you visited the site and may contain tracking and settings information. Flash cookies are stealthier than regular cookies. Flash can install cookies on your computer without your permission by default.[14]

Flash cookies are more persistent than HTTP cookies. While HTTP cookies are stored inside browser files and have a size limit of 4 kilobytes. Flash cookies have their own folder on the disk drive, which is not deleted when you use the standard "remove cookies" browser function. Flash cookies have a default size of 100 kilobytes, allowing them to store more tracking information and other settings. Flash cookies are managed through Adobe Flash Player settings, which can be accessed via Control Panel ➤ Flash Player (applicable to all Windows versions).

Some types of Flash cookies have the ability to re-create HTTP cookies after the user deletes them. Flash cookies also have the ability to access multiple browsers on the same computer, allowing them to monitor all online activities on a computer.[15]

FlashCookiesView (`www.nirsoft.net/utils/flash_cookies_view.html`) is a small utility created by NirSoft that allows you to display a list of Flash cookies that exist on your system and delete them.

Evercookies

According to its developer Samy Kamkar, an *evercookie* is a JavaScript-based cookie that can survive even after the user deletes HTTP and Flash cookies from his or her machine. It accomplishes its persistence by storing its data in several locations on a client browser/machine (for example, in an HTTP cookie, Flash cookie, HTML5 local storage, web history, Silverlight). If one of these locations is deleted, for example, by the user, the evercookie will detect this and regenerate itself.[16] Thankfully, the browsers and anti-malware software that exist today are now able to block or detect evercookies.

■ **Note**   Flash and evercookies are also known as *supercookies*.

ETags

ETags are another way of tracking users without using cookies (both HTTP and Flash), JavaScript, HTML storage, or IP addresses. This technique has been used by many web sites, but few people know about it. The *ETag*, or entity tag, is part of a Hypertext Transfer Protocol (HTTP) mechanism that provides web cache validation and is intended to control how long a particular file is cached on the client side.

ETags help a web browser to avoid loading the same web resources twice, such as when a user visits a web site that plays music in the background that changes according to a user's local time. On the first visit, the web server will send an ETag along with the audio file to the client browser, which will download the audio file and cache it. When the user visits the same web site again, the web server will inform the client browser that the audio file has not changed. As a result, the browser will use the local copy in cache, saving bandwidth and speeding load time. If the ETag is different, then the client browser downloads the new version of the audio file.

ETags can be exploited to track users in a similar way to persistent cookies, and a tracking server can continually send ETags to a client browser, even though the contents do not change on the server. By doing this, a tracking server can maintain a session with the client machine that persists indefinitely. To get rid of ETags, you must clear the browser cache content.

Digital Fingerprinting

A browser *fingerprint* is the set of technical information about a user's system and browser that can distinguish his or her machine online. This information includes the following: browser type, operating system (OS) version, add-on installed, user agent, fonts installed, language settings, time zone, screen size, and color depth, among other things.

Fingerprinting allows trackers to distinguish a user's machine even though cookies and JavaScript are disabled. A fingerprinting-specific browser is stateless and transparent to the user and machine.

The information collected from a digital fingerprint may seem generic and not enough to identify an individual machine online among millions of connected devices; however, if this information is combined, you can draw a comprehensive unique picture about each user machine, and later, this information can be linked to a real identity if combined with other PII data. This should effectively allow different outside parties to easily profile people without using traditional tracking techniques such as computer IP addresses and cookies.

The Electronic Frontier Foundation (EFF) published an excellent study in May 2010, detailing some of the various methods of fingerprinting a browser. See www.eff.org/deeplinks/2010/05/every-browser-unique-results-fom-panopticlick. The result concludes that the majority of Internet users can be profiled and tracked online using only minor technical information from their browsers. Although the study was conducted in 2010, its results are still valid now because of the transparent way fingerprinting occurs in digital devices.

There are two main types of device fingerprinting: script-based techniques and canvas.

Script-Based Fingerprinting

The majority of online trackers, especially the old-school ones, use this script-based technique in fingerprinting users' browsers. It works by loading a script (generally JavaScript) into the user's browser. Once the script is loaded successfully, it will execute to extract a wide array of technical information about the current browser and system configuration. The information extracted includes user agent, add-on installed, fonts installed, screen resolution, time zone, operating system type and version, CPU type, and many other details about the targeted system. A hash is then made based on the information the script has collected. That hash can help identify and track your computer like an IP address would.

You can use Flash, Silverlight, or a Java applet to perform the fingerprinting instead of JavaScript; they will all return the same result. The main defense against this technique is to disable JavaScript in your browser. However, this approach is not practical and may result in breaking a large number of web sites (the majority of web design frameworks are based on JavaScript to deliver functionality). Disabling Java will not cause problems like disabling JavaScript. In Chapter 4 we'll cover how you can fight against all types of browser fingerprinting.

Canvas Fingerprinting

Canvas is an HTML5 element originally developed by Apple; it is used to draw graphics (lines, shapes, text, images) and animation (e.g., games and banner ads) on web pages using a JavaScript API. Apart from web development, canvas features can be exploited by advertisers to fingerprint browsers and profile people accordingly.

Canvas fingerprinting is a new method for tracking users' online activities. It simply works by drawing an invisible image on the user's client browser. This image will be different for each user, and once drawn on the client browser, it will collect different technical information about the user's browser and machine. A hash is then made based on the information the canvas has collected. This hash will be consistent across all the web sites the user visits (the hash is generated from the canvas data); this will effectively record a user's browsing history.[17]

Although the collected information from canvas fingerprinting cannot be used alone to identify users, this fingerprint can be combined with other sources to identify you completely.

Browser fingerprinting is a powerful tool for tracking users along with IP addresses, cookies, and supercookies. This type of tracking (also known as *stateless tracking*) raises serious privacy concerns since it is hard to detect. In Chapter 4, we will show you mitigation strategies against all types of tracking techniques.

HTML5

HTML5 is the latest version of the Hypertext Markup Language (HTML) specification. HTML is used to define how browsers present web sites on their devices. HTML5 comes with new components that can threaten user privacy.

The HTML5 support for media, especially its ability to grant access to device microphones and webcams, can be exploited by outside intruders to invade your personal privacy. The HTML5 Geolocation API realizes location-based services via the Web by granting web sites the geographical location information of user devices. HTML5 expands the number of methods given to a web application to store information locally on the user machine and increases the size of data stored using a new feature called Web Storage as an alternative to cookies.

Search Engines

Search engines have the ability to track users' searches and tie it to their dedicated online profile. Information acquired by search engines can reveal a great number of details about its users and can easily become PII after combining it with other sources. For example, when a user uses Google to search for something while logged on to a Gmail account, the user's activity can be easily recorded and linked to the user's real identity. Nevertheless, even if the user is not logged into a Gmail account, Google can still link search terms used to a user's real account by using the IP address or any of the tracking techniques already mentioned. Please note Google offers a way to delete your previous search history and stop saving the new one in your account. Configuring Google for better privacy will be covered in Chapter 4.

For instance, keep in mind that normal search engines (which are not privacy oriented) can know a great number of details about your personality and habits from your searched terms, in addition to their ability to track your location. In Chapter 4, we will show you how to use different anonymous search engines.

Social Networking Web Site Tracking

We already covered how Facebook uses its Like button to track users online. Twitter does the same things with the Tweet button and so does Google+. You don't even have to be logged into your social network account for the tracking to occur.

BuiltWith found that 2,360,275 web sites are currently use the Facebook Like button.[18] In the same period, there are 1,372,583 live web sites using Twitter's Tweet button.[19]

Social networking web sites are considered a great source of information for both security services and advertisement companies. Their ability to track a user's actions across multiple web sites in addition to monitoring their habits, online friends, private messages, location, and all searches they conduct online imposes a great danger on a user's privacy.

Mobile Device Tracking

The majority of smartphones come equipped with different sensors such as a camera, microphone, and GPS. With the advance of technology, the computing power of smartphones has increased rapidly. Today, it is usual to find a smartphone with computing power that exceeds some laptops or tablet devices. This makes the smartphone act as a mini computer for a large number of users, where they store their personal e-mail, friends list, social networking accounts, phone log, personal pictures and video, and all sorts of personal data that comes in digital format, in addition to mobile device–specific information such as the IMEI number (which is used to distinguish the phone globally).

Location-based services (LBSs) are popular personalized services that are tightly associated with user privacy. Examples of LBSs include navigation services, local search services, traffic alert services, and localized weather services, in addition to many more that are especially useful for mobile device users.

In today's digital age, individuals are fond of their mobile devices because of their ability to simplify and socialize their daily lives. Individuals can share real-time and historical location information online to facilitate a social interaction or event, play games with other people around the globe, and purchase items online. Among other benefits, these mobile services also can quickly enable consumers to locate nearby stores and restaurants, find the nearest cash machine or gas station, share their current location by "checking in" at venues, and navigate to a desired location.

Imagine the amount of information that can be collected from your mobile device interactions, especially after combining the data with your real identity, which can easily be done on smartphones by their network operators.

It is important to understand what your mobile app or service is sharing about you before using its service; you must read its privacy policy agreement or other related disclosures that clearly state how location data and other information is collected and whether it is going to be handed to third-party affiliates.

Mining Big Data

Big data is defined as the gathering of a vast volume of data that is being exchanged over a digital communications medium like the Internet and GPS. The amount of big data is huge and cannot be handled by normal computers. Thus, it is stored on giant server-system databases. The data is then analyzed by scientists using specialized data-mining software that interprets and categorizes this data (e.g., according to user demographic and trends).

Giant companies like Google and Facebook are collecting such data to feed their ad network systems with customized user profiles in addition to predicting future trends. Intelligence agencies are also interested in big data to understand future world development directions and counter any risk toward national security before it happens. The NSA surveillance program named Skynet has been using big data–mining techniques to extract information about possible terror suspects. Skynet24 applies complex combinations of geospatial, geotemporal, pattern of life, and travel analytics to identify patterns of suspect activity.[20]

E-mail Tracking

E-mail tracking is a technique for monitoring the delivery of e-mail to the intended recipients. Most tracking technologies utilize certain features such as web beacons or digital time-stamped records to reveal the exact time and date that an e-mail was received or opened, in addition to the open rates, the volume of clicks on links in e-mails, and the number of downloads of e-mail attachments, as well the IP address of the recipient.

Some e-mail clients such as Microsoft Outlook and Mozilla Thunderbird have a read-receipt tracking mechanism. The sender needs to activate this option before sending an e-mail; however, the recipient has the option to either notify the sender that the message has been read or simply ignore sending the read request. In addition, not all e-mail applications or services support sending read receipts.

Many organizations employ an e-mail tracking mechanism to study recipient behavior on their advertisement e-mails. Marketers usually use cookies and web beacon techniques to track e-mail. For instance, if the e-mail sent is a graphical HTML message, the tracking software will embed a tiny, invisible tracking image (usually 1 pixel in size) within the content of the e-mail. When the recipient opens the e-mail, the tracking image will execute some code and send it back to the tracking software server, which will record user actions (whether an attachment was opened, whether any links were clicked, the IP address and country where the e-mail was opened, the number of times this e-mail was read) and store the information in a single database that allows marketers to collect each user action and profile it accordingly.

Please note that e-mail tracking cannot always be considered an accurate indicator that a message was opened or read by the recipient because of many technological considerations.

Open Source Intelligence

Open source intelligence (OSINT) refers to all data that is publicly available. This data can be used by different parties to gather intelligence about a specific target (the target can be a person, a company, or a nation).

OSINT includes all publicly accessible sources of information, such as the following:

- The Internet, which includes the following and more: forums, blogs, social networking sites, video-sharing sites like YouTube.com, wikis, Whois records of registered domain names, metadata and digital files, Dark Web resources, geolocation data, IP addresses, people search engines, and anything that can be found online

- Traditional mass media (e.g., television, radio, newspapers, magazines)

- Specialized journals, conference proceedings, companies profile, annual reports, company news, employee profiles, and résumés

- Photos and videos including their metadata

- Geospatial information (e.g., maps and commercial imagery products)

OSINT techniques and tools have rapidly developed with the advance of computing technology; nowadays, OSINT is used extensively by intelligence agencies to gain insight about future events to make their country's foreign-policy decisions.

OSINT is also used by business organizations to monitor trends on a global level and to gather competitor intelligence in order to become more effective.

Most OSINT tools and techniques are freely available online, and from a privacy perspective, such techniques can be exploited to gather data about a specific person or entity (also known as *footprinting*). This imposes a high security risk because anything published online will remain stored or hidden somewhere online even after deleting it, and the OSINT techniques will simplify extracting it.

To get some practical experience about how OSINT can be used to gather intelligence, visit the OSINT framework at http://osintframework.com. The OSINT framework focuses on gathering information from free tools or resources. The intention is to help people find OSINT resources that return free information.

We will not delve into OSINT techniques because the topic deserves a book on its own, but it is necessary to know about it and how it works to avoid posting sensitive information about yourself publicly. In Chapter 2 you will use some OSINT tools to learn your online exposure level.

Regulatory and Legislative Approaches Concerning Online Privacy

Data protection laws are commonly defined as laws designed to protect your personal information, which is collected, processed, and stored by automated means or intended to be part of a filing system.[21] Data protection laws cover safeguarding personal information stored in physical or electronic records.

Data protection laws are important in today's digital world. As the majority of people begin to shift many of their activities online, you can expect to have a large volume of personal data generated by their online tracks. Business organizations also record key information about their clients, staff, and business partners. All this data should be handled and stored according to strict rules to ensure that people's private information is kept safe.

Data protection laws are not alike in all countries. For example, EU laws are different from those implemented in the United States. Actually, even in the United States, there is no one rule that governs data protection across all states. Some states have stricter laws than others (California is an example). Despite these differences, a set of general protection principles must be ensured by business organizations globally to keep personal information secure.

- Collect only the data allowed by the laws (e.g., there's no need to request the customer's age if the law does not allow you to ask for it).

- Do not collect more information than you actually need for your purpose (e.g., there's no need to ask the user for his or her religion as a part of free e-mail service registration).

- Do not keep the data for longer than you need.

- You must assure that the information stored can be made available instantly on request, and the owners (the personal information owners) can access it to view, update, and delete their information.

- Ensure that staff members who handle user personal information are well trained to avoid any errors that may lead to a security breach of a user's PII.

- Make sure that personal information is stored in an encrypted format (for electronic data) and that it will be accessed only for legitimate purposes; you must also assure that the accessing of personal data by staff members is logged and stored for future audits.

Large business organizations usually have a special department to manage data protection issues, and small businesses can benefit from hiring consulting companies to stay in-line with data protection laws currently implemented. Data protection rules are usually enforced by a regulator or authority, often called a *privacy commissioner* (or *information commissioner*). Some commissioners work closely with government bodies; others do not. These commissioners have the ability to conduct investigations (in case of a data breach) and impose fines when they discover an organization has broken the law.

In this section, we will provide an overview of the major data protection laws issued globally and how they interact to safeguard your personal data on a global level. Links to external resources are offered at the end of the chapter to enrich your thinking about data protection laws globally.

Privacy Laws in the European Union

The Data Protection Directive (or Directive 95/46/EC) is an EU directive adopted in 1995 that regulates the protection of individuals with regard to the processing of personal data and to the free movement of such data within the EU countries. Despite its importance as a legal framework for protecting an EU citizen's privacy and human rights, it has been implemented differently in each EU country, according to its local jurisdiction. This led to the fragmentation of this law, making it less effective.

This directive covers all companies that do work in EU countries. It also applies to companies that are located outside the European Union and process data related to EU citizens. The directive can be found at `www.wipo.int/wipolex/en/text.jsp?file_id=313007`.

The General Data Protection Regulation (GDPR), adopted in April 2016, will replace the Data Protection Directive and is planned to be enforceable across Europe starting on May 25, 2018.

The GDPR's focus is on the protection of natural people with regard to the processing of personal data and to the free movement of such data within the EU countries. This regulation will unify data protection laws across the EU countries, forcing all companies that work (or aim to work) within Europe to follow strict rules when gathering or processing private information about EU citizens and residents.

As we already said, the GDPR will apply to all companies that offer goods and services to EU citizens. This includes companies that work outside EU countries and hold/process personal data of data subjects (whether they are individuals or companies) in EU countries.

For individuals younger than 16 years, online services will require parental consent before processing their personal data.

In the United Kingdom, the government has confirmed that the UK's decision to leave the EU will not affect the commencement of the GDPR.

The regulation will not apply to the processing of personal data used for protecting national security or law enforcement activities.

You can find more information about the protection of personal data in the EU on the European Commission web site (`http://ec.europa.eu/justice/data-protection/index_en.htm`).

Privacy Laws in the United States

The lack of comprehensive U.S. data privacy legislation has placed the Fourth Amendment at the heart of much privacy litigation. Privacy advocates and defense attorneys alike seek to uphold "probable cause warrants" as the baseline requirement for any searches of personal data records, but judicial interpretation of the Fourth Amendment has been hard to predict in cases where personal information is processed in digital form, outside the home, or by a third party (Pell and Soghoian, 2015).[22]

The U.S. legislative framework for the protection of personal information is still not harmonized across all the U.S. territories. For instance, there are about 20 national privacy or data security laws regulated primarily by industry, on a sector-by-sector basis. Many of the 50 U.S. states have passed laws mandating stronger protection of PII than the federal government requires. California, which is considered a pioneer in protecting user privacy, has six major privacy protection laws that cover all areas of user privacy such as protecting health information, identity theft, unsolicited commercial communications, and online privacy, in addition to general privacy laws.

At the federal level, the Federal Trade Commission (FTC) is the primary federal privacy regulator in the United States. It has the authority to enforce its privacy laws over the majority of organizations in the business sector across the United States. The main privacy regulations enforced by the FTC to protect consumer data in the United States include the following:

- *Children's privacy*: This act is called the Children Online Privacy Protection Act (COPPA). It prevents commercial entities from collecting PII about children without their parents' prior consent.

- *Consumer privacy*: This monitors online businesses to assure that their work does not violate their published privacy policy statement in terms of protecting a consumer's personal information.

- *Fair Credit Reporting Act*: This makes sure that consumer credit reports are not misused by companies in an unfair way to measure the trustworthiness of consumers when doing business or applying for jobs.

- *Data security*: This makes sure that any PII of consumers or employees stored by a business organization is protected well and used only for the purpose that it was gathered for. Companies should dispose of this data later securely and must give data owners the ability to access and modify these data upon their request. The FTC gives many free resources for businesses to comply with these rules (`https://www.ftc.gov/tips-advice/business-center/privacy-and-security/data-security`).

- *Red Flags Rule*: This requires some businesses to enforce an identity theft prevention program in their companies to detect any identity theft in their work and to report it instantly.

- *Privacy Shield*: This is a legal framework between the United States and the European Union to protect EU citizens when doing business or using services offered by U.S. companies.

- *Tech companies*: The FTC gives resources and advice for technology companies involved in the design and development of computer systems and mobile applications, web sites, or any software that is used to process or store consumer data to consider the privacy and security implications when designing these products or services.

To stay up-to-date with the most recent privacy laws in the United States, you can always check the State of California's Department of Justice site for the major privacy protection laws at the federal level (https://oag.ca.gov/privacy/privacy-laws) and the Federal Trade Commission portal (https://www.ftc.gov).

DLA Piper has issued an excellent guide about global data protection laws named "Data Protection Laws of the World Handbook," which is available for download as a PDF at https://www.dlapiperdataprotection.com/index.html#handbook/world-map-section.

As we have mentioned, the European Union and the United States have different privacy laws. The United States has always been criticized for not having one federal law that governs data protection activities across the entire states. This makes making cooperation with outside countries more difficult to achieve. However, at the beginning of 2016, officials from both the European Union and the United States agreed on a new framework for transatlantic data flows called the EU-U.S. Privacy Shield.

The EU-U.S. Privacy Shield Framework was designed by the U.S. Department of Commerce and the EU commission to provide a legal mechanism for companies processing the personal data of EU citizens to comply with the legal requirements of privacy laws in the European Union.

This act will govern how non-EU companies (from the United States only) can gather, store, and process an EU individual's personal data and will determine in what cases the U.S. government can have access to this data. It also includes close cooperation between U.S. government and EU data protection authorities (DPAs) through an annual joint meeting to monitor the implementation of this agreement. In the United States, the Privacy Shield Framework is administered by the International Trade Administration within the U.S. Department of Commerce, which took responsibility of enforcing this act among U.S. companies doing business with EU countries that acquire personal data from EU citizens. An overview of this act is available at https://www.commerce.gov/sites/commerce.gov/files/media/files/2016/fact_sheet-_eu-us_privacy_shield_7-16_sc_cmts.pdf.

In the future, we expect to see more cooperation on the data protection laws between different countries around the globe, especially between the United States and EU countries because of the increased number of companies that offer products/services across national borders.

Privacy Laws in Other Countries

As you saw, we have limited the discussion about privacy laws to the European Union and United States. These two are the greatest democratic blocks on Earth that already have—and are continually developing—strict rules to protect their citizens' private data. Of course, there are other countries that have their own laws that govern how a user's private data can be accessed and used. Singapore, Malaysia, and Canada are examples.

In Singapore, data is protected under the 2012 Personal Data Protection Act (PDPA). This act establishes a data protection law that comprises various rules governing the collection, use, disclosure, and care of personal data. It recognizes both the rights of individuals to protect their personal data, including rights of access and correction, and the needs of organizations to collect, use, or disclose personal data for legitimate and reasonable purposes.[23]

We can't cover data protection laws of all countries around the world in this book; however, the rule of thumb is clear regarding this issue. Whenever you want to travel to a country, you should check its privacy laws before reaching it. You can search online about this easily; the phrase *privacy laws in Canada* should return some results about private and public bodies that govern privacy laws in Canada. Autocratic nations usually do not have privacy laws, and even if they have one, they use it only for decoration. For instance, the majority of Arab states, Iran, China, and Pakistan do not respect the privacy of their citizens and visitors, so always make sure to leave all sensitive information at your home when traveling to such places!

Privacy Policies of Web Sites

Privacy policies are agreements where you need to specify what personal data you collect from your users and what you do with that information. It is common for any web site to post a privacy policy agreement when collecting data that can be used to identify an individual.

In the United States, there is no general law that mandates the existence of a privacy policy agreement on each web site or app. However, the majority of state laws insist on this issue either directly or indirectly. There are also some federal laws that govern the privacy policies in specific circumstances such as the following:[24]

- The Children's Online Privacy Protection Act (COPPA)

- The Gramm-Leach-Bliley Act

- The Health Insurance Portability and Accountability Act (HIPAA)

In California, which is considered the strictest state in the United States in implementing privacy policy regulations, there is a law called CalOPPA, which mandates the existence of a privacy policy agreement on all web sites or online services that collect "personally identifiable information through the Internet about individual consumers residing in California."

In the European Union, the Data Protection Directive and the ePrivacy Directive are regulating how to handle private users' data. They state that a privacy policy agreement must exist when a web site or a mobile application uses the personal data of individuals/users.

Please bear in mind that despite the majority of countries around the world mandating the existence of a privacy policy agreement on any commercial web site, app, or online service that collects personal information about their citizens, this does not mean that companies that have a privacy policy agreement will respect users' private data! A policy can contain many terms that violate a user's right to privacy (e.g., some web sites' privacy policy agreements mention that they have the right to give your non-PII to third-party companies for advertisement purposes). Unfortunately, the majority of users do not read privacy policy agreements because they are long and contain legal terms that may not be well understood by casual users.

Do Not Track

Do Not Track (DNT) is a web browser setting that requests that a web application disable its tracking of an individual user. When you choose to turn on the DNT setting in your browser, your browser sends a special signal to web sites, analytics companies, ad networks, plug-in providers, and other web services you encounter while browsing to stop tracking your activity.

It is not mandatory to obey DNT when enabled in browsers by websites owners and advertisers; till now there is no mandatory regulation that enforces implementing it.

To enable DNT in the Firefox browser, select Tools ➤ Privacy and check the option Use Tracking Protection in Private Windows (see Figure 1-2).

Figure 1-2. *Enabling tracking protection in the Firefox browser*

Opt Out

The term *opt out* refers to several methods by which individuals can avoid receiving unsolicited product or service information. This ability is usually associated with direct marketing campaigns such as e-mail marketing or direct mail.

In e-mail marketing, the concept of opt out is quite simple; when you receive a commercial or promotional e-mail that promotes services or products that you already subscribe to receive information from, the e-mail must contain a link to unsubscribe yourself from the marketer's e-mail list. All reputable companies include such a link in their e-mails and allow up to two business days to remove your e-mail completely from their list upon subscription. Users should be careful when clicking the Unsubscribe link. They should first check the e-mail carefully to see whether they have really subscribed to this service previously because some spammers may send such e-mails to a large number of automatically generated e-mails. When a user clicks the Unsubscribe link, the spammers will know that this e-mail is valid and they will target it with further unsolicited e-mails.

There are a number of different laws that guide the use of e-mail for commercial marketing purposes. In the United States, it's the CAN-SPAM Act (`https://www.ftc.gov/tips-advice/business-center/guidance/can-spam-act-compliance-guide-business`). In Canada it's the CASL laws (`http://crtc.gc.ca/eng/internet/anti.htm`), while in the United Kingdom it's a set of laws known as the Privacy and Electronic Communications Regulations of 2003 (`https://ico.org.uk/for-organisations/guide-to-pecr/electronic-and-telephone-marketing/electronic-mail-marketing`).

All of these laws stipulate that your e-mail campaigns must include a clear and conspicuous mechanism for opting out of receiving e-mail from you in the future, so it is mandatory to put an Unsubscribe link in every marketing e-mail. In addition, when your web site uses cookies for tracking, you must tell visitors to your web site how your site uses cookies and ask if they want to accept them. The information should be easy to understand by any user, as shown in the following quote for the LinkedIn web site:

> *This LinkedIn website uses cookies and similar tools to improve the functionality and performance of this site and LinkedIn services, to understand how you use LinkedIn services, and to provide you with tailored ads and other recommendations. Third parties may also place cookies through this website for advertising, tracking, and analytics purposes. These cookies enable us and third parties to track your Internet navigation behavior on our website and potentially off of our website. By continuing your use of this website, you consent to this use of cookies and similar technologies.*

What Is Anonymity?

Internet anonymity refers to conducting your online activities without revealing your true identity. This effectively means concealing your real IP address and prevents others from tracking you online in any method to reveal your true identity.

Anonymity can be used for good and bad purposes. An example of good anonymity is when using it by journalists in third-world countries to avoid being tracked and captured by their local authorities. On the bad side, criminals can use anonymity to conceal their criminal activities from law enforcement authorities.

We can differentiate between many kinds of online anonymity, such as using anonymous payments, sending anonymous e-mails, surfing the Web anonymously, and anonymous web hosting and blogging. Generally speaking, anonymous online services include all services that do not reveal the true identity of its users.

What Is the Difference Between Privacy and Anonymity?

Privacy and anonymity are two different concepts; however, both are essential in today's digital world. *Privacy* means that online communications are confidential and no third party is allowed to intercept them in any way. Following this definition, the main concern of privacy is to keep the content of the online communication private. For example, when sending an encrypted e-mail, you are assuring your privacy by encrypting the e-mail content.

Protecting the privacy of your online communications is easier than staying anonymous online. As we already said, privacy is concerned with keeping communication content private. This can be mainly done through applying strong encryption to contents and keeping the encryption keys in a safe place. Anonymity is more difficult to achieve and needs good experience in Internet technologies in order to apply it successfully.

To transfer top-secret information online, the best solution is to use a combination of both. Anonymizing your Internet connection will make tracking you difficult—and even impossible—while encrypting your messages (or files) using strong encryption algorithms and complex passwords will make it impossible to read your content if your e-mail gets intercepted in one way or another. In this book, you will learn everything you need to implement this combination effectively to protect your confidential communications.

Entities That Promote and Help People Retain Privacy Online

There are many organizations that are fighting to protect your right to privacy. Table 1-1 lists the most popular ones around the globe.

Table 1-1. *Global Nonprofit Entities That Promote a User's Right to Privacy*

No	Name	Web Site (URL)
1	EPIC	https://epic.org
2	EFF	https://www.eff.org
3	Privacy Alliance	www.privacyalliance.org
4	Privacy International (PI)	https://www.privacyinternational.org

Summary

In this chapter, you discovered various parties interested in having your private data, and the motivation behind them, which include the following:

- Advertisement companies

- Law enforcement and intelligence agencies

- Web analytics

Basically, there are two types of information generated by online traces: personality identifiable information (PII) and anonymous information. PII contains information that is strictly related to your personality such as name, e-mail, age, and the like. The other type is the anonymous information that contains data such as your IP address, web browsing history, and previous searches. Anonymous information can become PII when combined with other details (e.g., combining a user's IP address with his or her browsing history and Facebook account).

Web tracking technologies are used to collect, store, and connect user web browsing behavior records. Advertisers are continually adopting unique methods to track a user across many web sites so they can know a user's habits in order to predict future actions (mainly future purchases). Other parties also gather information in bulk, such as intelligence services and giant IT companies (Facebook and Google).

Different regulations exist to protect users against the invasion of their online privacy. The European Union has a more uniform legal framework to handle consumer privacy issues. However, the same is not available in the United States, which still has many privacy regulations adopted across its states.

In this first introductory chapter, you learned who is gathering your online information and what they are doing with it. We also talked about how this might affect you. For the rest of the book, we will cover the last question: how do you stop it?

Bibliography

Carly Nyst and Anna Crowe, "Unmasking the Five Eyes' global surveillance practices." Global SocietyWatch, 2014. `https://giswatch.org/en/communications-surveillance/unmasking-five-eyes-global-surveillance-practices`.

Brian Buntz, "The World's 5 Smartest Cities." Internet of Things Institute, May 18, 2016. `www.ioti.com/smart-cities/world-s-5-smartest-cities`.

Notes

1. Sam Thielman, "Yahoo Hack: 1bn Accounts Compromised by Biggest Data Breach in History." The Guardian, December 15, 2016. `https://www.theguardian.com/technology/2016/dec/14/yahoo-hack-security-of-one-billion-accounts-breached`.

2. Gartner, "Gartner Says 8.4 Billion Connected 'Things' Will Be in Use in 2017, Up 31 Percent From 2016." February 7, 2017. `www.gartner.com/newsroom/id/3598917`.

3. Gartner, "Gartner Says By 2020, More Than Half of Major New Business Processes and Systems Will Incorporate Some Element of the Internet of Things." January 14, 2016, `https://www.gartner.com/newsroom/id/3185623`.

4. PWC, "IAB Internet advertising revenue report 2015 full year results." https://www.iab.com/wp-content/uploads/2016/04/IAB-Internet-Advertising-Revenue-Report-FY-2015.pdf.

5. Network Advertising Initiative, "Understanding Online Advertising." https://www.networkadvertising.org/understanding-online-advertising/what-is-it.

6. Jianqing Chen and Jan Stallaert, "An Economic Analysis of Online Advertising Using Behavioral Targeting." *MIS Quarterly* 38, no. 2 (2014): 429-449.

7. Association for Psychological Science, "Marketing Is More Effective When Targeted to Personality Profiles." May 21, 2012. https://www.psychologicalscience.org/news/releases/marketing-is-more-effective-when-targeted-to-personality-profiles.html.

8. Jack Marshall, "Facebook Wants to Help Sell Every Ad on the Web." *The Wall Street Journal*, May 27, 2016. www.wsj.com/articles/facebook-wants-to-help-sell-every-ad-on-the-web-1464321603.

9. IP Location, "What is the difference between a static and dynamic IP address?" https://www.iplocation.net/static-vs-dynamic-ip-address.

10. Katriina_M, "Why does my IP address seem to be in a different country than expected?" F-secure, February 6, 2017. https://community.f-secure.com/t5/F-Secure/Why-does-my-IP-address-seem-to/ta-p/66063.

11. Kathryn Wynn, "Treating IP addresses as personal data is best approach for businesses, says expert." Out-Law.com, March 9, 2016. www.out-law.com/en/articles/2016/march/treating-ip-addresses-as-personal-data-is-best-approach-for-businesses-says-expert-/.

12. Personal Data Protection Commission, "Advisory guidelines on the pdpa for selected topics." Chapter 7, December 20, 2016. https://www.pdpc.gov.sg/docs/default-source/advisory-guidelines---selected-topics/ch-7---online-activities-(201216).pdf?sfvrsn=2.

13. InfoCuria, "Case-law of the Court of Justice, (Reference for a preliminary ruling — Processing of personal data — Directive 95/46/EC — Article 2(a) — Article 7(f) — Definition of 'personal data' — Internet protocol addresses — Storage of data by an online media services provider — National legislation not permitting the legitimate interest pursued by the controller to be taken into account)." http://curia.europa.eu/juris/document/document.jsf?text=&docid=184668&pageIndex=0&doclang=en&mode=lst&dir=&occ=first&part=1&cid=1406323.

14. Piriform, "Cleaning Flash cookies." https://www.piriform.com/docs/ccleaner/ccleaner-settings/cleaning-flash-cookies.

15. Techtarget, "Flash cookie." October 2014. http://whatis.techtarget.com/definition/Flash-cookies.

16. Samy Kamkar, "Evercookie." September 20, 2010. http://samy.pl/evercookie/.

17. Browserleaks, "Canvas Fingerprinting." https://browserleaks.com/canvas.

18. BuiltWith, "Facebook Like Button Usage Statistics." https://trends.builtwith.com/widgets/Facebook-Like-Button.

19. BuiltWith, "Twitter Tweet Button Usage Statistics." `https://trends.builtwith.com/widgets/Twitter-Tweet-Button`.

20. The Intercept, "SKYNET: Applying Advanced Cloud-based Behavior Analytics." `https://theintercept.com/document/2015/05/08/skynet-applying-advanced-cloud-based-behavior-analytics/`.

21. Privacy International, "Data Protection." `https://www.privacyinternational.org/node/44`.

22. Stephen Cobb, "Data privacy and data protection: US law and legislation." 2016. `www.welivesecurity.com/wp-content/uploads/2016/04/US-data-privacy-legislation-white-paper.pdf`.

23. Personal data protection commission Singapore, "Legislation and Guidelines." April 10, 2017. `https://www.pdpc.gov.sg/legislation-and-guidelines/overview`.

24. Children's Online Privacy Protection Rule (COPPA). `https://www.ftc.gov/enforcement/rules/rulemaking-regulatory-reform-proceedings/childrens-online-privacy-protection-rule`.

CHAPTER 2

▓ ▓ ▓

Essential Privacy Tips

What You Should Do Right Now

Privacy is not a new concept; it existed long before the current digital age. It is a natural reaction of individuals to maintain their rights in public and to be left alone. As you saw in Chapter 1, the legal right to privacy is constitutionally protected in most democratic societies. However, the recent revelations of mass surveillance programs in addition to the new bills issued in the United Kingdom and United States against protecting users' privacy cast doubt on whether your privacy is protected when online.

In today's digital age, information gathering is fast, easy, and less expensive than in the past. Huge technological advancements in computing technology make it easy to collect vast volumes of data and store it for later analysis.

With buzz words such as *hacking* and *cybersecurity* appearing in the press regularly and being common topics of conversation among everyday technology users, information security and privacy are at, or at least should be, at the forefront of people's minds.

In this chapter, we will present technical tips and best practices to assure your digital privacy when surfing the Web, sending e-mails, shopping online, banking online, and using social networking web sites. The practices covered in this chapter offer the first line of defense against online privacy threats. Advanced techniques in encryption, Windows hardening, data concealments, and many more will be covered thoroughly in the remaining chapters.

To better understand how you can maintain your online privacy, we'll first introduce the types of computer security threats that you face online.

Types of Computer Security Risks

The Internet is full of risks! Whenever you go online, there is a possibility that you will encounter a risk. There are different types of computer threats with varying associations of damaging effects. For example, some threats may damage or corrupt your installed operating system and force you to reinstall it. Another type may steal your credentials and saved passwords. Still other threats may not bring any harm to your PC; instead, they will track your online activities and invade your privacy.

Today, criminals are smarter than ever before, and malicious programs are more sophisticated. Modern malware can infect a target PC and remain undetected for a long time. The motive behind the majority of cyber-attacks nowadays is not to damage your machine but instead to steal your money, to access your private information, or to acquire your logon credentials.

In this section, we will briefly talk about the main types of security risks that you may encounter when going online.

© Nihad A. Hassan and Rami Hijazi 2017

N. A. Hassan and R. Hijazi, *Digital Privacy and Security Using Windows*, DOI 10.1007/978-1-4842-2799-2_2

Malware

Malware is short for "malicious software" and is any software employed to bring damage to computing devices (computers, smartphones, etc.) or the stored content (data or applications). Malware corruption can manifest in different ways, such as formatting your hard disk, deleting or corrupting files, stealing saved login information, gathering sensitive information (your files and private photos), or simply displaying unwanted advertisements on your screen. Many malware variants are stealthy and operate silently without the user's knowledge or awareness. Malware is a term used to refer to many types of malicious software such as computer viruses, worms, Trojan horses, spyware, ransomware, scareware, and adware.

Hacking

Hacking is the process of invading your privacy by gaining unauthorized access to your computing device. Hackers usually scan your machines for vulnerabilities (such as unpatched Windows updates) and gain access through them. After gaining access, they may install a keylogger or a Trojan horse to maintain their access, to begin stealing information, or to spy on user activities.

Pharming

Pharming is a cyber-attack intended to redirect users from a legitimate web site to a fraudulent site without their knowledge. Pharming can be conducted either by changing the hosts file on a victim's computer or by poisoning the Domain Name System (DNS) server records with false information to lead users to unwanted destinations. DNS servers are computers responsible for resolving Internet names into their real Internet Protocol (IP) addresses.

If the Windows hosts file gets infected with malware, it can change its contents and insert redirects, so when the user types the legitimate URL, the browser may then redirect to a malicious web site that has the same look and feel. When the user enters his or her username and password, the malicious web site will receive them instead of the original one, thus resulting in a compromised user account and credentials.

To mitigate such attacks, you can prevent hosts file modifications by following these steps:

1. Navigate to the %SYSTEMDRIVE%\Windows\Ssystem32\drivers\etc folder (SYSTEMDRIVE is where you installed Windows, usually at C:\).

2. Right-click the hosts file, select Properties, and select the Read-only attribute; finally click OK (see Figure 2-1).

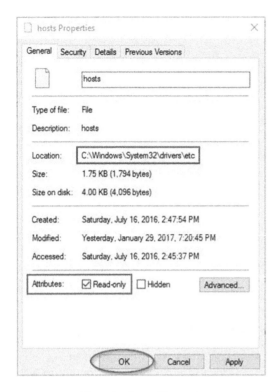

Figure 2-1. *Changing hosts file attributes to Read-only to avoid pharming attacks on Windows machines*

Phishing

Phishing messages come in different shapes, such as SMS messages, e-mails, and web site links (URLs), all of which are designed to look genuine and use the same format as the legitimate company. Phishing aims to collect user-sensitive details (such as banking information, passwords, and credit card details) by tricking the end user into handing the information to the attacker. Phishing is covered in detail later in this chapter.

Ransomware

Ransomware is computer malware that installs silently on the user machine. Its objective is to deny access to user files, sometimes encrypting the entire hard disk drive and even all the attached external disk drives. It then demands that the user pay a ransom to get the malware creator to remove the restriction so the user can regain access to the system and stored assets.

Most ransomware hits devices through phishing e-mails and pop-up advertisements. There are three major types of ransomware.

- The first one locks the system in a way that is not difficult for a technical person to reverse; it displays a message requesting payment to unlock it.

- The second type encrypts the whole disk drive, including any removable storage, and demand a ransom to decrypt it (but there's no guarantee of getting any data back).

- The third is a variant that pretends to be ransomware but is actually trickware, which can easily be removed. Figure 2-2 shows an example that was mounted against the iPad and iPhone.

Figure 2-2. *Sample trickware mounted against Apple devices*

Victims of ransomware usually pay the ransom through the bitcoin digital currency (more on bitcoins in Chapter 4).

Ransomware usually comes hidden in a legitimate file. When the user installs the legitimate program, the ransomware gets installed as well without the user's knowledge.

Ransomware is now the number-one security concern for organizations. As the number of attacks increase, it has become a global problem that threatens both individuals and companies. According to CNN, cyber-criminals collected $209 million in the first three months of 2016, meaning that at the end of 2016 this number may reach $1 billion. This number may be even bigger than that, though, because some victims may choose to pay and not report the crime.[1]

Adware and Spyware

Adware is used to collect information about you and your machine. It usually comes with free software or useful plug-ins or search bars for web browsers; once installed, it begins tracking your online activities and may then send it to outside parties. Many free games and free system utilities contain adware. As we already said in Chapter 1, few users read the end-user license agreements (EULAs) and simply click the "I agree" button without knowing that the freeware may contain adware (which is clearly stated in their EULAs).

Spyware in the form of a keylogger will seek to steal everything you type on your keyboard (usernames and passwords) and send it to its operator. Some spyware can facilitate installing a virus on your operating system, rendering it inoperable. Other forms can do this via the in-house/in-home Wi-Fi connection, communicating any acquired credentials and information into the hands of an awaiting actor.

Trojan

This type of malware can infect computer silently. It usually installs itself as part of a legitimate software installation. In fact, many Trojans work stealthily in the background and are undetectable by antivirus programs. Most of the popular banking threats come from a Trojan family like Zeus and SpyEye. Trojans can potentially gain access to all your system functions including the camera and microphone. They also have the ability to delete files and monitor your online activities and keystrokes or even to detect other Trojans that may be installed by other criminals and then to remove them, making the new resident Trojan the only active variant on the target system.

Virus

Computer viruses have been around now for at least two decades and are one of the oldest traditional risks known since the early days of personal computers. They have morphed through many variations of dangerous profiles. A *virus* is a malicious program that infects a target PC or its content with the objective to make the computer inoperable, thus possibly forcing drastic action like a reformat to return to its normal state. Some viruses cause more damage such as stealing your contact list and credentials and facilitating unauthorized access to your machine. Nowadays, viruses are not widely used because they have been replaced with other types of malware that enable attackers to generate revenue from their attacks such as ransomware.

Worms

The Morris worm, or Internet *worm*, was one of the first to be seen in the wild. In November 1988, it was distributed via the Internet and caused significant damage to the infected systems. This is now another type of old-school attack that is still widely used. However, unlike viruses, which aim to destroy or compromise the OS, the worm works to spread from one machine to another through internal networks or the Internet. Many types of worms attack the e-mail client (e.g., Microsoft Outlook or Thunderbird) and copy themselves to all contacts in the address book to further distribute their infection to new locations. Worms can make computers run slowly because they can consume your disk space and Internet bandwidth. Worm propagations can cause tremendous lost in revenue for companies when spread inside a company's intranet.

Wi-Fi Eavesdropping

No matter whether you are at home, at work, or at a public access point, hackers can intercept communication communicated through unprotected wireless networks and access points. Such attacks can result in intercepting all your online communications, including your usernames and passwords, and of course may provide access to your online banking details.

Scareware

Scareware is a form of malicious software that uses social engineering to cause shock, anxiety, or the perception of a threat in order to manipulate users into buying unwanted software.[2] For example, scareware can report to a user that his or her machine is full of spyware and other infections and he or she must act promptly and purchase an anti-malware solution (which is fake!). The idea here is to trick the user into purchasing something unnecessarily in order to take his or her money.

Distributed Denial-of-Service Attacks

A *distributed denial-of-service* (DDoS) attack is an attempt to make an online service unavailable by overwhelming it with traffic from multiple sources. Attackers build networks of infected computers, which could be millions of machines, known as *botnets*, by spreading malicious software through e-mails, web sites, and social media. Once infected, these machines can be controlled remotely by a *bot master*, without their owners' knowledge, and used like an army to launch an attack against any target.

Botnets can generate huge floods of traffic to overwhelm a target. These floods can be generated in multiple ways, such as sending more connection requests than a server can handle, manipulating the TCP flags (like the well-known Christmas Tree attack did), or having computers send the victim huge amounts of random data to use up the target's bandwidth.

Cyber-criminals don't have to make their own malware these days; they can purchase ready-made malware in the form of crime wave as a service (CaaS) that is ready to launch DDoS attacks against any web site they choose. An underground black market (we will talk about this later in the book) offers the Bot Malware Kit, which can be used to infect a large number of computers, create a botnet, and launch a DDoS attack for only $200.[3]

Rootkits

A *rootkit* is a dangerous type of malware; it can potentially gain full access (administrative access) over the system and has the ability to prevent normal detection programs (antivirus and anti-rootkit programs) from noticing its presence. Some dangerous rootkits attack at the hardware level (firmware rootkit), and removal may require hardware replacement or specialized intervention.

Juice Jacking

In this attack, an intruder will steal your private data through the USB charging port of your smartphone, tablet, or laptop when you connect your device to a public power-charging station such as the ones available in airports, conferences, and restaurants. Malware can also get installed using this technique. To counter such risks, do not charge your computing device in public charging stations; use personal power bank units instead.

Install Antivirus and Other Security Solutions

Installing an antivirus program is considered the first line of defense for any computer user. However, keep in mind that having an antivirus solution does not mean you are covered on the whole Internet security front. Unfortunately, some antivirus products try to give the impression (for marketing purposes) that they will completely cover all security holes once installed.

Traditional antivirus programs are useful against classical threats such as viruses, worms, some types of malware, phishing, and spam. But the end user may still need a specialist solution against spyware and ransomware in addition to a firewall solution for maximum protection. The majority of commercial antivirus solutions come with an integrated firewall; each product has its own configuration manual to explain how to use it. In this section, we will demonstrate how to use a free dedicated firewall from Comodo. All personal firewalls use the same configuration terms, so this should help you to configure yours easily. For now, we'll start by talking about computer antivirus software.

How to Select Your Antivirus Program

Antivirus software usually uses three basic methods for detecting, blocking, and removing viruses.

- Signature-based detection

- Heuristics detection

- Rootkit detection

Most personal antivirus solutions use a combination of signature-based detection and heuristic technology. Although most antivirus programs have a similar approach for detecting malicious software, some are better than others. To help you select the best one, we have created a number of criteria that should be met by your future antivirus solution.

- The antivirus program should detect and remove malware of all kinds (including ransomware or any other financial malware).

- It should be able to detect phishing attacks and dangerous web sites and deny access to them.

- It should be able to integrate with major e-mail clients (such as Microsoft Outlook and Thunderbird) to scan incoming and outgoing e-mails automatically in addition to filtering spam e-mails.

- It should be compatible with the currently installed operating system and programs.

- It should come equipped with a personal firewall.

- It should update itself automatically.

- It should be efficient in terms of discovering zero-day malware and updating its virus signature database instantly.

- If the antivirus has the ability to detect rootkits, this is an excellent extended feature.

- It should have a lower number of false positive alerts or false alarms (this happens when antivirus software recognizes legitimate software as malware).

- It should be able to protect your browser from outside attacks.

- It should have a DNS protection feature (more about DNS in Chapter 4).

- It should be lightweight and not consume high computing resources when scanning files or working in the background.

- It should not renew its license automatically without explicit approval.

- It should be affordable to you.

Microsoft has a free antivirus solution that provides protection against different types of computer malware called Microsoft Security Essentials (MSE). MSE has received generally positive reviews for its simple user interface, low resource usage, and freeware license. MSE can be installed on Windows 7; however, modern versions of Windows (Windows 8, Windows RT, Windows 8.1, Windows RT 8.1, and Windows 10) have Windows Defender built into Windows that helps guard your PC against viruses and other malware. Windows Defender surpasses MSE for having enhanced protection against rootkits and bootkits. If you're looking to protect an older PC running Windows 7, you can use Microsoft Security Essentials (http://windows.microsoft.com/mse/).

The main disadvantage of both MSE and the modern Windows Defender is the lack of a personal firewall. Despite this fact, these products are excellent choices for Windows. With regard to the firewall issue, you can install a separate solution from Comodo, as you are going to see later.

■ **Note** Install antivirus alongside Windows Defender. Windows Defender will automatically disable itself when you install a third-party antivirus program and then reenable itself again if you decide later to uninstall that third-party antivirus program. It's designed to get out of the way.

Other free antivirus solutions offer good basic protection for your Windows PC, as shown in Table 2-1.

Table 2-1. *Some Free Antivirus Solutions*

Antivirus	Main Feature	URL
360 Total Security	Its virus definition signature is based on four antivirus engines (360 Cloud Scan Engine, 360 QVMII AI Engine, Avira, and Bitdefender).	`https://www.360totalsecurity.com/` `en/features/360-total-security/`
Avast	This captures emerging threats (real-time analysis of unknown files).	`https://www.avast.com/en-us/index`
AVG AntiVirus Free	This provides basic protection against viruses and other malware.	`www.avg.com/ww-en/homepage`

If you want to purchase a paid antivirus solution (always recommended as they offer more comprehensive protection), you can always check the Independent IT-Security Institute web site at `https://` `www.av-test.org/en/`, which conducts regular tests to find the best antivirus solution for different operating systems (including smartphones) according to specific technical and security criteria.

Anti-exploit

An antivirus program by itself is no longer an adequate security measure on its own. Emerging threats require you to install additional solutions for full protection. Anti-exploit programs help you survive against sophisticated attacks such as Flash and Silverlight exploits and Browser vulnerabilities. Anti-exploit tools also provide protection against zero-day malware.

The Enhanced Mitigation Experience Toolkit (EMET), available at `https://www.microsoft.com/` `en-us/download/details.aspx?id=50766`, is a free product from Microsoft. EMET anticipates the most common techniques that adversaries might use in compromising a computer and helps protect by diverting, terminating, blocking, and invalidating those actions. EMET helps protect your computer systems even before new and undiscovered threats are formally addressed by security updates and anti-malware software.

Anti-spyware

Running anti-spyware software for computer safety is considered to be just as important as having antivirus software. Spyware is a kind of malware that tracks your online activities and sends it to third parties. The more dangerous spyware can steal everything you type on your keyboard and send it to its creator. Antivirus solutions have the ability to detect different kinds of spyware; however, it is advisable that you have a dedicated solution for spyware removal for maximum protection.

Spybot S&D (`https://www.safer-networking.org`) is a popular free program used to detect and remove different kinds of adware, malware, and spyware from your computer system. Spybot S&D (the free edition) is not an antivirus tool. It can, however, run alongside antivirus software to enhance the security of your PC. The paid edition comes supplied with antivirus functionality.

Anti-malware

As we said previously, malware includes all types of malicious software that can damage your operating system and stored files. Every day a large number of malware programs are launched online. The security solutions we already talked about can stop many types of malware, but it is recommended that you have a dedicated solution to stop malware attacks only. Spybot S&D (the free edition) comes with an anti-malware functionality, but there is another famous program for detecting malware called Malwarebytes (https://www.malwarebytes.com). The free edition can detect and remove malware and advanced threats in addition to removing rootkits and repairing the files they damage. Malwarebytes doesn't require advanced configuration. Install it and you are ready to go, making it a preferable solution for beginners.

░ **Warning**   It is not recommended that you install Spybot and Malwarebytes at the same time because they both have anti-malware functionality.

Firewalls

A *firewall* monitors and controls the incoming and outgoing network traffic and helps you to screen out hackers, viruses, and worms that try to reach your computer over the Internet. All Windows versions, beginning from Windows XP SP2, have a firewall built in and turned on by default. However, this firewall has some limitations compared with third-party firewalls. (For example, it monitors incoming traffic only, while letting outgoing traffic flow freely; also it does not offer an easy-to-use interface for its advanced features.) You can access Windows Firewall (in all Windows versions) from Control Panel ➤ Windows Firewall.

The primary function of a firewall is to block unrequested incoming and outgoing connections. It allows you to set access permissions for each program on your computer. When one of these programs tries to connect to the Internet, your firewall will block it and launch a warning message unless it recognizes the program and verifies that you have given it permission to make that sort of connection. By doing this, your firewall prevents any currently installed malware from connecting to the outside world to spread viruses or to communicate with hackers to invade your machine.

░ **Tip**   To better configure the advanced features of the built-in Windows Firewall, you can install a tiny program called Windows Firewall Notifier (https://wfn.codeplex.com) that helps you to better visualize Windows Firewall functions.

The majority of the paid versions of antivirus solutions come equipped with a personal firewall, but if you opt to install a free edition, then you need to have a dedicated personal firewall installed on your machine. There are many free firewall solutions for Windows; however, configuring a firewall could be a daunting task for beginners, so it is better to install one that is easy to configure and provides maximum protection. The free Comodo firewall has such characteristics.

Because of the importance of a robust firewall on every computer accessing the Internet, we will describe how to set up and configure the Comodo firewall in some detail. Before beginning the installation of Comodo firewall, though, make sure that your current antivirus software doesn't have its own firewall activated as part of it. Also, make sure to deactivate the built-in Windows Firewall.

HOW TO DISABLE THE BUILT-IN WINDOWS FIREWALL IN WINDOWS (ALL VERSIONS)

1. Go to Control Panel ➤ Windows Firewall.

2. In the left panel, click "Turn Windows Firewall on or off."

3. On the next screen, select to turn off Windows Firewall for both private and public networks (see Figure 2-3).

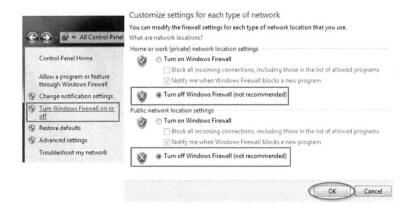

Figure 2-3. *Turning off Windows Firewall*

4. Click the OK button and you are done!

Install the Comodo firewall by following these steps:

1. Download the Comodo firewall from `https://www.comodo.com/home/internet-security/firewall.php`. The current version of the Comodo firewall is 10. After downloading the program, execute the installer to begin the installation wizard. The first screen in the wizard asks you to select your installation language. In our case, we are selecting English. Then click the I AGREE button to move to the next step.

2. Comodo may ask you to set Yahoo as your default home page and search engine. In our case, we are unchecking this option. Click Next to continue.

3. The next wizard has two tabs. The first one asks whether you want to send anonymous program usage information and whether you want to use cloud-based behavior analysis. Uncheck both options.

4. The next tab asks you whether you want to install the additional components, which are Comodo GeekBuddy (for technical support) and Comodo Dragon Web Browser. In this case, we are unchecking both. Now click the Install button to begin installing the firewall (107MB). This may take some time depending on your Internet connection speed.

5. Upon finishing, the final wizard window will ask you to enter your e-mail if you want to receive offers and news from Comodo. In our case, we are selecting not to receive anything. Click the Finish button. Restart your computer to finish the installation.

6. After Windows restarts, Comodo will detect your current network connection and ask you about your location. In this case, select "I am at Home."

7. The Comodo firewall desktop icon appears in the system tray. To access the firewall settings, double-click this icon.

▪ **Note** The default settings of Comodo are suitable for most users; however, we prefer to use custom rules in order for interactive protection to investigate all incoming and outgoing connections.

---

8. Once Comodo's main interface appears, click Settings (see Figure 2-4).

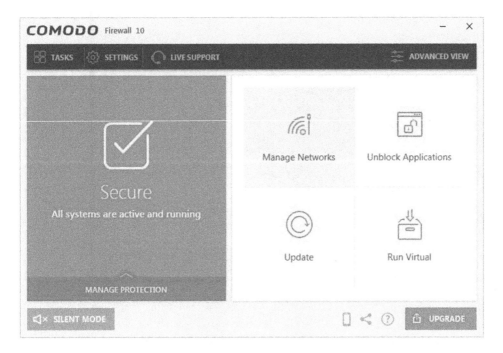

Figure 2-4. *Comodo program main interface*

9. Go to Firewall ➤ Firewall Settings and check Enable Firewall (Recommended). From the drop-down menu, select Custom Ruleset. Finally, click the OK button to accept the new settings (see Figure 2-5).

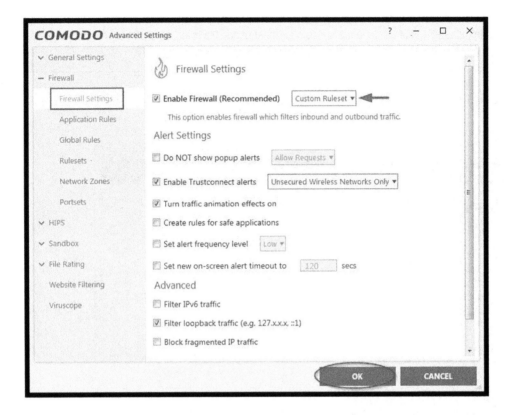

Figure 2-5. *Modifying the firewall settings to become a custom ruleset for interactive protection*

10. After implementing the new setting, every time the Comodo firewall receives a connection request, it activates a pop-up firewall alert prompting you to either allow or block access to your system to and from the Internet (see Figure 2-6).

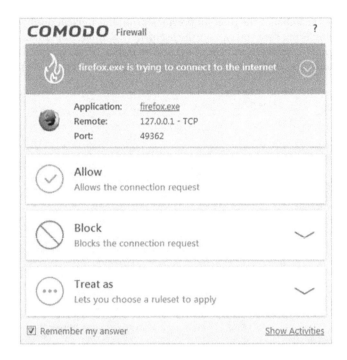

Figure 2-6. *Example of Comodo firewall alert when trying to access the Internet using Mozilla Firefox*

It is advisable to be strict in allowing programs to connect to the Internet. Do not hesitate to stop any suspicious program from connecting to the Internet. If you suspect any program, you can simply click its icon to open the Properties window and learn more about the process or program requesting access (see Figure 2-7).

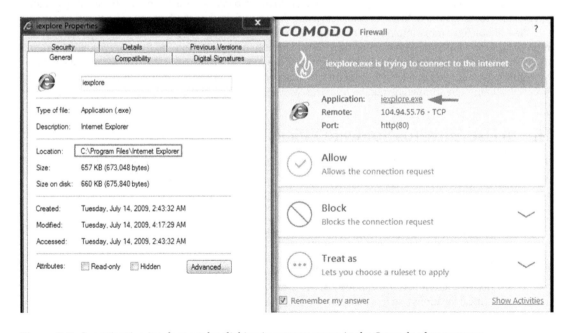

Figure 2-7. *Investigating iexplore.exe by clicking its process name in the Comodo alert message*

You can further configure application rules and change the rules for previously running applications by going to Settings ➤ Firewall ➤ Application Rules. From here you can see the list of firewall application rules currently activated on this system. Select any one (by selecting its check box) and then click Edit to further customize its online behavior (e.g., allowing outbound traffic while denying inbound traffic) (see Figure 2-8).

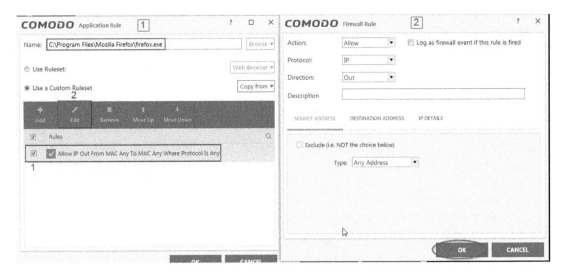

Figure 2-8. *Configuring specific application firewall rules (Firefox in this case)*

The Comodo firewall comes with a default host intrusion prevention system (HIPS) ruleset that works "out of the box," providing extremely high levels of protection without any user intervention. For example, HIPS automatically protects system-critical files, folders, and registry keys to prevent unauthorized modifications by malicious programs. Advanced users looking to take a firmer grip on their security posture can quickly create custom policies and rulesets using the powerful rules interface.

We will not delve more into how to configure the Comodo firewall. We cover its basic usage here to impress upon you the importance of having a firewall on your computer. You can find everything you want to know about the Comodo firewall in the help section of the product online page (`http://help.comodo.com`). We highly encourage you to have a firewall installed on your PC before going online because there are many threats that cannot be stopped by regular antivirus/anti-malware software.

Tips to Use Antivirus Software Efficiently

Here are some tips to follow in order to achieve the maximum efficiency when using your antivirus software:

- Do not install two antivirus programs at the same time. They may be in conflict, slow down your machine, or cause instability problems in your computer.

- Make sure your antivirus program is updating itself automatically. If you are suddenly disconnected from the Internet, make sure to update it manually when you have your connection back.

- Perform or schedule a full scan for the entire system. Antivirus programs usually perform automatic scans; however, this scan doesn't cover all system areas (only critical locations), so it is advisable to run a full system scan each week for maximum protection.

- Be cautious before executing any software downloaded from the Internet. It is better to execute such programs on an isolated virtual machine before installing them on your work PC.

- Do not open e-mail attachments before scanning them using your antivirus program. Executable programs and scripts should not be opened at all when sent through e-mails.

- Do not insert removable media (such as USB stick drives, DVDs, CDs, external hard disks, and SD cards) from unknown sources into your computer. Many viruses reside on such removable media and can infect your computer even when you have an antivirus program installed.

HOW TO DISABLE THE AUTORUN FEATURE OF WINDOWS

The Windows Autorun feature is turned on by default on most Windows versions, allowing programs to run from an external device as soon as they are attached to a computer. Because malware can exploit the Autorun feature to infect your computer and spread to others, it is highly recommended that you disable the Autorun feature. (The AutoPlay feature in Windows is part of Autorun.)

To disable the AutoPlay feature in Windows (applicable to all versions from 7 to 10), go to Control Panel ➤ AutoPlay and uncheck the "Use AutoPlay for all media and devices" box.

Passwords

People's choice of passwords continues to pose a huge security risk. Recent data breaches of user personal data and account passwords show that a large number of users are still using risky passwords to secure their accounts. According to SplashData's 2015 "Worst Passwords List" (compiled from more than 2 million leaked passwords during the year), the two most commonly used passwords by online users were *123456* and *password*, both of which have remained at the top of the list since it first started in 2011. The report also shows that despite many users attempting to create more secure passwords, the majority are based on simple patterns that would be easily guessed by hackers. Examples include 1234567890, 1qaz2wsx (the first two columns of the main keys on a standard keyboard), and qwertyuiop (the top row of keys on a standard keyboard); these all appeared in the top 25 list.

In this section, we will give guidelines and tools for creating strong passwords.

Create Secure Passwords

Here are some tips to create secure passwords:

- The password should be at least 15 characters in length for maximum security.

- The password should contain at least one lowercase letter, one uppercase letter, one number, and one symbol (e.g., # % &).

- The password shouldn't be your username or even part of it.

- Do not use your spouse's, family member names (including your name), or pet's name as part of your password.

- Do not share the same password between your spouse or friends (have two e-mails with the same password).

- Do not use your gender or birth date/place as part of your password.

- Do not use places names for your password (country, city, street name, school, or university name).

- Do not use famous people's names as your password (e.g., famous movie actors, political leaders, public figures, singers).

- Avoid sequences when creating passwords (consecutive letters, numbers, or keys on the keyboard such as 123456 or asdfghjkl).

- Do not use the same passwords for two different accounts (e.g., your bank account password and your private e-mail password should not be the same).

- Change your password once every three months.

- Do not use the same password again (e.g., when you change your e-mail password, do not return and use any password you were using during the last year).

- Do not use dictionary words as your password or part of it.

- Do not use real words from foreign languages as your password.

- Use a password manager to organize and protect passwords, generate random passwords, and automatically log into web sites.

- Don't store your passwords in an unencrypted text file or Microsoft Excel spreadsheet or any other file type that is not encrypted. Also, never write down your password on paper. If you want to take your password with you and you are afraid that you may forget it (because it is complex), then use a portable password manager and keep it on your smartphone or on your USB stick drive.

- Do not let your web browser save your entered passwords.

- Do not use tools to automatically generate your password for top important accounts (e.g., bank accounts and medical record accounts). For such important accounts, follow the rules already mentioned and create something from your mind.

- Do not send your password if someone requests it from you. Many social engineering attacks involve making users trust the attacker and getting them to share their passwords.

- Whenever you hear about a data breach in press, instantly change your affected account password.

- Do not ever type your password on a computer that does not belong to you.

Password Generation Tools

Obviously, it is important to change your passwords continually and to use strong, complex passwords that can be difficult or impossible to crack using brute-force, dictionary, or guessing attacks. Many users may fail to create such complex passwords or may simply repeat and use a portion of the old password to create the new one, which is considered an insecure practice. In this section, we will give you some tools and services that can help you to generate strong and complex passwords.

- Free Password Generator (https://www.securesafepro.com/pasgen.html) is a free, lightweight tool for generating secure and complex passwords. It has a portable version and can run on all Windows versions.

- PWGen (http://pwgen-win.sourceforge.net) is an open source professional password generator capable of generating large numbers of cryptographically secure "classical" passwords, pronounceable passwords, pattern-based passwords, and passphrases consisting of words from word lists. It uses a "random pool" technique based on strong cryptography to generate random data from indeterministic user inputs (keystrokes, mouse handling) and volatile system parameters. It also has some interesting features because it can encrypt, decrypt, and clear the clipboard so that no information is intercepted when copying passwords out of this program.

Many web sites offer online password generation services. However, we prefer not to use such services because your password can be intercepted while traveling to your PC (even though some of these services encrypt the password before sending it to you or simply use a script to run locally on the user's client machine).

■ **Tip**   Most password manager tools contain a password generation utility. So, you can opt to use one tool for both generating your secure passwords and storing them directly in a safe encrypted database.

Now you may wonder that after you have successfully created your strong passwords, how can you keep them all in a safe location? The next section will answer this.

Password Managers

As you already saw, the majority of users use weak passwords and repeat using them across different web sites. This bad practice happens because humans have difficulty remembering long, complex passwords, especially if they have many accounts with different passwords. The solution for this problem is to use a password manager.

A password manager allows you to store all your online accounts' login details in one place. When you want to log in to any service/web site, all you have to do is copy the username/password to the login form. A password manager encrypts the database that contains your login information and protects it with a master password. This is the only password you have to remember.

WARNING! AVOID USING BROWSERS' BUILT-IN PASSWORD MANAGER

Major web browsers have their own built-in password manager; however, they can't compete with a dedicated program specialized for this purpose. Internet Explorer, Chrome, and Opera store their saved passwords in unencrypted form, meaning that anyone can crack them (see Figure 2-9) unless the entire disk drive has been encrypted.

One exception is Mozilla Firefox, which allows you to encrypt your saved passwords using a master password. However, the Firefox password manager lacks many functionalities found in a traditional password manager program.

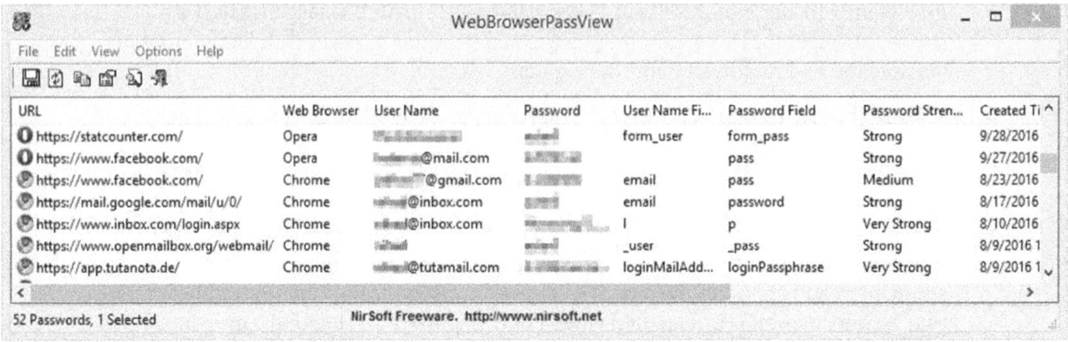

Figure 2-9. *Saved passwords in major web browsers can be extracted using portable tools. WebBrowserPassView from NirSoft reveals saved passwords in the Chrome and Opera browsers.*

It is always preferable to use open source tools, especially when dealing with security software. Open source tools can be audited for backdoors, thus providing confidence to its users. The following sections highlight open source password managers that also have a password generation feature.

KeePass Password Safe

KeePass Password Safe (http://keepass.info) is a free open source password manager. You can take a look at its full source and check whether the encryption algorithms are implemented correctly. KeePass has a portable version so you can run it from your USB stick. It has been ported onto different platforms such as macOS, iOS, Linux, and Android.

Master Password

Master Password (https://ssl.masterpasswordapp.com) has a unique approach to generating user passwords. Its passwords aren't stored in an encrypted database or uploaded to a secure cloud service. Instead, they are generated on the fly using the following parameters: your name, the site you are going to use the password for, and your master password (which is the main password used to log in to the Master Password program). This unique approach to password creation/management guarantees that your passwords will not get intercepted as you synchronize your account between devices (for example, your smartphone and PC). In addition, you do not need any repository to store these passwords. All you need to do is install the Master Password tool on each device you want to use and then enter your name and site names and you are ready to go (see Figure 2-10).

Figure 2-10. *Sample password generated using the Master Password tool*

Password Safe

Password Safe (`https://www.pwsafe.org`) is an open source program that allows you to easily and quickly generate, store, organize, retrieve, and use complex new passwords, using password policies that you control. The original version was designed by renowned security expert Bruce Schneier. Password Safe is designed to be extremely hard to crack using brute-force attacks, and it encrypts all user data in memory when using it.

You can copy a username and password from your saved entries by right-clicking the entry, without needing to access and view the record itself.

The password managers introduced in this section are all offline (except for Master Password, which uses a stateless approach) and store users' passwords in a safe location on the device being used. We still find that storing user passwords on your own computing device or a USB memory stick is the most secure solution for keeping such important information away from outside interception.

In addition to storing your credentials safely, password managers can make you more resistant to many types of keyloggers because they can securely send your password directly to the form fields in your browser without needing the user to type usernames or passwords for the keylogger to pick up. Password manager software is considered a type of encryption software, and it can be vulnerable to different attack types (both hardware and software based). We will cover these attacks and suggest countermeasures in Chapter 5.

■ **Warning**   Password managers don't completely protect against keyloggers that actually scan the forms in web browsers. It also cannot protect you against malware that has direct access to your computer clipboard.

Secure Your Online Browsing

Your web browser is your window to the entire world. From here you can log in to your social media accounts, access your bank account, buy products and services, and check your e-mails, in addition to anything else you do online. The wealth of information that exists in web browsers makes them attractive for cyber-criminals. Thus, it is necessary to tweak your browser security settings to make it less vulnerable to outside attacks.

There are many desktop browsers; the market share is mainly divided between Microsoft Internet Explorer (IE), Mozilla Firefox, Safari, Opera, and Google Chrome. IE and its successor Edge come preinstalled on the Windows OS; however, we always encourage users to use open source software to assure maximum security when working online. Mozilla Firefox is still considered the only true open source browser among the main browsers already mentioned, so in this book we will cover using this browser only.

In this section, we will give useful basic tips to secure your online browsing. In Chapter 4, we will cover advanced configuration for Firefox to harden it against online threats.

Turn On Private Browsing

Most modern web browsers have a privacy feature called *private browsing* that lets you browse web sites without your history being tracked locally on your computer. When this is enabled in Firefox, Firefox will not record your visited pages, cookies, temporary files, and searches. Firefox will also activate tracking protection, which will block parts of web sites that try to track your browsing history across multiple sites.

To enable private browsing in Firefox, go to the Firefox menu at the top-right corner of your browser window and then click New Private Window (see Figure 2-11). You can also use the Ctrl+Shift+P keyboard shortcut to access it directly.

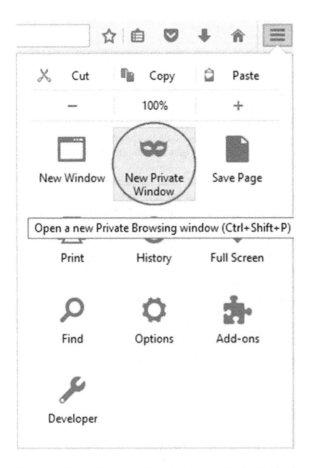

Figure 2-11. *Setting New Private Window in the Firefox browser*

A new Firefox window will appear showing you what is saved and what is not saved while browsing in this mode.

As we said, Firefox will also enable tracking protection, which blocks common advertising trackers, social sharing trackers, and analytics trackers. If you want Firefox to be more aggressive in blocking all trackers, you can enable this feature from the Firefox menu (see Figure 2-11). Select Options, go to the Privacy tab, click the Change Block List button, and select "Disconnect.me strict protection. Blocks known trackers. Some sites may not function properly." Finally, click Save Changes (see Figure 2-12).

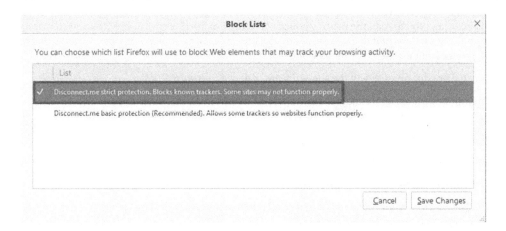

Figure 2-12. *Enabling aggressive tracking protection to block all online trackers using Mozilla Firefox*

Keep in mind that activating strict protection may break the functionality of some web sites, so if this happens and you want to disable protection for a specific web site, click the little shield icon in the address bar and then click "Disable protection for this session" (see Figure 2-13).

Figure 2-13. *Disabling tracking for a specific web site when you are in private mode*

Read Web Site Privacy Policies

When you join a social networking web site or buy something online, you are asked to agree to the terms of use and to read and agree to the privacy policy agreement before proceeding. Such policy agreements will usually contain information on how the web site will collect data from your computer and how the web site will share it. Because the privacy policy agreement is long and full of legal terms, people tend not to read it at all.

Another misconception about privacy policies is that users assume having a privacy policy on a web site means that their personal information is protected. In truth, many privacy policy agreements contain terms that violate users' rights to privacy.

We always encourage you to read the privacy policy agreement in full (for critical services and software) or at least the important sections of it to be aware of any violation against your personal data. To make things simpler for you, just look out for these key items while reading:

- What type of information will the site/software collect about you?

- Will your personally identifiable information (PII) or anonymous information be shared with third-party affiliates?

- Will your information will be disclosed overseas?

- Can you opt out from this agreement later?

- Where will your information be stored?

- Who has access to your information (check all possible parties, including law enforcement and security services)?

- Can you access the service later to update or delete your personal information?

- Can you make a privacy complaint?

- When will your information be discarded or deleted? Some sites store information for specific periods of time, while some store your information indefinitely.

- What kind of security measures will protect your information?

- Focus on everything written in capital letters.

- Use Ctrl+F to conduct a search for the following keywords in the agreement: *third party*, *affiliate*, *opt out*, *arbitration*, *contents*, *advertisers*. When finding any of these words, read the corresponding section carefully.

- When signing your agreement, make sure that `https://` appears in the browser bar to indicate a secure connection.

These tips will help you read the privacy policy agreement quickly, but they may not prevent you from signing a bad agreement; nevertheless, it's still better than signing an agreement without reading it!

Disable Location Information

Sure, it sounds like a great idea to check into your favorite bar or restaurant on Facebook, Yelp, Google+, and more, but a simple click with your smartphone could unknowingly put you in trouble. Major social networking web sites give you the ability to "check in" and reveal your current location on a map. For example, many people "check in" with their Facebook account at home to announce some events (e.g., a birthday party), which will reveal the user address publicly. The same person can later announce he or she is at a restaurant or going on a vacation; for thieves, this means an empty home ready for robbery.

Robbery is not the only danger of revealing your location through the check-in feature; your child's safety can be at risk. If your child also performs regular check-ins, this will reveal the current location of your family members and will simplify attacking them if you or they become a target someday. It is highly advisable to deactivate location services in your social networking app, teach your children to do the same, and ask them not to reveal their location using written status updates either.

To disable the location service in the Facebook app (on Android), open the Facebook app, tap the menu button, and select Account Settings ➤ Location ➤ Location Services ➤ Turn it OFF.

Each version of Android, iOS, and Windows Phone has its own settings to disable location services. As a rule of thumb, you can search for *disable location services X* (substitute your operating system version or phone model for the *X*) to find a detailed guide on how to disable it on your phone/tablet.

Another important feature that must be turned off on your smartphone is recording geotagging information, which contains the GPS coordination of your current location when a photo has been taken. This feature is sometimes useful, but, for instance, it could reveal your address information if you take pictures in your home or work office.

The GPS information stored with your shots is part of the Exchangeable Image File (EXIF) data. This is metadata about the image file itself and does not appears to the naked eye; it contains different technical metadata information such as the time and date of each photo and the camera used to take it (see Figure 2-14).

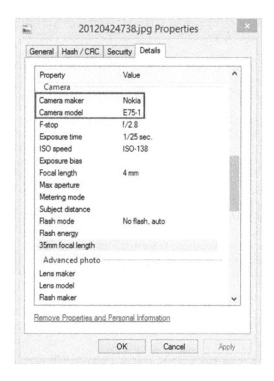

Figure 2-14. *Metadata of a JPEG image showing mobile phone and camera type that took the shot*

You can disable the "location tag" on your smartphone, thus preventing it from recording your current geolocation on all future shots. To do this on an Android phone, turn on the camera, go to Settings ➤ Location tags, and turn it off (see Figure 2-15).

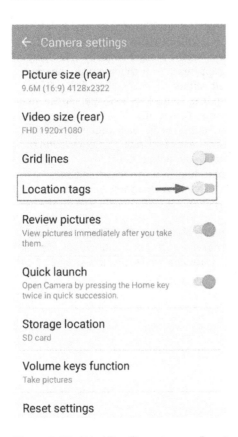

Figure 2-15. *Disabling "Location tags" on Android smartphones*

On iOS, go into Settings, tap Privacy, and then tap Location Services; toggle the Camera option to off. If you cannot find the specified setting on your smartphone, search for *disable location tags in X* (with your smartphone or OS type instead of the *X*).

Some social networking web sites strip out geolocation information and other metadata automatically before publishing it online. Twitter and Facebook do so, but some web sites do not. So, to stay in the safe zone, always turn location tags off and read the next section to learn how to remove metadata of different digital file types.

Remove Metadata from Digital Files

Metadata is a data about data. In technical terms, it contains hidden descriptive information about the file it belongs to. For example, some metadata included in a document file might include author name, date/time created, and comments.

From a privacy perspective, users are mainly concerned about the metadata that exists in digital images, but keep in mind that metadata exists in almost all digital files such as documents, video and audio files, and web pages. Metadata usually comes stored in the digital file; however, some file types store it in a separate file.

There are three types of image metadata.

- *Technical metadata*: This data is usually generated by the capturing camera. It contains information such as camera type and brand name, date/time when the photo was captured, geolocation information (if enabled) of the captured image, and the ID number of the device.

- *Descriptive metadata*: This data is added by the user using a specific software program to add details about the captured images. For example, the user can add the photographer name, comments, title, and caption, among other things.

- *Administrative data*: This data is added manually by the image creator to protect the photo; such data may contain copyright information and the contact address for licensing.

EXIF is a standard that specifies the format for images, sound, and ancillary tags used by digital cameras (including smartphones), scanners, and other systems handling image and sound files recorded by digital cameras.[4]

EXIF data is embedded within the image file and works with JPEG images only. EXIF metadata can contain geolocation metadata in addition to a wide array of technical information.

Other metadata standards include the Extensible Metadata Platform (XMP) and the International Press Telecommunications Council (IPTC). XMP is a metadata standard developed by Adobe Systems. It's based on XML and was designed to allow the exchange of standardized and custom metadata for digital documents and data sets. Hence, it's a format that can be used to describe any kind of asset, not limited to pictures (e.g., support video, audio, and PDF files).

IPTC is an older meta-information format, which is slowly being phased out in favor of XMP. The newer IPTCCore specification uses the XMP format. IPTC information can be found in JPEG, TIFF, PNG, MIFF, PS, PDF, PSD, XCF, and DNG images.[5]

It is advisable to check the metadata of all images before uploading it to the Internet to avoid leaking private information about yourself and the device. There are many freeware tools that can view and edit a digital file's metadata; we'll begin with digital images.

Exif Pilot (`www.colorpilot.com/exif.html`) is a free EXIF editor that allows you to view, edit, and remove EXIF, EXIF GPS, IPTC, and XMP data in addition to adding new tags and importing and exporting EXIF and IPTC to/from text and Microsoft Excel files (see Figure 2-16).

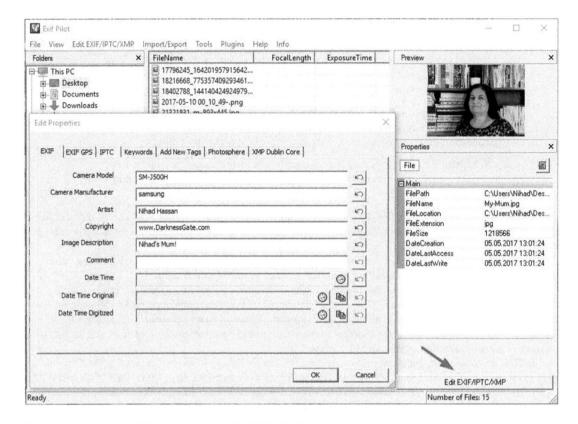

Figure 2-16. *Using Exif Pilot to view and edit EXIF/IPTC tags*

Other free tools that can be used to remove image metadata are GIMP (`https://www.gimp.org`) and XnView (`www.xnview.com/en/`).

Windows comes supplied with a built-in function that allows you to view and remove some metadata associated with documents and digital images. However, keep in mind that Windows may not be able to remove all EXIF tags, so if you intend on sharing important files, always use the suggested third-party tools already mentioned.

To remove EXIF using Windows, right-click the image, select Properties, and go to the Details tab. At the bottom, click Remove Properties and Personal Information to open the EXIF removal tool. The tool lets you either create a copy of the image with all metadata removed or pick and choose which properties to erase from the selected file (see Figure 2-17).

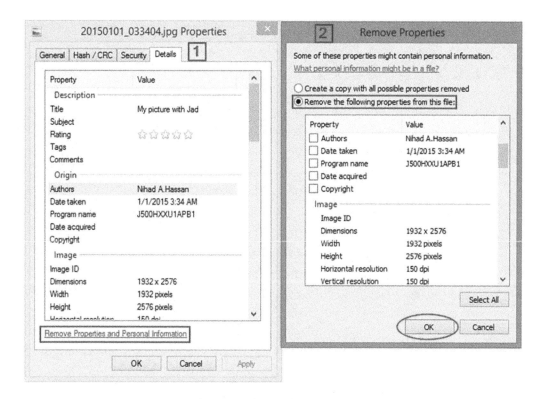

Figure 2-17. *Removing EXIF metadata using the Windows built-in function*

As we already said, Microsoft Office documents, PDF files, and audio and video files all have metadata associated with them. We will cover how to remove them quickly in a moment.

To clear metadata from PDF files, Adobe has a feature called Sanitize Document. After clicking it, you can remove all hidden metadata from the intended PDF file (see Figure 2-18).

Figure 2-18. *Clearing PDF file metadata*

Please note that not all versions of Adobe Reader support the sanitization feature. If your currently installed version does not support it, you can use a third-party tool for this purpose such as ImageMagick (`https://www.imagemagick.org/script/index.php`) or Pdf Metadata Editor (`http://broken-by.me/pdf-metadata-editor/`).

To view/edit and remove audio file metadata, use Mp3tag (`www.mp3tag.de/en/`). This is a powerful and easy-to-use tool to edit the metadata of audio files. It supports batch tag-editing of ID3v1, ID3v2.3, ID3v2.4, iTunes MP4, WMA, Vorbis Comments, and APE tags for multiple files at once, covering a variety of audio formats.

To remove a video file's metadata, use MediaInfo (`https://mediaarea.net/en/MediaInfo`).

To remove metadata from Microsoft Office documents, do the following: for Microsoft Office 2010, 2013, and 2016, you can check the document metadata by selecting File and then going to the Info tab. The Properties panel will be on the right side; from here you can remove document metadata by clicking the Properties button and selecting Advanced Properties (see Figure 2-19).

Figure 2-19. *Removing Microsoft Office document metadata*

In Microsoft Office 2007, you need to click the Microsoft Office button and then select Prepare ➤ Properties to edit the document metadata.

Another issue you need to consider when sending Microsoft Office documents to outside parties is deleting other hidden metadata. Fortunately, Microsoft Office provides a functionality for deleting hidden metadata. You can access this feature in Microsoft Word 2013/2010/2016 from File ➤ Info ➤ Check for Issues ➤ Inspect Document. In Microsoft Word 2007, you can access this feature by clicking the Office button and selecting ➤ Prepare ➤ Inspect Document.

Make Sure to Log Out

Whenever log in to your social networking account, your e-mail, or an online retail account, make sure to log out when finished. Web sites usually put the login/logout links at the top of the web site. If you are using Firefox in private mode, it will log you out automatically when you close it. Giant companies like Facebook and Google can track your online activities and link them back to your real identity (on Facebook or Google ID) easily when you remain logged in while you browse the Internet or conduct regular searches. The same thing happens to smartphone applications; the majority of users remain logged in to their Facebook app while browsing the Internet on their mobile device. This practice is bad and will reveal much about your personality and online habits, as we mentioned in Chapter 1.

How to Know Whether a Web Site Is Secure

Millions of dollars are spent daily on web sites such as Google, Amazon, and eBay. These giant companies use the latest technology to protect their assets and customers from cyber-criminals, but when comes to new web sites and online stores, you should be careful that the web site is secure before giving any information or making any purchase. The following are some quick tips that you can use to tell whether a site is secure.

Check the Web Site SSL Certificate

SSL certificates are small data files that digitally bind a cryptographic key to web site details. When installed on a web server, the certificate activates a padlock and the Hypertext Transfer Protocol Secure (HTTPS) and allows a secure connection between the company server and the client machines. Upon installing the SSL certificate, the URL of the web site will begin with `https://` instead of `http://` (the *s* stands for "secure").

To get an SSL certificate, a company must undergo a validation process. There are different levels of validation. Some require only a valid domain name; others require more information about the company behind the certificate. The lowest validation level requires that you prove that you have the right to use the domain name that you are trying to secure (usually done through checking the Whois record of your domain). This type of validation is not secure because an attacker could buy an SSL certificate and bind it to a web site dedicated to conducting phishing attacks.

A more stringent validation will require (in addition to domain validation) you to submit official documents about your company such as a business license/certificate, public records filing for a new business entity, certificate of payment of business tax, or any official documents that can validate your business legitimately. This kind of validation is called *extended validation* (EV) and uses the highest level of authentication and a rigorous verification process. You can tell when a site is using an EV certificate because the address bar will be green, and the security status bar will reveal detailed information about the company operating the web site when you hover the mouse over it (see Figure 2-20). EV certificates incorporate some of the highest standards for identity assurance to establish the legitimacy of online entities.

Figure 2-20. *Sample web site protected with EV SSL certificate*

Check the Domain Name

Cyber-criminals create web sites that are identical to an existing one and try to trick people into logging in or purchasing items from it. These web sites are designed to look completely legitimate and like an existing web site.

It is highly advisable to type the URL of your intended web site directly in the address bar of your browser instead of clicking links that come in e-mails, especially e-mails that ask you to update your bank, PayPal, or online store account details. For example, a criminal could buy the domain name Go0gle.com and set up a web site that looks just like the Google.com home page. Then the user could buy an ordinary SSL certificate (that only needs domain name validation) and try to trick users into signing in to their Google account to receive a prize by sending the fake URL through phishing e-mails. When the user clicks the fake URL and accesses his or her Google account, his or her credentials will travel to the attackers, and the fake web site will forward the user to the real Google web site to avoid raising suspicion.

Legitimate Web Sites Do Not Have Pop-Ups

Most reputable retailers don't use pop-ups; they know that customers strongly dislike them and that using pop-up ads may turn customers away.

Know That Legitimate Web Sites Do Not Send Spam

Reputable web sites don't send you spam e-mail unless you specifically signed up to get information from them or their partners. Be cautious and do not click links in spam e-mails.

Check the Physical Address

Reputable retailers usually put their physical address and phone number on the Contact Us page or in the footer or header of the web site.

Other Indicators of Fake Retailer Web Sites

Here are some other indicators:

- If you are shopping for products online and find a store that offers very low-priced items, be suspicious. Such web sites could be a scam to steal your money.

- Always look for a return policy and shipping policy. Reputable retailers have such documents clearly on their web sites.

- Fake web sites usually do not accept credit cards; they ask for debit cards or for checks. This is because they want to stay anonymous and do not have a legitimate presence to make agreements with credit card companies to accept online purchases.

- The overall design of the web site should be consistent and professionally developed. Broken pages and inconsistent colors or themes across pages should raise suspicion about the web site. Credible web sites have excellent design and support mobile devices.

Do Not Install Pirated Software

As software prices increase, many users illegally download pirated software from the Internet to save costs. Such software usually comes with an executable program named Crack or Patch to unlock the pirated program trial version and make it work like the paid one. Running executable programs to unlock legitimate software is dangerous, especially because many pirated program instructions ask the user to turn off antivirus software to avoid any conflict while installing. The pirated software might be disguised malware that will install silently upon executing it. This will effectively jeopardize your personal security.

Another risk is disabling updates. Users are forced to stop automatic updates of pirated software to avoid being discovered by the developer company. For example, when you install a cracked version of Windows or any security solution (e.g., an antivirus solution), you may not be able to update it regularly like the original version. This will leave your software or OS vulnerable to different risks.

If you prefer to use freeware programs downloaded from the Internet, it is highly advisable to use your antivirus solution to scan them before executing them. To become more confident, you can scan the downloaded program with free scan services, which comes in handy when you want to scan a specific file/program using multiple antivirus engines.

VirusTotal (`https://www.virustotal.com`) is a free service that analyzes suspicious files and URLs and facilitates the quick detection of viruses, worms, Trojans, and all kinds of malware. All you need to do is enter the web site URL you want to check or to upload the file/program to see whether it is clear from malware threats.

Update Everything

Be careful to configure Windows to install automatic updates; your web browser and antivirus should both update automatically.

To configure Windows (applicable to Windows 7 and 8) to install updates automatically, go to Control Panel ➤ System. On the bottom left, click Windows Update. On the left side, click "Change settings," and from the drop-down menu, select "Install updates automatically (recommended)" (see Figure 2-21).

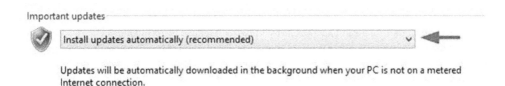

Figure 2-21. *Configuring Windows 8 to install updates automatically*

In Windows 10, automatic updates are enabled by default.

E-mail Security

E-mail is the most used service through the Internet; it is widely used for both business and private communications. Using it unwisely or without appropriate protection can make you susceptible to different online threats. Here are some important tips to consider when using your e-mail service:

- Do not access your primary e-mail account using free, open Wi-Fi access points in public places.

- Use encryption when using an e-mail client (e.g., Mozilla Thunderbird) and make sure to encrypt the connection between your computer and e-mail server.

- Create multiple e-mail accounts. Dedicate one e-mail to sign up for free offers and services, keep one for private use, and use another for your daily work. There are many providers that offer free e-mail services; Google and AOL are among them.

- Do not use free e-mail service for mission-critical work. Giant free e-mail service providers such as Google (Gmail) and Microsoft (Live) scan e-mail contents to deliver targeted advertisements to their users.

- Encrypt all your mission-critical e-mails. Chapter 5 will cover e-mail encryption.

- Do not publish your primary e-mail address online; instead, use another account for public use.

- Make sure that your antivirus solution can scan inbound and outbound e-mails in your e-mail client and can stop spam and phishing scams.

- Do not open e-mail attachments from unknown senders. If a friend on your contact list sent you an e-mail with an attachment, make sure to scan it first for malicious software.

- Beware of phishing scams that use fraudulent e-mails and fake web sites, masquerading as legitimate businesses, to trick unsuspecting users into revealing private account or login information. To be safe, if you receive an e-mail from a business that includes a link to a web site, make certain to type the web site URL in the address bar manually. We will cover phishing in more detail in the next section.

- Do not send sensitive documents (e.g., a Social Security number, a copy of your passport, credit card information, medical records) via e-mail without appropriate encryption.

- Do not reply to spam e-mails. If you reply, the spammers will know that your e-mail is valid, and they will target you with more spam and maybe phishing attacks.

- Do not use your personal e-mail account for your work because most business organizations have Internet usage policies that allow them to monitor all Internet traffic passing through the organization's internal network. If you use your personal e-mail account for business work, they will have the right to access your e-mail and check its content. On the other hand, if you forward some sensitive business documents to your personal e-mail, your company could take legal action if it suspects you of corporate espionage or misuse of sensitive in-house information.

WARNING! LIST OF FILE EXTENSIONS THAT SHOULD NOT BE OPENED WHEN SENT AS AN E-MAIL ATTACHMENT

E-mail is still considered the preferred tool for cyber-criminals to spread their malicious software. In addition, many worms spread automatically from one PC to another using e-mail. Most average Internet users think that executable files (with an .exe extension) are the only dangerous file type that they should avoid opening when received through e-mail. Unfortunately, this information is not complete, as there are a large number of file types that can be used to execute malicious code on Windows computers. The following are the most dangerous file formats that you should not open when sent as an attachment:

EXE, MSI, MSP, PIF, APPLICATION, GADGET, HTA, CPL, MSC, JAR, CMD, VB, VBS, VBE, JSE, PS1, PS2, MSH, MSH1, MSH2, MSHXML, SCF, LNK, INF, REG, JS WSC, WSH

Microsoft Office files can contain malicious code in the form of macros. If an Office document extension ends with an .m, it can contain macros (e.g., .docm, .xlsm, and .pptm). Be careful and do not run Office macros sent from unknown senders.

Finally, do not open zip files protected with passwords (a password is usually sent in the body of the e-mail). Some attackers use this trick to prevent antivirus programs from investigating the encrypted archive file, which can contain malware ready to launch after being opened.

Social Engineering

Social engineering is a kind of attack that uses psychological tricks (social tricks) over the phone or uses a computing device to convince someone to handle sensitive information about himself or herself or an organization and its computer systems (see Figure 2-22).

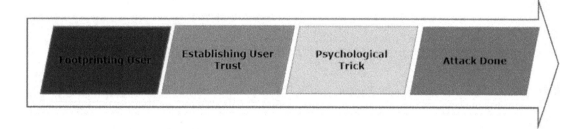

Figure 2-22. *Social engineering attack life cycle*

Hackers exploit a human's natural tendency to trust in order to acquire sensitive information in order to gain access to computing systems and information. There are many techniques already employed to conduct social engineering attacks; the most common type is phishing.

Phishing

The United States Computer Emergency Readiness Team (US-CERT) defines *phishing* as follows:

> *"...an attempt by an individual or group to solicit personal information from unsuspecting users by employing social engineering techniques. Phishing emails are crafted to appear as if they have been sent from a legitimate organization or known individual. These emails often attempt to entice users to click on a link that will take the user to a fraudulent website that appears legitimate. The user then may be asked to provide personal information, such as account usernames and passwords, that can further expose them to future compromises. Additionally, these fraudulent websites may contain malicious code."*[6]

What Does a Phishing E-mail Message Look Like?

Certain characteristics distinguish phishing e-mails from legitimate ones. Here is a list of the main ones:

- Many phishing e-mails use urgent or threatening language in the subject line (e.g., they threaten you about account closure if you do not act promptly). Such e-mails ask you to send your details, fill in online forms, or click a link to renew your subscription or to update your personal details. This could be for your e-mail service, bank account, or any of your social networking accounts.

- They make job offers or talk about work-from-home opportunities with high salary and simple requirements.

- They offer prizes, like a lottery. Some phishing e-mails say that your e-mail won the lottery and you must send your personal details, including bank account, to receive the funds or tax repayment.

- They offer business deals with promises of great profits.

- They are business e-mails with programs or executable code attached to them. Businesses usually do not send programs to execute on client machines.

- Some immigration firms claim an ability to give you a U.S. visa or other country's visa and request your personal details or ask for a tiny payment to submit the application for you.

- Phishing e-mails usually contain grammatical errors and seem unprofessionally written.

- Phishing e-mail addresses come from a different domain name than the company presents. For example, an e-mail sent from a free service (Google or Outlook) asking you to update your PayPal account details is a phishing scam.

- They contain links that take you to web sites other than the company they are pretending to represent.

Whenever you suspect an e-mail to be a scam, do not reply to it. To check whether it is a phishing e-mail, rest your mouse (but don't click) on the links contained in the e-mail to see whether the address matches the link that was typed in the message or the sender domain name.

Some attackers may use short URL services to mask the real phishing URL sent to the user. Services like Bitly (`https://bitly.com`) and TinyURL (`https://tinyurl.com`) allow users to shorten any URL. If you suspect that a short URL could be a scam, you can expand it using a free online service like the one at `http://checkshorturl.com` to see the destination.

You can also check whether the link is safe before clicking it by using free online services such as Norton Web Safe (`https://safeweb.norton.com`) and ScanURL (`http://scanurl.net`).

Phishing is not only limited to e-mails or a digital medium; many phishing attacks are done through phone calls. Phishers will say anything to cheat people out of money. They seem friendly and usually have some previous information about you. They call you by your first name and ask about your life and family to gain your trust. Many of them claim to work for companies you already deal with; others may first send you an e-mail asking you to call them later on their free phone line.

Phishing attacks can also target employees in giant companies. A good example is when an attacker tries to gain some sensitive information about a specific person. If the attacker knows the targeted person's phone number, he or she can pretend to be that person and call the targeted user's mobile phone operator technical support and ask for an account reset because he or she forgot the online password. If the trick is successful, the attacker can access the targeted user's online account and gain sensitive information about him or her that can be used to impersonate him or her or to launch further attacks.

Here are some countermeasure steps against phishing attacks:

- Do not give your credit card, bank details, or other sensitive personal information over phone calls or through e-mails. Some phishers may have part of your personal information and ask you to confirm it; beware of this trick and do not give any information or confirm your details.

- Refuse to answer calls from telemarketing people. Some of them could be genuine; however, it is preferable to avoid them for security purposes.

- Do not give information to charity organizations that you do not know. Some attackers may pretend to be working in a charity to steal your money or to gain more information about you.

- Do not give information about the company you work for. This also includes revealing information about it online (e.g., on social networking sites).

- Pay attention to the URL of a web site. A phishing web site may look identical to a legitimate site, but the URL may use a variation in spelling or a different domain (`.com` becomes `.org` or `.info`).

- Do not click hyperlinks or links attached in the suspected phishing e-mail, especially when you want to check your bank account. Always type the bank URL directly in the web browser address bar.

- Check your bank account regularly to make sure it is safe and no illegal transactions have been made.

- If you suspect that a phishing e-mail could be a legitimate one, try to contact the company behind the e-mail directly using its web site's Contact Us page. Do not use the Contact Us e-mail or link supplied as part of the suspected e-mail because it could be false and part of the phishing attack.

- Do not install programs or download files sent as attachments in e-mails from unknown senders.

- Do not access your important accounts on public computers, and use a virtual keyboard where applicable.

- Always discard pop-up screens and never enter information using them.

- Make sure the web site you deal with to enter your personal information is protected by an SSL certificate (HTTPS).

- Phishing is not limited to one avenue. Although most phishing attacks target bank accounts, there are many that target social networking sites and other companies such as eBay and PayPal.

- Consider the anti-phishing working group at `www.antiphishing.org` for a list of previously recorded phishing attacks. ISIT Phishing (`http://isitphishing.org`) checks phishing URLs using heuristic technology coupled with machine learning.

- Enhance the security of your computer by keeping your antivirus software up-to-date, update your Windows machine continuously, and do not ignore any warning raised by your web browser or e-mail service provider about any a suspected phishing e-mail/web site.

- Organizations should invest in educating their employees about cyber-security attacks. If employees learn how to protect their data and the company's confidential data, they'll be able to recognize a social engineering attempt and mitigate its consequences.

- Business organizations should have a data classification policy, where only the employees who really need to access sensitive data are given access to it.

If you suspect that you are a victim of a phishing attack, contact the Federal Trade Commission and raise a complaint at `https://www.ftc.gov/complaint`. You can report identity theft at the same page if you suspect that someone or a company is misusing your private data. You can also file a complaint on the FBI web site at `https://www.ic3.gov/complaint/default.aspx`.

NOTE! AUTHENTICATION ICON FOR VERIFIED SENDERS

Spammers can "spoof" a message to make it look like it's sent by a real web site or company that you might trust. To help protect you from such messages, Google tries to verify the real sender using e-mail authentication. As an additional security measure, you can enable the "Authentication icon for verified senders" option. After enabling it, you will see a key icon next to authenticated messages (see Figure 2-23) from trusted senders, such as Google Wallet, eBay, and PayPal.

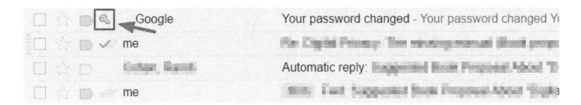

Figure 2-23. *Activating "Authentication icon for verified senders" to distinguish original senders from spoofing e-mails*

To enable this feature in a Gmail account, do the following:

1. Access your Gmail e-mail at `https://mail.google.com`.

2. Access the Gmail Settings in the top right.

3. Click the Lab tab.

4. In the "Authentication icon for verified senders" section, select Enable.

5. At the bottom of the page, click Save Changes.

Other Social Engineering Attack Types

Social engineering attacks are a preferred method to gain access to sensitive information in a relatively easy way compared with technical attacks such as brute-force or man-in-the-middle attacks. Phishing is the most common technique currently used to trick users into handing over their sensitive information; however, there are other techniques used to perform social engineering attacks. The following are the most popular:

- *Shoulder surfing*: This is trying to gain sensitive information from users while they perform their regular tasks. For example, it means capturing user passwords by watching them type them on the keyboard.

- *Dumpster diving*: This attack tries to gain sensitive information from materials thrown in the trash. Many organizations discard different types of papers without proper shredding (e.g., calendar of meetings, users list, system usage manuals). In fact, some organizations get rid of old computers without properly destroying them or securely wiping data on the hard disk. An attacker can gain important information by looking in the garbage or recovering data from old computers' hard disks.

- *Role-playing*: In this kind of attack, an attacker will impersonate technical support staff at some company and try to take sensitive information from users to gain illegal access to their accounts.

- *Keyloggers/Trojan horses*: Here, an attacker tricks the user into installing malicious software on his or her machine (e.g., through an e-mail attachment or freeware downloaded from the Internet). The installed tool will record everything the user types on the keyboard and send it back to its operator.

- *OSINT*: Open source intelligence (OSINT) is where attackers investigate publicly published information about a specific company or person to gain intelligence. Different tools exist to perform these attacks such as Maltego (`https://www.paterva.com/web7/`) and Social-Engineer Toolkit (SET) (`https://github.com/trustedsec/social-engineer-toolkit`).

As you can see, there are different kinds of social engineering (SE) attacks, and all try to gain unauthorized access through exploiting the "human factor," which remains the weakest element in computer security. Educating users about SE risks is still the best countermeasure technique against such attacks.

Secure Home Wi-Fi Settings

Most individual users connect to the Internet using a dedicated router (usually an ADSL router). All home computing devices and appliances are connected using this single device. Most users prefer to use a wireless connection instead of cables. A wireless connection is easy to set up and does not require physical space. However, a wireless connection is promiscuous and should be considered less secure than its wired equivalent of communication and, if not correctly secured, may be intercepted and compromised more easily by outside hackers. In this section, we will give you simple guidelines to secure your home Wi-Fi network settings to become less vulnerable to outside attacks.

First, you need to access your router's settings page. This usually done by typing a router control panel address in your browser and then entering the default username and password at the prompt. The default comes supplied with your router manual (e.g., D-Link uses `http://192.168.1.1` to access its settings).

NOTE! FIND YOUR ROUTER DEFAULT LOGIN INFORMATION

You can check your router's default login and password at `www.routerpasswords.com`. All you need to do is to select your router brand name and then search for the specific router model name (see Figure 2-24).

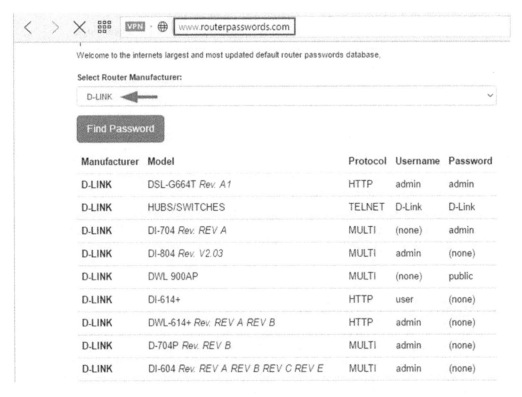

Figure 2-24. *Checking for your router's default username and password on* www.routerpasswords.com

After you are at the router's settings page, you must change your router administrator password. Most routers use the default login *admin* and the password *password*. Change the default password to something difficult to crack.

Change the Network SSID Name

Each router comes with a default name (SSD or wireless network name), which is usually the name of the manufacturer (e.g., D-Link). Changing this name to something else (don't use your personal information; use something ordinary and not related to you personally) will help you to prevent outsiders from knowing which router belongs to you.

You can also hide your Wi-Fi SSID completely. (Router settings allow you to hide your Wi-Fi network from prying outsiders. Note that once you do this, you'll stop seeing the network pop up in your own devices' Wi-Fi lists, and you'll need to type the SSID into each device you want to connect to.)

■ **Warning**   Even after hiding your network name and not broadcasting your network presence, hackers can use some tools to capture your network even when it is in the hidden state. Tools such as InSSIDed (www.metageek.com/support/downloads/#downloadInssider), WirelessNetView (www.nirsoft.net/utils/wireless_network_view.html), and Homedale (www.the-sz.com/products/homedale/) can capture hidden wireless networks.

Enable Wi-Fi Encryption

When you are at your router's settings page, go to Wireless setup ➤ Wireless security and select a strong encryption standard to secure your Wi-Fi transmission. For instance, WPA2 is the most secure one (see Figure 2-25). Finally, enter a passphrase to protect your Wi-Fi connection (this passphrase is used by all devices that want to use your Wi-Fi connection; it is different from the first password used to secure your router's settings area).

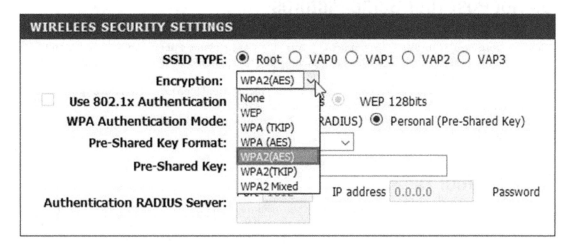

Figure 2-25. *Enabling strong encryption standard for Wi-Fi connection using D-Link router*

Filter MAC Addresses

All computing devices (laptops, tablets, desktops, and smartphones) have a MAC address. This is a unique address hard-coded on the network interface card of each device capable of interacting with the Internet. You can go into your router settings (usually the MAC filter area) and type in the MAC addresses of only those devices you want to allow on the network. This will effectively help you to restrict access to your local network.

▓ **Warning**   Please bear in mind that hackers can spoof MAC addresses and gain full access to your Wi-Fi network. They can achieve this by sniffing your device MAC address using a free tool like Nmap (https://nmap.org) and then spoofing the MAC address on their attacking device using a free tool like Technitium MAC Address Changer (https://technitium.com/tmac/).

Update Firmware

Make sure to update your router firmware continually. Manufacturers release updates to counter future vulnerabilities, and leaving your router without an update is a security hole.

Cover Your Laptop Webcam

This tip is from FBI director James Comey, who recently recommended that we all cover our webcams with tape for security reasons. Comey believes that doing so is a simple step for people to "take responsibility for their own safety and security."[7]

Do Not Post Your Selfie Pictures

Taking pictures of yourself (*selfies*) while raising your fingers (displaying the peace sign, for example) in the photo can pose a real security risk to your privacy. Nowadays, smartphone cameras are so accurate and can produce pictures with so much detail that these pictures can be magnified using special computer programs to extract user fingerprints.

Professional hackers can harvest the Internet for such pictures and then extract user fingerprints to use in different criminal scenarios. Creating false passports or security access cards is one of them.

So, if you have pictures posted online where your finger appears clearly, delete them immediately to avoid identity theft.

Back Up Your Data

Backing up is a way to protect your sensitive data when a failure happens to your computing device. It is essential to have at least three copies of your data off-site and to protect these copies with a password so you can retrieve your important data in the case of system failure, virus attack, or natural disaster.

Most business organizations have backup plans already in place. They back up their data daily and in some instances after each transaction to assure a high level of security and trust.

Individual users can either back up their data to the cloud or use tapes and external hard disk drives for this purpose. We prefer to use external disk drives and tapes to back up our confidential data. This is the safest method because storing data in the cloud, especially sensitive information, may not always be a good choice for security-conscious people.

░ **Note**   Consider using an iStorage FIPS-140/2 password-protected device to secure all of your backup files and important data assets.

For individuals, it is essential to maintain a backup schedule of your important files. It is recommended that you have at least two copies stored on two different backup media (e.g., one stored on tape and another on an external hard drive). Backup media should be stored in a secure, safe location and must be protected with a strong password (review our password creation guidelines). There are many free backup software applications for Windows systems. The following are the most popular ones:

- Comodo Backup (`https://www.comodo.com/home/backup-online-storage/comodo-backup.php`): This is a free backup solution that is easy to use by ordinary computer users; it walks you through a wizard and asks you exactly what you want to do. It can back up data to a local drive, optical media like a CD/DVD/BD disc, network folder, external drive, or FTP server; it can also be sent to a recipient over e-mail. The backup can be divided into pieces and protected with a password. Recovering data is easy and needs only a few clicks.

- Cobian Backup (www.cobiansoft.com/cobianbackup.htm): This is a multithreaded program that can be used to schedule and back up your files and directories from their original locations to other directories/drives on the same computer or other computer in your network. FTP backup is also supported in both directions (download and upload). Cobian works silently in the background to check your backup schedule and perform the required tasks.

These backup programs do not have the ability to perform a backup on specific programs. For instance, e-mail clients such as Thunderbird and the Mozilla Firefox browser contain important information that must be backed up on a regular basis. MozBackup (http://mozbackup.jasnapaka.com) is a simple utility for creating backups of Mozilla Firefox, Mozilla Thunderbird, Mozilla Sunbird, Flock, SeaMonkey, Mozilla Suite, Spicebird, Songbird, and Netscape profiles. It allows you to back up and restore bookmarks, mail, contacts, history, extensions, passwords, cache data, and so on. It's an easy way to do Firefox and Thunderbird backup.

Web Sites That Create a False Identity

Some web sites may ask you to provide personal information about yourself to register with or use their services. The Internet is a hostile place, and you cannot guarantee that a web site that requests this information is 100 percent secure or respecting the law and not handing such information to third-party affiliates. There are many web sites that generate alternate valid personal information that you can use to register with the web sites that you do not trust 100 percent.

A fake identity generator can generate everything you need to become a new digital citizen. This includes phone, web site, e-mail, username, password, account security questions, fake credit card and Social Security numbers, occupation, company, physical traits, and more. Here is a list of the most popular identity generation web sites:

- www.fakenamegenerator.com

- https://names.igopaygo.com/people/fake-person

- www.elfqrin.com/fakeid.php

Using a fake identity generator is against the law when providing personal details for legitimate web sites. It is strongly advised to limit this usage to web sites that you do not trust and noncritical services that ask for personal details without an acceptable reason.

▓ **Warning**   Hackers misuse fake ID generation tools to gain unauthorized access to sensitive data. According to the BBC, Facebook user Aaron Thompson exposed an online thief who gained access to his account simply by sending the support team a fake passport to unlock the account.[8]

The trick was successful, and the attacker gained unauthorized access to a legitimate Facebook account. This clearly shows you the danger of using a fake ID and false government paper in the digital world to hack into honest people's accounts.

Best Practices When Using Social Networking Sites

Social media is a part of our daily lives. Often, when we talk about social media, we tend to think of Facebook, Twitter, and LinkedIn. People tend to post many details about their personal lives on social media sites. These services attract cyber-criminals who aim to perform malicious actions such as identity theft and footprinting users to direct customized attacks against them later.

Covering all the privacy settings of the main social media sites is a daunting task and requires a book on its own. However, there are general guidelines that can be followed to create a balance between using social media sites and keeping your information confidential.

Facebook is the biggest and most popular social media site, so we will cover its security settings in some detail. First, you need to access your Facebook settings by clicking the downward arrow in the top-right corner of the screen and then clicking Settings (see Figure 2-26). You must be logged in to your account to access this page.

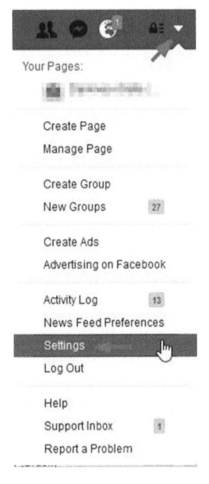

Figure 2-26. *Accessing the Facebook settings page*

This will open General Account Settings page of your Facebook profile, where you can download a copy of your Facebook data. On the left side of the page, click Security to access the Facebook security panel.

Security Section

The Login Alerts setting allows you to get an alert (e-mail or SMS) when anyone logs into your account from an unrecognized device or browser.

The Two-Factor Authentication setting enables two-factor authentication (you need a security code generated automatically) when logging in to your Facebook account using a new browser. You have the following options to receive this security code:

- You can receive an SMS message on your cell phone.

- You can use a Universal 2nd Factor (U2F) security key to log in through USB or NFC.

- You can use Code Generator in your Facebook mobile app to reset your password or to generate Login Approval security codes.

- You can use recovery code (pregenerated security codes; you can keep them with you on paper) to access your account when you do not have your mobile phone with you.

The Where You're Logged In setting allows you to see all the places where you are currently logged in. You can also terminate the session of any device currently logged into your account that you do not recognize.

The Deactivate Your Account setting will disable your profile and remove your name and photo from most things you've shared on Facebook. Some information may still be visible to others, such as your name in their friends list and messages you sent. You can reactivate the account at any time you want.

There are other settings, but they are all self-explanatory.

Privacy Section

The next section that you should access and configure properly is the Privacy settings (which resides below the Security section on the left side of the Settings page). This section shows you the basic privacy settings and helps you make sure that your profile and the content you share are viewable only by the audience you select (see Figure 2-27).

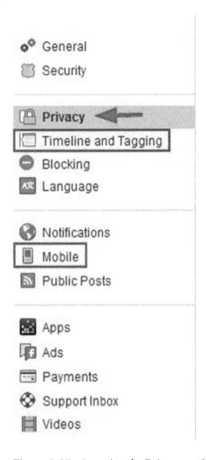

Figure 2-27. *Accessing the Privacy section in the Facebook settings*

The "Who can see my stuff?" group of settings lets you edit who can see your future posts. It is recommended that you set the default sharing option to Friends.

The "Who can look me up?" group of settings allows other people to look you up using your e-mail address and phone number. It also determines whether search engines from outside Facebook can link to your Facebook profile directly. This setting is important because it will determine how outsiders can find you online; select the best privacy setting commensurate to your needs.

The next important section is Timeline and Tagging Settings. It contains the following settings:

- The "Who can add things to my Timeline?" group has two settings. The first one is "Who can post on your Timeline?" The recommended setting is "Only me." The next one is "Review posts friends tag you in before they appear on your Timeline?" The recommended setting is Enabled.

- "Who can see things on my Timeline?" has three settings. The first one is "Review what other people see on your Timeline." This tool lets you see what your Timeline looks like to the public or a specific friend. The second setting is "Who can see posts you've been tagged in on your Timeline?" The recommended setting is Friends. The third one is "Who can see what others post on your Timeline?" The recommended setting is Friends.

- "How can I manage tags people add and tagging suggestions?" has three settings. The first one is "Review tags people add to your own posts before the tags appear on Facebook?" The recommended setting is Enabled. This is an important privacy option because if someone adds a tag to one of your posts, his or her entire list of friends will see the post and not just the friends you've selected. Enabling this option will allow you to review the tag first. The recommended option for the next two settings is Friends.

The last groups of settings we are going to cover is the Mobile section; click it on the left side of the Settings page.

Enter a mobile phone and verify it. This setting is important to protect your account from theft attempts. If your browser is not recognized, you will receive a confirmation code via text message to log in to your Facebook account.

We covered the Facebook security settings in some detail because of Facebook's widespread usage, but keep in mind that social media sites exist to simplify sharing and making connections between people online. It is essential to use such services wisely and avoid releasing your personal information or work details online. Make sure to activate Two-Factor Authentication and have some sort of second authentication (e.g., your mobile phone and password) for maximum security. It is also advisable to keep your browser, antivirus, and anti-malware programs up-to-date. Do not use the same password twice on Facebook and remember to log out when you're done.

Remember what we said in Chapter 1: anything that goes online will remain there, even after deleting it. Be cautious before posting anything online, especially your personal pictures and private data.

■ **Note** You can view your Facebook account activity log by going to `https://www.facebook.com/me/allactivity`.

Protect Your Children Online

Today, most kids these days are well versed in the tech-savvy art of computing. Most children own a smartphone or a tablet and use it to access the Internet. As we've already mentioned many times, the Internet is a dangerous place to let kids surf without proper advice and precautionary measures. For instance, it is crucial to educate your kids about Internet threats to help them enjoy the Web safely and keep your family protected in today's digital age.

Internet Dangers for Kids

Here's a list of possible Internet dangers for kids:

- *Pornography*: Viewing porn pictures and movies by kids may affect their look on life and will change their sexual attitudes and beliefs. This can have a huge negative impact on your child's social life and health.

- *Cyber-criminals/cyber-bullying*: People may trick your children in giving sensitive information about their family to conduct different crimes later.

- *Gaming*: Many online games involve playing with other unknown people online. In addition, these games can include sexual content, violence, and crude language. You can see the same dangers in public chat rooms.

- *Social media sites*: Most kids have social media accounts (especially on Facebook), and posting personal pictures and revealing geolocation positions online can pose a great danger to kids and their entire family. Social media sites facilitate making friends online, but you cannot trust all people online in today's digital age, and your kids may easily fall victim to cyber-criminals.

- *Health effects*: Using a computer for long hours will affect a kid's health. The risk of eye strain, wrist strain, and other injuries increases when using computers for long hours. It is crucial to limit the amount of time your kids spend on computing devices.

- *Internet addiction*: This has become a modern heath problem. Spending long hours online will heavily affect your kid's personal life (offline life).

This does not mean your child may encounter these threats when going online. However, knowing about the dangers can help you and your kids make smart decisions online.

Now, we'll give some countermeasures to protect your kids online.

Teach Your Kid About Internet Dangers

It is important to have a discussion with your kids and teach them about Internet safety. Your kids certainly do not know what is waiting them when going online; it is your responsibility to educate them well on how to use the Internet following safety rules.

Here is a list of rules that your children should understand and agree to follow when using the Internet:

- They will not post personal information about their parents or any family members online without clear consent from their parent. This includes home address, parents' work address and contact information, geolocation information, and anything else that is considered private.

- If they come across something inappropriate online, they should immediately inform their parents or guardian and close the page (e.g., seeing porn material).

- They should not make friends online or chat with strangers without their parental consent.

- They will not post pictures/videos about family to social media sites without parents' consent.

- They will not respond to e-mails or chat messages that pop up from unknown people; they always must inform an adult to check such issues.

- They will not install games or freeware on their computing device.

- They should understand that anything that goes online will remain there, even after deleting it.

- They will not use the Internet extensively and must follow their parents' advice on the amount of time they can spend online daily.

- They should not share their passwords with others, even their close friends, and must store these passwords in a location that their parents can access (e.g., a password manager).

Written rules and discussions are effective means to communicate with your kids; however, some technical measures will also help you enforce these rules.

Parental Control Software

Parental control software helps parents to monitor and track their children's online activity. You should block dangerous sites and protect kids from online bullying or even the potential of an approach from a pedophile. There is software already available for this purpose; many of them are free and have excellent features. The following are the most popular ones.

Microsoft Family Safety Account

For Windows 8 and 10, you can sign up for a family safety account. You can have multiple accounts (one for each child) and link them all to your family account (`https://account.microsoft.com/account/ManageMyAccount`). All you need to have is one Microsoft account (ID) and to sign in with it on your Windows PC. To activate this option in Windows 10, follow these steps:

1. Click the Windows 10 Start menu and select Settings (see Figure 2-28).

Figure 2-28. *Accessing Settings in Windows 10*

2. The Settings window appears; select Accounts.

3. Make sure you are signed into your Microsoft account (see Figure 2-29).

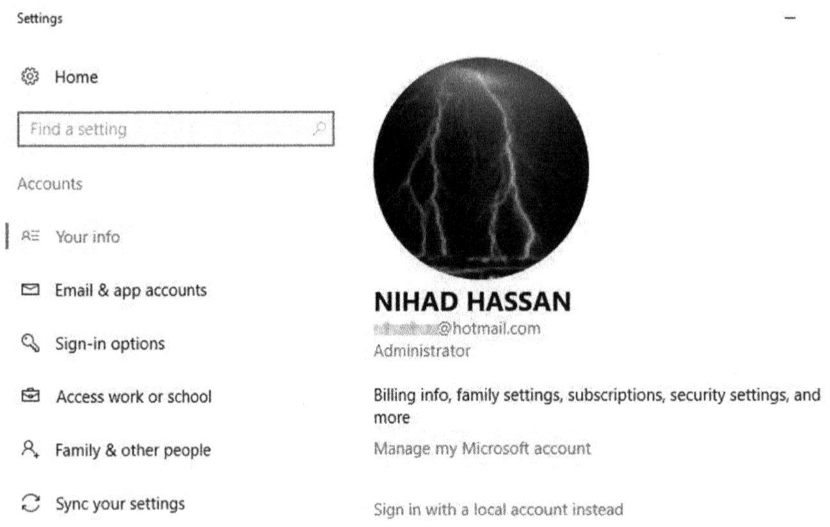

Settings   −

⚙ Home

Find a setting   🔎

Accounts

A≡ Your info

✉ Email & app accounts   **NIHAD HASSAN**
                                   ▓▓▓▓▓▓@hotmail.com
🔑 Sign-in options   Administrator

📧 Access work or school   Billing info, family settings, subscriptions, security settings, and
                                   more
👤 Family & other people   Manage my Microsoft account

🔁 Sync your settings   Sign in with a local account instead

Figure 2-29. *Making sure you are signed into your Microsoft account*

4. In the left panel, click "Family & other people." After that, click "Add a family member."

5. A pop-up window appears. Select the option "Add a child" and enter the child's e-mail. Click the Next button (see Figure 2-30).

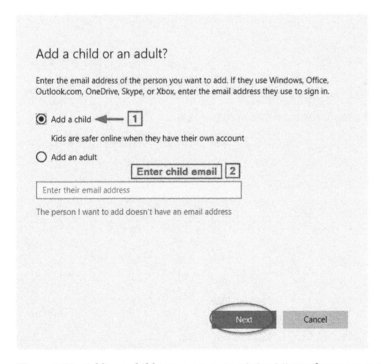

Figure 2-30. *Adding a child account to your existing Microsoft account to activate parental controls on Windows 10*

6. The next window asks you to confirm your choice; click the Confirm button.

7. The final window informs you that an invitation has been sent to your child's e-mail. To activate parental control on the child's account, your child needs to accept the invitation (see Figure 2-31) and then access his or her Windows account using this registered e-mail (Microsoft e-mail, Outlook, Live, or Hotmail).

Figure 2-31. *Invitation sent to child account to activate parental control*

Now, after your child has been successfully added to your family, you can access the Family Safety web site at `https://familysafety.microsoft.com` and log in with your Microsoft account credentials to view reports and edit the family safety settings for each child. You can also review the privacy settings for each child, add another child, and add another parent (e.g., your spouse) to monitor your child's activities.

Configuring a Windows safety account offers great features for parents to monitor their kids' online activity.

- Parents can add a small amount of money to a kid's Microsoft account to facilitate online shopping with small limits. No credit card is needed when your child wants to make online purchases, and Microsoft will set age limits on their purchases.

- If your kids are using a Windows mobile phone, parents can track them online and see where they are.

- Microsoft will generate online activity reports about all your kids' online activity. It can also block their access to specific apps, games, and web sites.

- It will also limit how much time your children can stay online.

It is highly advisable to use the Microsoft family safety account for your children; it is supported in modern Windows versions and offers a comprehensive solution to protect your children online.

If you do not like the Microsoft approach to protect your children's safety online, you can use third-party software for this purpose. There are many parental applications available, and some have great features for free. You can always search for parental software and compare their features. We will mention one free popular solution in the next section.

K9 Web Protection

This is a free Internet filter and parental control application for your home Windows or Mac computer. Its main features include blocking web sites, forcing safe searches on all major search engines, setting a time restriction on computer usage, and protecting against adult and malicious web sites. You need to register to get the free license to use this software. You can find K9 Web Protection at www1.k9webprotection.com.

Bear in mind that parental controls cannot block everything bad online, but they can help you to better monitor your children's activities online and assure that your discussion with them about Internet dangers is properly understood and followed.

Set Up a Family-Safe DNS

Another technical method to prevent viewing porn and malicious web sites is to use a safe DNS service. DNS works transparently in the background to convert human-readable web site names into computer-readable numerical IP addresses. By setting a safe DNS on your Windows PC, you can assure, to a large extent, that bad web sites will not open when your kids use the Internet.

There are many family-safe DNS providers; we will demonstrate how to use a popular free service called OpenDNS Family Shield, which comes preconfigured to block adult content without user intervention. Later we will show you how to use a simple program that can change between different safe DNS providers.

To configure your Windows to use OpenDNS Family Shield, follow these steps:

1. Go to Control Panel ➤ Network and Sharing Center and click "Change adapter settings" on the left side. Right-click the network connection you're using and select Properties.

2. Highlight Internet Protocol Version 4 (TCP/IPv4) and click Properties.

3. Select "Use the following DNS server addresses" and type the OpenDNS addresses **208.67.222.222** and **208.67.220.220** in the "Preferred DNS server" and "Alternate DNS server" fields (see Figure 2-32).

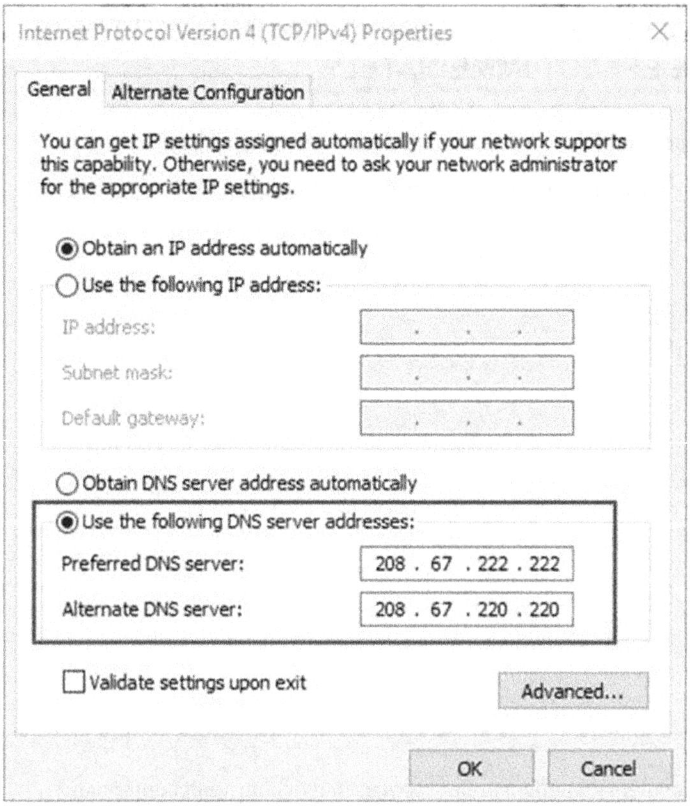

Figure 2-32. *Using a custom DNS server for your current connection*

4. Click OK, then Close, and then Close again. Finally, close the Network Connections window.

> # NOTE! ENSURE THAT YOUR NEW DNS CONFIGURATION SETTINGS TAKE EFFECT IMMEDIATELY

Open the command prompt as the administrator (right-click it and select Run as Administrator).

Run the following command at the command line and hit Enter (see Figure 2-33):

```
ipconfig /flushdns
```

Figure 2-33. Flushing DNS on Windows to force new DNS settings to take effect immediately

There are other family-safe DNS providers that offer similar services in blocking adult content and fraudulent web sites. Examples include Yandex.DNS (https://dns.yandex.com) and Norton ConnectSafe (https://dns.norton.com). Configuring Windows to use the DNS of these services is like what you already did previously. However, there is a tool that can simplify this process and change between different DNS services automatically.

DNS Angel (see Figure 2-34) is a portable freeware application for changing the DNS setting automatically in Windows. You can download it from www.sordum.org/8127/dns-angel-v1-4/.

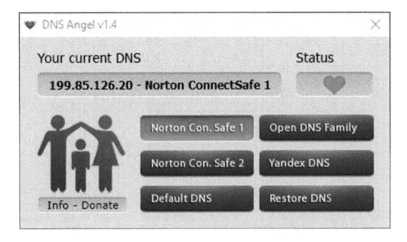

Figure 2-34. DNS Angel used to change between different DNS services automatically on Windows

■ **Warning**   You can configure your router to use a safe DNS. This will effectively allow you to use the same settings on all connected devices on your local network. However, local DNS settings in Windows will override the one inserted in your router, so if your tech-savvy kid changes the DNS setting on the local machine, this will override the one used on your router. To prevent your children from changing the DNS setting on Windows, create a limited user account for them without administrator access.

Track Yourself Online

It is important to track yourself online on a regular basis. This helps you to find where you are showing up online and what others are saying about you. This section covers the free online services that can help you with this.

Google Alerts

Google Alerts is a notification service offered by Google; it works by sending an e-mail to the user when it finds new results such as web pages, newspaper articles, blogs, or scientific research that matches the user's entered search terms. You must be logged into your Google account to create a new alert.

You can set up a new alert at https://www.google.com/alerts. In the box at the top, enter a topic you want to follow. You can create as many alerts as you like and adjust the settings to be notified on a daily, weekly, or "as it happens" basis (see Figure 2-35).

Figure 2-35. *Setting up Google Alerts to get notified when your search terms are mentioned online*

The free people search engine at `https://pipl.com` is another web site to search about yourself and other people online. It allows you to search by name, address, or e-mail and has the most comprehensive database of people profiles online.

Auditing Facebook Profile

Many users have been using Facebook for a long time. Some people have thousands of likes and posts on their Timelines. Humans have a tendency to forget their previous online actions, though. For instance, any person who previously posted his or her political opinion or comment (aggressively) may find that it will be more suitable to hide previous online actions for many reasons. Performing a check on every post and action conducted on Facebook is a daunting task, especially if the user has been active on Facebook for a long time.

Stalkscan (`http://stalkscan.com/en/`) is a free online service that allows anyone to look up any Facebook user's public information. It is a great auditing tool for Facebook profiles and allows any person to see previously posted images, comments, events attended in the past in addition to future events planning to attend, places where they "checked in," and everything they "like" online (posts, video, pictures, etc.).

This tool shows you just how easy it is to find any public information on Facebook, so be careful before posting anything publicly online.

Check Whether Someone Has Taken Your Personal Picture

Sometimes you may encounter a case where someone took your personal pictures (or your child's pictures) from your Facebook profile and used them on a profile or blog without your consent or even used them for the wrong reasons. Reverse Image Search helps you to find any photo you have uploaded to the Internet along with a list of all other web sites where this photo appears.

TinEye (`https://www.tineye.com`) is a reverse search engine with more than 17.4 billion images indexed (at the time of writing). You can upload the image you want to search for online or simply enter its URL, and TinEye will find all the locations and web sites where this image is located.

Google has a similar service to search for images online. To use it, follow these steps:

1. Go to `https://images.google.com`.

2. In the search bar, click the camera icon (see Figure 2-36).

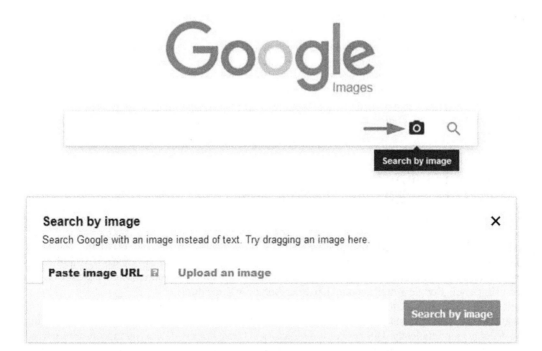

Figure 2-36. *Using a Google image search to find all instances of a selected picture online*

3. You can either upload a picture from your computer or enter its URL to search for it.

4. Google will return every instance of that image it can find.

Another free service to conduct an image search is `https://www.imageraider.com`. This web site allows you to search popular search engines like Google, Bing, and Yandex to find all web sites using your photos.

A good practice when publishing personal photos online is to watermark them. This allows you to prove ownership of your photos. There are many tools and online services that offer watermarking for free. `https://www.watermarquee.com` offers free online watermarking, as does Picasa (retired but available) at `http://filehippo.com/download_picasa`.

Check Your Data Breach Status

Almost every week the press announces a data breach that hit a major web site. To tighten your security, it is essential to check whether your account was among the ones that got breached. Fortunately, there are many free services to check whether your account was compromised.

`https://haveibeenpwned.com` is a free resource for anyone to quickly assess whether they may have been put at risk because of an online account being compromised or "pwned" in a data breach. It is run by security researcher Troy Hunt, who tracks data breaches. To use this web site, enter the e-mail address or username in the search box to check whether you have an account that has been compromised in a data breach.

You can also sign up for alerts tied to your e-mail address so you can be notified as soon as another breach is detected by clicking "Notify me" at the top of the page.

`https://breachalarm.com` offers a similar service; it allows you to check anonymously if your password has been posted online and sign up for e-mail notifications about future password hacks that affect you.

It is highly advisable whenever you hear about a data breach in the press and you have accounts at a company that has been breached that you change your affected account's password. Checking the previously mentioned sites to see whether your account was stolen is a good thing, but it is important to act promptly and change your affected account's password. Remember, do not use the same password on two different accounts.

Delete All Your Online Profiles

If you decide to delete your online presence from the Internet and return to the "offline age," there is a free service that can help you achieve this. Deseat.me is a service that lets you see all the web sites you're signed up for and asks if you'd like to delete them or unsubscribe. It asks for your e-mail address and password so it can scan for the sites you're signed up to. The sign-in must done using a Google account (using Google's OAuth protocol); this makes this service limited because it requires users to have a Google e-mail address that is used for all their online accounts. This will result in discarding online accounts where the user registered using a non-Google e-mail account like Microsoft or AOL account.

Another value-add security service that can help you to find all major web sites that you may have accounts at is `http://backgroundchecks.org/justdeleteme/`. It is not like Deseat.me in terms of searching for online accounts automatically. This service is a directory of direct links to delete your account from web services. It offers a direct link and some information on how to disable your account for each listed online service.

Remove the Offending Content

Sometimes your personal information is made available to the public without your consent, or it may happen that someone writes something inappropriate or false about you that may affect your reputation and you want to remove it. Removing the offending content or even personal data is not an easy task online. The nature of the Internet allows the information to be replicated quickly. (For example, posting a photo to your Facebook Timeline will make it appear on all your friends' feeds, and if some of your friends share it using the public state, it can replicate and appears in the timeline of millions of people.)

Removing yourself completely from the Internet is extremely difficult, and no one can guarantee 100 percent successful removal. However, you can minimize your online footprint in many ways and remove offending content.

We already covered how to delete yourself from major social media sites, but remember, you may have been using some less famous sites in the past and forgotten about it. The same thing applies to shopping web sites (e.g., Amazon and eBay). Your information is still available and must be deleted to minimize your online footprint.

To delete old accounts, you need to handle each one separately. Each one should have an option in the settings area to cancel, remove, and deactivate your current account. If you have problems deleting it, you can search the Internet for information on how to remove it using *how to remove my X account* (replace the *X* with your account provider name). For example, use *how to remove my Reddit account* and Google will return detailed instructions accordingly.

If you cannot delete your account or the account providers don't supply such an option, change your real information to something fake or random.

Data collection sites are another threat to your online privacy. These web sites gather your information from primary sources, such as public records from government entities, social media sites, Whois records of registered domain names, and any source that is publicly available. They sell this information to interested third parties and to advertisement companies. There are plenty of data collection web sites (Intelius, LexisNexis, PeopleFinders, Spoke, WhitePages, BeenVerified, DOBSearch, Pipl, Radaris, Mylife, Wink, LookUp, PeekYou, and Waatp, to name a few!), and removing yourself from them is a daunting task. This is why we always emphasize thinking twice before posting personal information about yourself online. For instance, we will give an example of how to remove yourself from one of these web sites. Unfortunately, not all data collection sites have similar removal procedures. You need to check each one's privacy policy agreement to see how you can remove yourself from it.

To remove your record from the Intelius database, go to `https://www.intelius.com/optout.php`. Fill in the form and submit your details (you need to provide an acceptable ID to validate your ownership of the data you want to remove).

There are some companies that will offer to delete your personal information from the Internet for a price. We will not endorse anyone for this task; you can always search online about such companies and compare their features and prices.

If someone has written something bad or offensive about you and you want to remove it, you need to follow different procedures than what you have already learned about. For instance, if you encounter a blog post about you and it contains inaccurate information that may damage your personal or business reputation, you can ask the web site that publishes it to remove it. Here is a list of methods you can use to remove false, unlawful, and damaging information from the Internet:

- Most web sites that allow its users to post their opinions or to make online reviews about products and services have set guidelines (often called *community* and *review guidelines*) that must be followed by all users when posting content. If someone violates their policies, you can "flag" or "report" the content to the site moderator, who will act to see whether this content is violating the site's terms of use. For example, Amazon allows its users to report abuse about any item review if you find it inappropriate (see Figure 2-37).

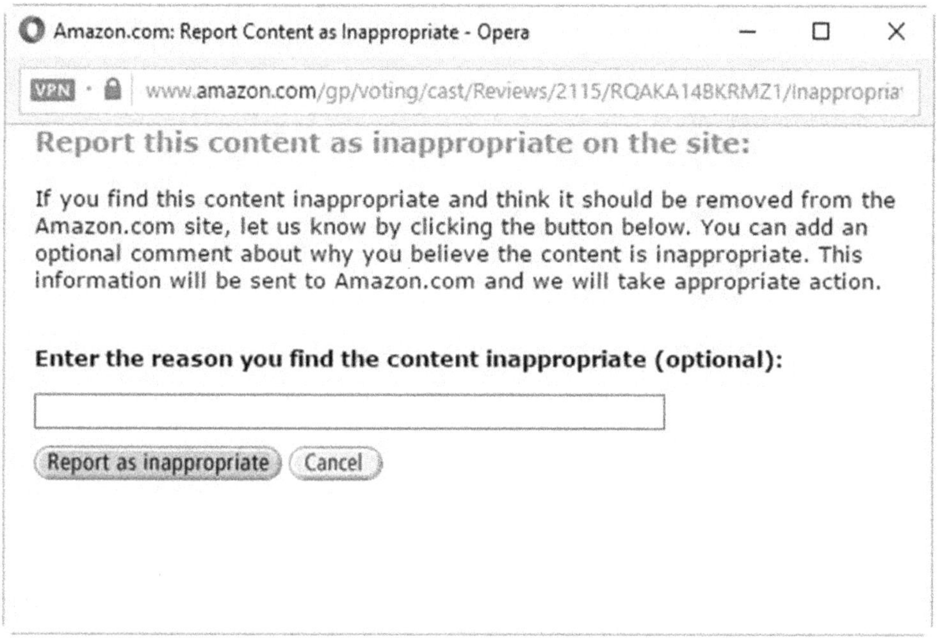

Figure 2-37. *Users can report abuse about any customer review posted on Amazon.com if inappropriate*

- If you have images or other copyright content that has been copied and used elsewhere without your consent, you can ask the web sites that host this content to remove it. If they do not respond, you can file a complaint according to the Digital Millennium Copyright Act, which preserves your rights when it comes to content that belongs to you.

- You can make direct contact with the web site owner asking to remove the damaging content. Of course, you should have a legal reason for this. It is advisable to contact the people in charge, not the person who wrote the damaging post. You can find out who is responsible for a web site by going to its About Us and Contact Us page. If you do not find the proper contact you are searching for, you can send your e-mail to the site webmaster (check to get the webmaster contact information at www.whois.com/whois/).

NOTE! WHO IS HOSTING THIS?

If you can't contact the person responsible for the web site that published the damaging content about you, you can try to contact the web site hosting service that hosts the site. Their contact information can be obtained by going to www.whoishostingthis.com/ and entering the URL of the web site. The hosting provider name will appear along with the URL (see Figure 2-38). Try to contact them directly because the hosting providers are more efficient in removing illegal content from their networks than web site owners.

darknessgate.com
is hosted by OVH
SAS

Hosting provider: OVH SAS
WHOIS: Click Here
IP Address: 193.70.110.132
Name Servers:
ns1.tsken.net
ns2.tsken.net

Figure 2-38. *Using whoishostingthis.com to find the name of the hosting provider of a specific web site*

- If the content contains your sensitive information, you have the right to get it removed. Google allows users to remove their personal content from its search results. To see the Google removal policy, check this page: `https://support.google.com/websearch/answer/2744324`. To remove information from Google, go to `https://support.google.com/legal/troubleshooter/1114905`. You can check what Google accepts you to remove (see Figure 2-39). To remove nude pictures of yourself from Google search results, visit `https://support.google.com/websearch/troubleshooter/3111061#ts=2889054%2C2889099%2C2889064%2C3143868%2C6256340%2C6256363`.

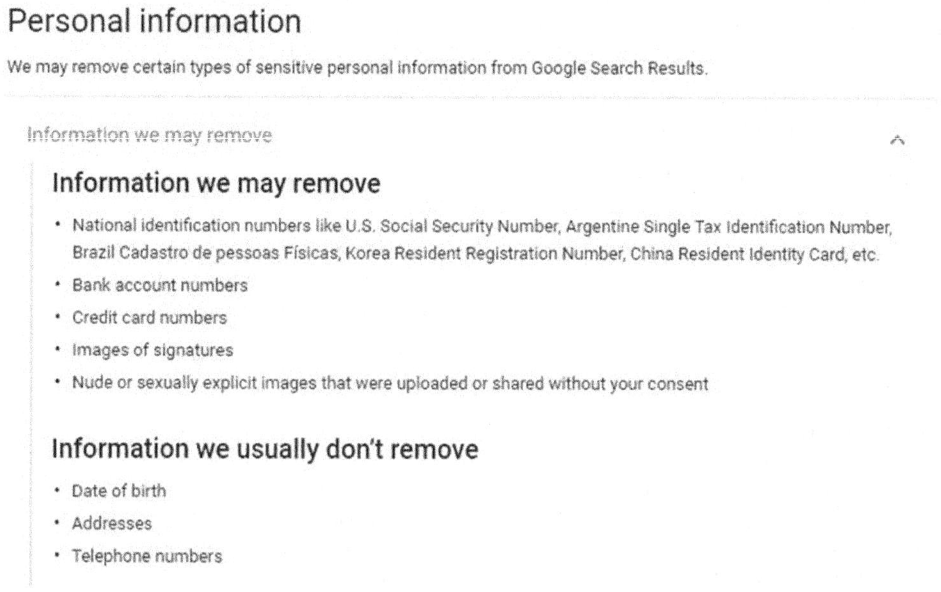

Personal information

We may remove certain types of sensitive personal information from Google Search Results.

Information we may remove ⌃

Information we may remove

- National identification numbers like U.S. Social Security Number, Argentine Single Tax Identification Number, Brazil Cadastro de pessoas Físicas, Korea Resident Registration Number, China Resident Identity Card, etc.
- Bank account numbers
- Credit card numbers
- Images of signatures
- Nude or sexually explicit images that were uploaded or shared without your consent

Information we usually don't remove

- Date of birth
- Addresses
- Telephone numbers

Figure 2-39. *Information that can be removed by Google*

- If you have personal old information published online and you successfully manage to remove it but it still appears in Google search results (because Google cached it), you can ask Google to remove this old content by filling out the form at `https://www.google.com/webmasters/tools/removals?pli=1`.

- The final method to lower the impact of offending content about you is to push such content from Google's first-page results. You can achieve this by posting content online and optimizing it with proper search engine optimization techniques to make it appear in the first Google result page.

▪ **Note** Remember, you cannot fight over someone's opinion because you simply do not like what he or she said about you. The freedom of speech is protected in democratic countries, and you cannot do anything about this.

Cloud Storage Security

More and more companies are adopting cloud storage solutions to reduce the costs of storing and processing data locally. Cloud storage solutions help employees access data anytime and from anywhere using any device type with low IT overhead. As more enterprises shift their data to the cloud, companies should take considerable steps to improve their cloud storage security and keep their sensitive data secure.

With the wide adoption of cloud storage solutions and the reduction of its costs, individuals also are more willing to save their sensitive data in the cloud. To secure cloud storage accounts, the following security measures should be implemented:

- Use strong passwords to secure your cloud accounts. These passwords should be stored in a safe location (e.g., using password manager software). At the beginning of this chapter, we thoroughly covered how to create and store passwords.

- Enable two-factor authentication to access your cloud account. For example, use a password and your phone to receive a security code.

- Use antivirus/anti-exploit software and keep them up-to-date along with your Windows OS.

- Cloud storage providers allow you to share specific files with your friends/colleagues. When you provide access permission, take care to revoke this access when sharing is no longer needed. It is advisable to give other people read-only access permission.

- Storing your data in the cloud does not mean it is 100 percent secure. It is highly advisable to keep a backup copy of all data in a safe location off-site.

- Do not upload anything to the cloud without encrypting it first locally! Some cloud storage providers offer the encryption feature to encrypt/decrypt your data while in the cloud before granting you access. This is not suitable for paranoid security people, as cryptographic keys will be stored by the cloud provider and can be compromised or taken by other third parties (e.g., intelligence agencies), which will put your data at risk. In Chapter 5 we will teach you everything you need to know to secure your data through encryption techniques.

- Even after encrypting your data, it is not preferable to use cloud storage to store sensitive data.

- Encrypt the connection between your machine and the cloud storage provider, and do not use a public Wi-Fi connection to upload your data to the cloud without proper encryption (e.g., using a VPN connection; more on that in Chapter 4).

- Do not upload business documents to free cloud storage or free file-sharing services. Some employees may make this mistake and upload sensitive business data to cloud providers that don't meet minimum security standards. This will effectively put company data at risk.

- Always read the privacy policy and terms of service agreement of the cloud provider to make sure that no terms are violating your privacy when using the service.

When it comes to security, remember that technology depends on human factors to make it work well. Be careful to not reveal sensitive data about your accounts (e.g., via social engineering attacks) and do not give applications installed on your mobile phone access to your confidential data.

■ **Note**   MyPermissions (`https://mypermissions.org`) is an app that allows you to know how many apps have access to your personal information on your smartphone.

On August 31, 2014, a hacker's invasion of dozens of celebrities' iCloud accounts led to the embarrassing leak of nude photos of about 100 celebrity women and one man. The hacker took advantage of a security flaw in Apple's online backup service, iCloud. Many online services lock someone out after several unsuccessful attempts to log in, but Apple's Find My iPhone app and iCloud did not. That has been changed by Apple in the aftermath of the nude celebrity photo scandal.

The attack was successful because most celebrities were using weak passwords and using the same password to secure their iCloud account and Find My iPhone app. The hacker first found the Find My iPhone app password and then used the same password to access the iCloud account.[9]

Internet of Things Security

Network-connected devices such as mechanical equipment, computing devices, and other services that can access and share data across the Internet constitute the Internet of Things (IoT). Nowadays, everything is connected to the Internet, from refrigerators to air-conditioning systems to coffee makers While these IoT devices can make our lives easier, they also create new security risks if compromised by malicious hackers.

Poorly secured IoT devices such as web cameras, baby monitors, and other home appliances can pose a great risk to individuals and the nation. As we already mentioned in Chapter 1, on October 21, 2016, a series of distributed denial-of-service (DDoS) attacks caused a widespread disruption of legitimate Internet activity in the United States. This huge attack was caused by exploiting vulnerabilities in a large number of IoT devices across the globe.

While the benefits of IoT are undeniable, the reality is that security is not keeping up with the pace of innovation. To enjoy the benefit of IoT devices, a set of security measures must be implemented by individuals and companies to avoid turning the IoT innovation into a catastrophe.

- Do not connect your device to the Internet unless there is a need for this. For example, if connecting your refrigerator to the Internet does not bring additional benefits to you, disconnect it. It is also advisable to turn such devices off when you are not going to use them frequently (e.g., turning off router when you are on a vacation).

- Isolate IoT devices in a separate network. Create a new virtual network and let your IoT devices use it. This will effectively help you to isolate your computing devices (which contains your personal data) from other home appliance devices.

- Use a strong, complex password for each IoT device. Do not use the same password on two devices.

- Change the device's default username and password. IoT devices come with default usernames and passwords known by hackers; you must change these before connecting your device to the Internet.

- Many IoT devices rely on cloud storage providers to store their data in the cloud. Make sure to read the device manual carefully and know what kind of data is going to the cloud. Enable encryption of the data before the device uploads it to the cloud. If you suspect that your data is not secure, do not use this device type and trade it for something else more secure.

- Businesses should prevent their employees from bringing their IoT devices to work. Wearable IoT devices such as smart watches, head-mounted displays, and others can impose a security risk on sensitive company data.

- Read the manual of the IoT device before connecting it to the Internet. Most devices allow you to enable encryption, which can add an additional layer of security to your device.

- Keep your IoT device up-to-date by visiting the device settings; you can also register your device on the manufacturer's web site to get regular updates. The device manufacturer may discover a security flaw and launch a patch to close the security hole. Make sure to close it before hackers exploit it.

- Disable Universal Plug and Play (UPnP). UPnP allows devices on your home network to discover each other; this allows outside hackers to take control of your local network if they successfully manage to compromise one device. UPnP can be easily disabled in your router settings.

- If your IoT device supports Telnet and SSH services, make sure to disable them. This will prevent hackers and malware from gaining access to your device through such services.

- Secure your Wi-Fi network as we already mentioned previously because most IoT devices will connect through a wireless connection.

- Purchase IoT devices from companies with a reputation for providing secure devices.

IoT adoption will increase in both speed and scope and will impact virtually all sectors of our society. It is crucial to study the features of IoT devices before buying them, especially the security features (in terms of the amount of sensitive data collected and the costs of remedying the security vulnerabilities). You should also make sure to configure the IoT device properly, as we already mentioned, to strengthen it against outside attacks.

WARNING! SECURITY RISKS OF (IOT) WEARABLE DEVICES

Wearable technology is on the rise for both personal and business use; such devices include any electronic devices that can be worn on the human body. Examples include smart watches, glasses, contact lenses, e-textiles, smart fabrics, and many more. These wearable devices can perform many of the same computing tasks as mobile phones and laptop computers.

Wearable devices impose great security risk on both individuals and business organizations. The following risks are associated with wearable technology:

- A majority of wearable devices don't encrypt their data by default. This will leave user data at risk.

- They can be used as spying instruments. Some wearable devices such as smart watches can record voice and video in addition to taking pictures. Sensitive business data can be leaked in this way.

- Many wearable devices can be synchronized with other computing devices such as tablets and smartphones through Wi-Fi and Bluetooth. This creates a wide open possibility for hackers to attack such weak secure connections.

- Medical devices can leak sensitive information about their users' health status if attacked by malicious hackers.

- Some wearable devices have GPS sensors and can record your geolocation data.

- Wearable devices are relatively easy to steal and lose. After falling into the wrong hand, it can reveal sensitive data about its owner.

It is strongly advised that companies prevent employees from bringing wearable devices to work, and if a company allows its employees to use such devices at work, it should prevent them from connecting them to the company's internal network. They should have a policy that governs the usage of such devices at work.

Physical Security Threats and Countermeasures

No matter how much effort you spend to secure your digital devices by following all the precautionary steps already mentioned, you could still find everything vanished before your eyes if your computing device or hardware gets stolen or unauthorized physical access to it took place while it was unattended. Physical threats are not only from theft; other threats include natural disasters, breakage, power surges, poured coffee over the computer, and anything else that can damage your computing equipment and prevent you from accessing the information stored on it.

Performing an IT security risk assessment should be an important part of any company's IT security precautions. It helps businesses to understand and quantify the risks to IT and the possible consequences each could have.

To counter such threats, business should create a plan to act promptly when something goes wrong. To begin, a company's IT staff members should first list all its IT equipment, then they should assess the risk to each individual item, and finally they should access each item's importance in terms of how much damage it will bring to the company if a failure takes place.

IT equipment includes the following and more:

- Computers (desktops)

- Portable devices (laptops, netbooks, tablets, personal digital assistants, USB [flash] drives, compact discs, smartphones)

- Servers

- Backup storage devices (tapes, external HDD)

- Printers and multifunctional devices (MFDs)

- Photocopier and photo printer

- Projectors

- Digital camera

- Digital duplicator

- Telephone handset

- Internet-connecting devices such as routers, switches, hubs, wireless access points

Now you should assess how the following risks would affect each item already mentioned; this will also help you to assess each item's importance on the overall business functions and continuity.

- Theft and loss of hardware devices

- Damaged equipment because of excessive heat, high humidity, water, or any liquids

- Damaged equipment (computers may fall on the ground and become damaged)

- Natural disaster (fire, flood, earthquake, tornados)

- Software failure

- Intentional destruction of data (e.g., vandalism and arson)

- Malware attacks (e.g., ransomware that encrypts disk drives and prevents access to stored data)

Your next step is to risk-assess the potential of these occurrences and the impact for each incident and overall business continuity. This will help you create a complete scenario on what is tolerable and what is not.

Individuals also suffer from physical threats. Theft and hardware defects can prevent them from accessing data stored on computing devices. For example, laptops that are left unattended without being secured by a cable lock can be quickly stolen. In today's digital age, most individuals carry at least one portable computing device with them. To secure mobile devices, use these tips:

- When using your laptop in public places, secure it by using a cable lock attached to a heavy object (e.g., desk, table, lighten column in gardens).

- Do not leave your office without locking it when you have portable devices left inside it.

- Do not store your company's sensitive files on your computing device without proper permission, and make sure to encrypt everything if you can store such data on your device.

- Do not store your sensitive/personal data on mobile devices without proper encryption. For instance, if you take personal pictures with your mobile phone, make sure to shift this data to your computer at home on a regular basis.

- Use a password to protect your mobile device from unauthorized access.

- Do not leave your device unattended in public places.

- Do not turn your Bluetooth connection on in public places, and if necessary, run it for a short period of time to receive or send urgent files.

- Turn off Wi-Fi when you are not using it. Be careful when using public hotspots and encrypt your connection using VPN.

- Keep a written record of the make, model, serial number, MAC address, and other pertinent information about your portable device in case it gets stolen.

Disposing of Old Computers

There is a large amount of computer equipment that is simply thrown away because people don't have the time to get it ready to donate or the equipment is no longer desirable to any consumers. You should make sure that your computing device's hard disk is wiped securely and does not contain any sensitive data that can be recovered later using forensic analysis techniques.

Most ordinary computer users do not know that deleting files from a hard disk, emptying the Recycle Bin, and even formatting the hard disk drive will not erase the data completely. There are many recovery tools that can be employed to recover this data. For instance, use these tips before selling or throwing away your old computing device:

- Ensure you destroy data stored on a disk completely using specialized software (also known as *disk wiping*). Data on the disk includes your main visible data and remnants of data left after deleting old files. Both should be cleaned completely.

- For Windows machines, you can turn on BitLocker encryption of all disk partitions, set a complex password, and then format the disk. This will make recovering data near impossible. We will show you how to use encryption techniques in Chapter 5.

- Use physical destruction techniques to destroy the hard disk drive/solid-state drive when you want to achieve the maximum security possible.

NOTE! TOOLS TO WIPE YOUR DISK DRIVE

Different programs are available to destroy the data stored on disk drives. Here are the most popular ones:

Eraser (`https://eraser.heidi.ie`): This program removes sensitive data from your hard drive by overwriting it several times with carefully selected patterns. Eraser is free software, and its source code is released under the GNU General Public License.

BleachBit (`www.bleachbit.org`): This program includes advanced features such as shredding files to prevent recovery, wiping free disk space to hide traces of files deleted by other applications, and acting as a privacy guard.

Another cheap physical method to destroy your old hard disk completely, without using a degausser, which considered expensive for individual user, is to use a hammer and smash your disk drive into small pieces.

The security risks of recovering sensitive data from disk drives are applicable to more than just computers because there is a lot of IT office equipment that stores and processes data; recovering such data can impose great security risk on companies if it falls into the wrong hands. An example is an office copier or multifunction printer; whenever documents are copied or sent to the printer, they are backed up to a hard drive inside the copier. This isn't a problem, but if the printer suffers from a technical problem and needs to be sent for maintenance (or simply resold or sent for parts) and if the data stored (or remnants of it) in the printer's hard drive is not erased securely, this will effectively expose your sensitive documents that were previously printed to danger.

Mobile phones also store a considerable amount of sensitive information about their users. When getting rid of your old device, it's important to take steps to help ensure that no sensitive data is left for recovery.

All smartphones have a setting that allows you to return the device to its factory reset. This will wipe all data stored on your device. To know how to do this for your device, search for the topic on the device manufacturer's web site or consult the device manual.

> **Warning**   Do not trust the reset function. This does not assure the removal of all the stored and potentially sensitive data objects.

The second thing you need to erase in your smartphone is the SD card; you can remove the SD card from the phone, attach it to your computer, and erase it securely using one of the tools already mentioned to erase data on a computer's hard drive.

> **Note**   Data destruction techniques in Windows will be covered in the next chapter.

Educate Yourself About Cybersecurity

As technology becomes more intertwined with our daily lives, it provides convenience but also increases our exposure to threats and risks. No one can predict to what heights such risks can reach. There are many security threats online that are still impossible to detect by security software. You, the user, are still the first and last line of defense against cyber-criminals trying to access your private data.

The importance of educating yourself about cybersecurity cannot be stressed enough; the more you know and understand about this domain, the better your chances of staying protected are. Your cyber-knowledge is essential to your safety and privacy on the Internet. The following resources will help you to stay up-to-date with the latest online threats and will broaden your knowledge about the subject. Of course, you can always search online for anything you came across and do not fully understand.

- Read specialized books about cyber-security and digital privacy. It is preferable to read books that offer practical guidelines with adequate theoretical information. A great example is the book you are reading right now!

- Watch cybersecurity online courses; there are many for free, and they offer excellent content suitable for ordinary Internet users. Check out the author's portal for a list of such courses: www.darknessgate.com/category/technical-training.

- Check out Internet resources. Many web sites offer detailed information and best practices on how to protect yourself online. The following list includes some of them:

  - www.darknessgate.com

  - https://staysafeonline.org

  - https://myshadow.org

  - https://www.digitaldefenders.org/digitalfirstaid

  - https://www.google.com/safetycenter/everyone/start

- Stay up-to-date on the latest recent online threats (this may not be practical for nonexperienced users). The following web sites offer such services:

  - https://www.fireeye.com/current-threats.html

  - http://map.norsecorp.com

Use Free and Open Source Software

As software prices become higher, some people may tend to install illegal programs (patched and cracked programs) on their computers to reduce costs. We already discussed the danger of installing illegal software, as the majority contains malware and other software that can track user activities online and even send keystrokes to malware operators.

This book will cover the Windows OS only when talking about operating system tools and functions. It is not practical to advise you to use an open source OS like Linux to save the cost of Windows! However, what most users care about when buying new software are the programs (productivity programs) that they are going to use to get their job done. There is plenty of free and open source software (FOSS) that can replace paid software. Microsoft Office and other drawing programs from third-party companies can be easily replaced with something free and open source instead of installing illegal software with security risks. Table 2-2 lists the main free alternatives to Windows commercial programs needed by most users.

Table 2-2. *Free Alternative Software for Windows*

Program Name	URL	Task
FreeOffice	`www.freeoffice.com/en`	Alternative to Microsoft Office
LibreOffice	`https://www.libreoffice.org`	Alternative to Microsoft Office
PeaZip	`www.peazip.org`	File archiver utility
PortableApps	`http://portableapps.com`	+300 apps covering all areas
GnuCash	`www.gnucash.org`	Personal and small-business financial accounting software
Thunderbird	`www.mozilla.org/thunderbird`	Free e-mail application
GIMP	`https://www.gimp.org`	GNU image-editing program
Pidgin	`www.pidgin.im`	Instant messaging

Summary

This was a long chapter full of advice on how to deal with today's online threats. We began by talking about the importance of installing security software on user computers. There are many products out there that perform great functions; however, they are not all equal in protection. We gave you some selection criteria to help you select the best solution according to your current needs.

Selecting a strong and complex password is vital to protecting your digital accounts. Unfortunately, many people still underestimate its importance. We focused on this and gave guidelines and tips.

The first thing most computer users do after logging into their machines is to open the web browser to access the Internet. Your web browser knows a lot about you, and we gave fast tips to secure your browsing sessions. In later chapters we will cover more techniques for safe browsing.

We also talked about e-mail security and social engineering attacks. Such attacks have become more sophisticated, and many people and companies' employees have fallen victim to them.

Children's online security is vital to parents, so we covered practical tips and suggested tools to monitor and protect children from cyber-threats.

Cloud storage, Internet of Things devices (IoT), and physical threats create risks for your sensitive data and online activities; we mentioned threats and suggested countermeasures to mitigate such threats.

We ended this chapter by stressing the importance of educating yourself to become more computer security literate. Being properly educated can only help in making an informed decision when figuring out how to properly protect your digital assets.

Cybersecurity is no longer buried far away in the tech section of newspapers and web sites. It has become first-page headline news and will remain so for the foreseeable future. Computer security is concerned with protecting computing systems and the data that stores and processes it. Without proper knowledge of the main areas of computer security, businesses cannot do their jobs, and individuals cannot benefit from the technology revolution to enjoy their modern lives.

Protection is never 100 percent, but knowledge is everything. In the coming chapters, we will delve more into the technical side of digital privacy to teach you how you can use a plethora of tools and techniques to protect your personal information and prevent identity theft against the ever-evolving cyber-threats.

Bibliography

National Resource Centre for Free and Open Source Software (NRCFOSS), "Benefits of using FOSS." http://nrcfoss.org.in/resources/benefits-of-using-foss.

State of California Department of Justice, "Online Privacy." https://oag.ca.gov/privacy/online-privacy.

Dmitri Vitaliev, "Digital Security & Privacy for Human Rights Defenders." Frontlinedefenders.org, February 23, 2016. https://www.frontlinedefenders.org/en/resource-publication/digital-security-privacy-human-rights-defenders.

Notes

1. David Fitzpatrick and Drew Griffin, "Cyber-Extortion Losses Skyrocket, Says FBI." CNN.com, April 15, 2016. http://money.cnn.com/2016/04/15/technology/ransomware-cyber-security/).

2. Luis Ayala, *Cybersecurity Lexicon*. New York: Apress, 2016. p. 139.

3. Betanews, "Want to launch your own DDoS attacks on a website? $200 will get you everything you need." Betanews, July 23, 2014. http://betanews.com/2014/07/23/want-to-launch-your-own-ddos-attacks-on-a-website-200-will-get-you-everything-you-need/.

4. Camera & Imaging Products Association, "CIPA DC- 008-Translation- 2016." July 2016. www.cipa.jp/std/documents/e/DC-008-Translation-2016-E.pdf.

5. The Sudbury Neutrino Observatory Institute (SNOI), "IPTC Tags." April 7, 2015. www.sno.phy.queensu.ca/~phil/exiftool/TagNames/IPTC.html.

6. US-CERT, "Report Phishing Sites." https://www.us-cert.gov/report-phishing.

7. Violet Blue, "The FBI recommends you cover your laptop's webcam, for good reason." Engadget. https://www.engadget.com/2016/09/23/the-fbi-recommends-you-cover-your-laptops-webcam-good-reasons/.

8. BBC, "Facebook 'hack' victim exposes passport scam." BBC, June 29, 2016. www.bbc.com/news/technology-36661557.

9. Alan Duke, "5 Things to know about the celebrity nude photo hacking scandal." CNN, October 12, 2014. http://edition.cnn.com/2014/09/02/showbiz/hacked-nude-photos-five-things/.

CHAPTER 3

■ ■ ■

Windows Security

How to Secure Your Windows Box

The operating system (OS) is what all your applications run on. In fact, you cannot run any program except firmware (which contains hardware-specific information) on your PC without installing an operating system first. No matter what precautions you've taken to secure your PC, if your OS gets compromised, all the applications running on it will become vulnerable, and all the data stored on its hard drive will be exposed to unauthorized access.

Cyber-threats targeting the operating system can arrive from two sources.

- *Logical threats from malware*: These generally come after installing or executing some malicious code, usually downloaded from the Web.

- *Physical threats*: Here the attacker or the device (e.g., USB memory) gains direct access to your computer to perform a crafted, malicious action.

Configuring your operating system to be more secure should be your first step when protecting your digital privacy and security, before accessing the Internet or installing any security software. This chapter will give you recommendations and best practices for configuring your Windows machine to become more secure and resistant to external unknown and known threats. Please note the recommendations in this chapter are not exhaustive, as you can implement more than what is covered here; in addition, you can ignore some according to the threats you are currently facing.

We will begin by giving general hardening techniques for the Windows OS. Later in the chapter, we will cover privacy settings related to Windows 10 only.

Harden Your OS

Before we begin sharing our recommendations to secure Windows machines, it is necessary to discuss the best hardware to integrate with the security features available in modern Windows editions (Windows 10 and newer).

Windows 10 comes equipped with enhanced security features for encryption and authentication. This is in addition to its native support to stop sophisticated malware such as bootkits and rootkits from attacking the native system before Windows can boot. Windows 10 is the most secure version of Windows ever created, and it is highly recommended that you stop using the older versions (such as 8, 7, Vista, and XP). To use the modern security features in Windows 10, though, your hardware needs to support the following security features (or at least some of them):

- Trusted Platform Module (TPM) version 2.0.

- Unified Extensible Firmware Interface (UEFI). This is the BIOS replacement.

© Nihad A. Hassan and Rami Hijazi 2017
N. A. Hassan and R. Hijazi, *Digital Privacy and Security Using Windows*, DOI 10.1007/978-1-4842-2799-2_3

- Fingerprint scanner.

- Integrated smart card reader.

- Kensington lock slot to physically secure your PC in public places (i.e., chain your computer to a desk with a cable).

- If the computer manufacturer offers the PC with Windows preinstalled on it, make sure that the Windows edition supports BitLocker drive encryption (Windows 10 supports BitLocker on Pro, Enterprise, and Education editions).

- When installing Windows, it is highly recommended that you buy the latest version with an edition that supports BitLocker drive encryption. Currently, the newest version is 10.

A retinal scanner and 3D camera for facial recognition are highly recommended so you can activate the advanced biometric features of the Windows 10 Hello feature. However, their existence in modern computers is still limited.

■ **Note**   We have not described the intended benefits of each recommended security component mentioned in the previous list. In Chapter 5, we will discuss the benefit of the features in detail and how they can help you secure your Windows machine.

You can buy some advanced hardware security components separately and integrate them with your computer. For instance, you can buy a card reader and pair it with any computer via USB. Some motherboards support adding a TPM microchip. Consult your computer manufacturer's manual or web site for such upgrade possibilities.

The previous features will make a computer cost more, so if your current computer satisfies your needs and you are not planning to replace it soon, the following measures (and all the recommendations in the book) will help you to secure your PC to a great extent despite the absence of the previous hardware components.

■ **Note**   It is always advisable to start with a clean install of your Windows OS without any extra programs before making security configurations. Many computer manufacturers add extra programs (sometimes named *bloatware*) when selling computers with Windows preinstalled. Make sure to uninstall these programs or reinstall Windows using your original CD/DVD.

■ **Warning**   Create a new system restore point before implementing the tweaks in this chapter so you can safely revert your changes in case something goes wrong.

Lock Your PC Using a USB Drive

In addition to using the regular Windows authenticator username and password when logging into Windows, it is recommended that you use USB authentication as a second authentication method for an older computer that cannot be protected using enhanced Windows 10 features. It works by storing a security key on a USB drive, which must be inserted into the computer whenever you want to unlock Windows.

USB Raptor allows you to lock your PC using a USB flash card. It is a free program with many advanced features. You can find it at `https://sourceforge.net/projects/usbraptor/?source=typ_redirect`.

Turn On Automatic Updates

The automatic updates feature for the Windows OS should always be turned on. In fact, the Windows 10 automatic updates feature is turned on by default and cannot be stopped easily.

Use a Less-Privileged User Account

Surfing the Internet, checking e-mails, using Microsoft Office, having Skype conversations, and doing other regular tasks do not require administrative privileges. It is always recommended that you use a limited user account for your daily tasks. This will effectively protect your computer from malware installed inadvertently; it will also limit hackers' ability to invade your system as they will have the same restricted account you are currently using.

▓ **Warning**   Disable the Windows guest account immediately. This account can be exploited by attackers to invade your system. To disable this account (in all Windows versions), go to Control Panel ➤ Administrative Tools ➤ Computer Management. In the left pane, click Local Users and Groups, double-click the Users folder in the right pane to open it, right-click the Guest account, select Properties, and select "Account is disabled." You should also disable the built-in Administrator account and then create another account with another name and give it administrative permissions. Protect the new administrator account with a strong, complex password.

Configure Windows Backup

It is highly recommended that you back up your operating system on a regular basis. Partitions that contain your sensitive data should be backed up to three different locations. In Chapter 2 we mentioned some backup tools; however, Windows offers a free backup feature that can be accessed from Control Panel ➤ Backup and Restore (Windows 7). This utility will allow you to back up your Windows drive onto an external drive. The feature is available in Windows 7, 8, and 10. However, Windows versions 8 and 10 have another backup utility called File History, which can also be configured to back up your personal files to an external drive or network location.

▓ **Note**   File History backup-specific folders relate to the current Windows user account by default (e.g., Desktop, Contacts, OneDrive, and so on). To configure it to back up other folders or drives, you should use the File History app. Go to Settings ➤ Update & Security ➤ Backup and then click "More options" in the "Back up using File History" panel to include more locations in your backup.

Disallow Remote Assistance

This feature allows you or another user to access your system remotely over the Internet or across local networks. Obviously, hackers can exploit this feature to gain unauthorized access to your machine. It is advisable to turn it off unless you are using it regularly.

To disable it in Windows 10, go to Control Panel ➤ System, select "Advanced system settings," and go to the Remote tab. Then deselect the option "Allow Remote Assistance connections to this computer." In the same dialog, make sure that the option "Don't allow remote connection to this computer" is selected in the Remote Desktop section (in Windows 10).

Manage Restore Points

In Windows XP and all later versions, Microsoft offers the Volume Shadow Copy Service (VSS), which is an application that coordinates the creation of a consistent snapshot of data at a specific point in time for each volume where it is activated. This helps Windows to recover if some of its files get corrupted and you need to restore the good version from one of its previous restore points.

Restore points can also hold files and folders created by the user. For example, if a user deletes a Microsoft Office document from his or her desktop, the user can still recover an old version of this document from a previous restore point.

Windows restore points can be beneficial to restore Windows to a previous stable state. With regard to your privacy, however, you should understand that they can also be used to recover older versions of your personal files/folders. Hence, the privacy danger comes from an adversary exploiting this feature to recover old, deleted files from your computer. Bear this fact in mind when activating the system restore feature for a specific volume.

There are some cases where it is beneficial to browse the old restore point contents without performing a full recovery. You may need to recover a specific file or folder or make sure that your deleted files are really gone forever without deleting the entire restore point.

ShadowExplorer (`www.shadowexplorer.com`) is a free utility that allows you to browse old restore points easily. You can view and extract individual files and folders with a simple point-and-click interface. All you need to do is to select the volume that you have a system restore activated for and then select the point that you want to browse. Right-click the file or folder you want to recover and select Export to save it in your desired location (see Figure 3-1).

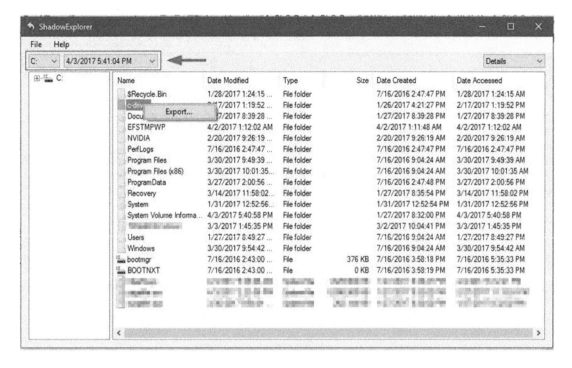

Figure 3-1. *Using ShadowExplorer to browse old restore points*

Make Hidden Files Visible

Windows hides some files and folders by default to prevent users from accidentally deleting them. From a privacy viewpoint, malicious programs come hidden in the same way to prevent a user from discovering them. Therefore, it is necessary to know how to reveal hidden files in Windows.

On Windows 10, go to Control Panel ➤ File Explorer Options. In Windows 7, select Control Panel ➤ Folder Options and go to the View tab. Select the option "Show hidden files, folders, and drives." Another setting you need to change in the same window to view the hidden system files is "Hide protected operating system files (Recommended)." Remove the check mark and you are done.

File extensions also are hidden by default in the Windows OS. This can make it harder to recognize potentially malicious files, which can lead to users executing malware inadvertently. For example, an executable malware file could have the extension file.doc.exe and display a Microsoft Word icon; in this case, only the .doc extension would appear, making this file look legitimate. To view the file extension in Windows, from the same window as mentioned previously, deselect the option "Hide extensions for known file types."

Set a Screen Saver Password

You should set a screen saver password so that Windows will lock your computer when you are not at it. To set a password for your Windows screen saver, go to Control Panel ➤ Personalization. At the bottom of the window, click Screen Saver. In the Screen Saver Settings dialog, select the box "On resume, display logon screen."

■ **Note** You can lock your Windows system immediately by pressing Windows Key+L.

Freeze the Hard Disk

Freezing software allows a Windows user to restore his or her operating system to a previous stable state within seconds each time the computer restarts. For example, if you are using a Windows PC with an administrative account and your computer gets infected with malware, all you need to do is to restart your machine and the malware will automatically be removed from your machine (regardless of whether you have already installed an antivirus program!). Enterprises can use such utilities to secure their computers and servers from malware threats and wrong configurations and restore them instantly to their original states.

RollBack Rx Home Edition (free for personal use) is a program for freezing Windows machines. You can find it at http://horizondatasys.com/rollback-rx-time-machine/rollback-rx-home/.

Set a Password for BIOS/UEFI

Many cyber-attacks rely on booting the victim's machine from a USB stick or CD/DVD drive to steal sensitive files or to bring damage to the victim's computer by wiping clean the computer hard drive. By setting a password on your computer BIOS, you can stop many threats in addition to preventing others from changing BOIS settings. Each motherboard manufacturer has its own menu to set this password, usually in a Security section. You should first boot to BOIS/UEFI and then activate this option.

Disable Unnecessary Ports/Protocols

Each open port on your Windows OS is considered a threat that an attacker could exploit to invade your system. In Chapter 2, we recommend installing a firewall and setting it to "Interactive mode." In this mode, any ingoing or outgoing connection will be suspended until the user allows or denies access.

Many tools are already available to monitor Windows ports and show which ones are open and what protocols they use. Such information is necessary to help you determine whether a specific port should remain open or you need to close it.

CurrPorts (www.nirsoft.net/utils/cports.html) is network-monitoring software that shows all open TCP/IP and UDP ports in addition to information about each port that includes the process/application that opened this port, the full path of the process, and other process-related information.

For advanced network protocol analyzing, especially for enterprises looking to get in-depth information about what is passing across their networks, Wireshark (https://www.wireshark.org/download.html) is highly recommended.

Disable Unnecessary Services

Like open ports, unused services should be disabled under Windows because they pose a potential security vulnerability in the computer system. You can stop Windows services by going to Control Panel ➤ Administrative Tools ➤ Component Services. Click Services on the left pane; all services available on your current computer should appear in the right pane. Each one's startup type will also be displayed.

If you want to investigate the running services on your computer and see what files are running as part of each service, Sysinternals offers two utilities for this purpose.

- Process Explorer (`https://technet.microsoft.com/en-us/sysinternals/bb896653.aspx`) shows detailed information about each running process on Windows in addition to all the associated DLL files and handles that each process opened. A new feature offered by this tool is its ability to query VirusTotal.com for each process or file running on the user PC. This will effectively help users to fight against malware not recognized by their antivirus solution.

- Process Monitor (`https://technet.microsoft.com/en-us/sysinternals/bb896645.aspx`) shows the currently running files and applications on your computer and their associated registry keys and memory threads.

Data Destruction Techniques

In today's digital age, data destruction is considered an integral part of any high-quality data management program. Most jurisdictions in developed countries require organizations and companies that handle private data to destroy it securely to protect individuals and businesses from the potential impact of a data breach or inadvertent disclosure. In Chapter 2 we talked briefly about the importance of wiping the hard drive before selling or disposing of your computing equipment. We suggested some techniques and tools for the safe removal of data. In this section, we continue the discussion of the safest methods to dispose of digital data securely.

Data destruction is an important step in covering your digital tracks. It is concerned with making your data (including remnant data) unreadable and impossible to recover from storage units. There are three types of hard drive destruction techniques: physical, degaussing, and logical destruction (sanitizing). Before describing each technique, let's first talk about the different types of hard drives in use.

There are mainly two types of hard drives used in computers.

- *Hard disk drive (HDD)*: This is the traditional (mechanical) hard disk drive. It uses a metal platter (or platters) made of glass or aluminum coated with magnetic material to store data.

- *Solid-state drive (SSD)*: This is a more advanced version of a drive. It does not contain any moving parts and stores data on small microchip units, similar to USB flash drives. Data can be accessed on an SSD even though the electricity is not powered on. An SSD is faster than an HDD, but it is more expensive.

In terms of data recovery, recovering data from the HDD is relatively easy and can be achieved with free tools by a novice user. On the HDD, when Windows deletes a file, all it really does is mark the space on the hard drive that your deleted file occupied as free. In other words, it only deletes the pointer to this file. This operation helps to speed up the deletion process, saving valuable time. For example, deleting a 10GB file requires the same time as writing 10GB of data to your hard drive. By removing only the pointer to the deleted file, its space will be freed up immediately (theoretically, of course); however, data that belongs to the deleted file blocks will remain on the disk and will not be removed until Windows needs to write new data in that place.

The previous discussion is applicable to HDDs only. Recovering data from an SSD is more difficult than HDD and impossible in many cases. For instance, an SSD uses a different mechanism when handling deleted files. All modern SSDs utilize the TRIM command, when enabled. This command will remove deleted file data blocks instantly, allowing for another file to take up that space. This speeds up the writing process the next time the OS needs to write data onto the drive. There are many approaches to implementing TRIM on SSD devices, depending on the OS in use. Some operating systems will execute TRIM instantly after each file deletion, while others will execute TRIM at regular intervals.

NOTE! HOW TO CHECK TRIM IS ENABLED IN YOUR WINDOWS PC

Launch a command-line prompt as an administrator and type the following command; then press the Enter key:

```
fsutil behavior query DisableDeleteNotify
```

After executing this command, if the result of `DisableDeleteNotify` is 0, this means TRIM is already enabled. If it is 1, this means you need to enable it by typing the following command and then pressing Enter:

```
fsutil behavior set DisableDeleteNotify 0
```

Rerun the first command; you should see the `DisableDeleteNotify` result become 1.

In the same way, you can disable TRIM by typing the following command and then pressing Enter:

```
fsutil behavior set DisableDeleteNotify 1
```

Now that you have a fair understanding of the differences between HDDs and SSDs, we can talk about how to destroy data completely when using both drive types. The following techniques are used to achieve this:

- *Physical destruction*: In this type, digital storage media (such as hard drives, memory sticks, magnetic tapes, CDs, DVDs and Blu-ray discs, and credit cards) is destroyed physically to avoid recovery. This technique is usually used by intelligence agencies such as the CIA in its Sensitive Compartmented Information Facility (SCIF) operational environments, and business organizations using this technique can assure the safe disposal of storage devices and avoid any possible recovery of classified and high-grade data assets. The equipment used to destroy these devices is a *hard drive shredder* or *destroyer*.

- *Degaussing*: This technique works by exposing the HDD or any magnetic storage devices to the powerful magnetic field of a degausser to destroy stored data magnetically. A degausser works on magnetic storage devices only and will prove ineffective when used to destroy data on the SSD or USB flash memory because data in such devices is not stored in magnetic coating material like their HDD counterparts. SSD devices should be destroyed physically to assure the safe destruction of stored data. Obviously, devices exposed to degaussing cannot be reused to store data.

- *Logical destruction of data (sanitizing)*: This is the most commonly used technique by individuals and many organizations to assure the safe destruction of data. It works by using specialized software to cover the old data and remnants of data with random characters written by the wiping tool. There are many techniques already used to destroy data digitally in this way; some are more secure than others. However, what you should know when using such a technique to destroy data is that it cannot guarantee 100 percent removal of all data on your drive. Some advanced recovery techniques that are hardware based are still able to capture your old data, or at least parts of it (but doing so is costly and time-consuming). The main advantage of software wiping is that your storage device can be reused again to store data, unlike the previous two methods. Software wiping tools come with some disadvantages; for instance, they need time to finish because they must write random data multiple times (several passes) over all the available sectors on the hard drive. In addition, this technique assumes that your hard drive is working and writable in order to write the random data into it. Another challenge to wiping software comes when using it to wipe data stored using the RAID technology. This technology offers fault tolerance by mirroring data onto multiple disk drives in different physical locations. In such a situation, the wiping tool should track all mirrored data across all enterprise storage servers.

Different standards have been developed to wipe data (logical data destruction) on hard drives. Table 3-1 shows the most popular ones.

Table 3-1. *Algorithms Used to Wipe Data on Hard Drives*

Erasing Technique	Security Level	Overwriting Passes	Pattern Used	Requires Verification
HMG Infosec Standard 5	High	3	All 0s, then all 1s, and finally randomly generated 1s and 0	Yes.
DoD 5220.22-M	High	3	All 0s, then all 1s, and finally a random character (with verification after each write)	Yes.
Bruce Schneier's algorithm	High	7	All 0s, then all 0s, and finally random characters five times	Some implementations of this technique require at least one verification after the first or last pass.
German standard BSI/VSITR	High	7	All 0s, then all 1s, then repeat that six times, and a final pass that writes random characters	No.

Different programs exist to wipe your hard drives, and the majority support more than one wiping standard. Table 3-2 lists the most popular ones (free tools only).

Table 3-2. *Tools Used to Securely Wipe Your Hard Drive Data*

Program name	URL	Comments
DBAN	`https://dban.org`	The free version supports HDDs only.
Eraser	`www.heidi.ie/eraser/`	Open source; supports SSD.
CCleaner	`www.piriform.com/ccleaner`	Drive wiper and Windows trace cleaner.
SDelete	`https://technet.microsoft.com/en-us/sysinternals/sdelete.aspx`	Erases data according to DOD 5220.22-M .

For SSD drives, the majority of SSD manufacturers offer utilities to erase data securely from their drives. You can check your SSD drive manufacturer's web site for such utilities. Table 3-3 gives direct links to some of them.

Table 3-3. *Specific Manufacturer Tools Used to Securely Wipe SSD Drives*

Tool Name	URL
Intel Solid State Drive Toolbox	`https://downloadcenter.intel.com/download/26574?v=t`
Corsair SSD Toolbox	`www.corsair.com/en-eu/support/downloads`
Samsung Magician	`www.samsung.com/semiconductor/minisite/ssd/download/tools.html`
SanDisk SSD	`https://kb.sandisk.com/app/answers/detail/a_id/16678/~/secure-erase-and-sanitize`

If you have a drive from a different manufacturer, search online for it using the phrase *SSD secure erase tool X*, replacing the *X* with the SSD maker.

NOTE! WINDOWS PROVIDES A BUILT-IN COMMAND-LINE UTILITY TO OVERWRITE DELETED DATA TO AVOID FUTURE RECOVERY

All data that is not allocated to files or folders is overwritten using three passes. The first pass writes all 0s (0x00), the second pass writes 255 (0xFF), and the third pass writes a random number. To launch this tool, open a command prompt as the administrator, type `cipher /w`, and then specify the driver or folder that identifies the location of the deleted data that you want to overwrite (see Figure 3-2).

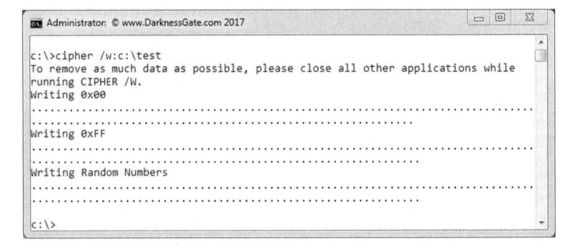

Figure 3-2. *Using Cipher.exe on Windows to overwrite deleted data space on selected folder*

Now, we will discuss how to configure Windows to stop recording your activities when using it. Windows records almost any task you do when using it, for instance, installing and uninstalling programs, launching a web browser to surf or to check e-mails, and conducting searches for a file or folder, as well as all errors generated from Windows and other software (e.g., memory dumps). These and more are all recorded somewhere on the hard drive. There are many privacy programs that can perform automatic checks of Windows digital traces in order to delete them; a good privacy tool for Windows is BleachBit (https://www.bleachbit.org). In addition to its main feature of deleting records of user actions in Windows, it has the ability to wipe clean your traces in thousands of applications (including all major web browsers).

Automated privacy tools are perfect for all users and offer an easy way to destroy your digital traces. However, to achieve the maximum privacy possible, it is recommended that you prevent Windows from recording some types of data about your computer usage. This way, you do not need to worry about data that does not exist in the first place!

Disable the Recycle Bin

When you delete a file, Windows will move it to the recycle bin. To force Windows to delete the file directly without sending it to recycle bin, right-click Recycle Bin (usually it resides on the Windows desktop), select Properties, and select the option "Don't move files to the Recycle Bin. Remove files immediately when deleted." Then click the OK button. Bear in mind that this technique does not guarantee the secure removal of deleted files. You still need to use one of the tools already mentioned to overwrite the deleted files sector area on the hard drive.

Disable UserAssist

Windows keep tracks of all programs launched on your PC since its installation date, including the number of launch times and other attributes. It also stores links you open frequently. To disable UserAssist, go to the registry and delete all entries under the following key:

HKEY_CURRENT_USER\Software\Microsoft\ Windows\CurrentVersion\Explorer\UserAssist

---

■ **Note** You can access the Windows registry editor by pressing Windows Key+R, then typing regedit in the Run dialog, and finally pressing Enter.

NirSoft has a good tool for viewing/deleting UserAssist keys; you can find it at www.nirsoft.net/utils/userassist_view.html.

Delete Previously Connected USB Devices

Windows keeps a history of all connected removable USB storage devices (thumb drives, iPods, digital cameras, external HDDs, SD cards, etc.) in different registry keys. Each key offers a different set of information for each connected USB device. If you want to view all this information in addition to many useful USB device manipulation functions in one location, use a free portable tool from NirSoft called USBDeview (www.nirsoft.net/utils/usb_devices_view.html).

Disable the Windows Prefetch Feature

This feature boosts Windows performance by predicting which application a user is likely to launch and then loads the necessary files to RAM to speed the launch time. A copy of each prefetched application will remain in the following folder: C:\Windows\Prefetch. Access this folder and delete everything in it. You can also disable the prefetch feature as follows: press Windows Key+R, type services.msc in the Run dialog, and press Enter. Search for a service named *Superfetch* and double-click to access it. Change "Startup type" to Disabled. Then click the OK button.

Disable the Windows Thumbnail Cache

Windows stores thumbnail images of major graphics file types in a thumbnail cache file called thumbs.db within each folder that contains such files. This file can reveal information about previous files on your system even though you have deleted them. To disable this feature, go to Control Panel ➤ Folder Options (in Windows 10 it is called File Explorer Options), go to the View tab, and select the option "Always show icons, never thumbnails." Click the OK button.

NOTE!

Thumbs.db files are hidden. You need to show hidden file/folders as you learned previously to see these files. Then you can delete each one manually if you want.

To delete all Thumbs.db files on a particular partition (for example, on the C:\ drive), right-click the drive on Windows File Explorer and then select Properties. Select the General tab and click the Disk Cleanup button. Select Thumbnail and then click the "Clean up system files" button (see Figure 3-3).

Figure 3-3. *Deleting all thumbnail images under the Windows partition (C:\ drive)*

Other Areas You Need to Consider

Other Windows features produce digital data that might include sensitive information about your computer usage, such as Windows restore points, the Windows hibernation file, the Windows paging file (virtual memory), and Windows error dump files. All these features can hold data that may violate your privacy or even crack your disk encryption if they fall into the wrong hands. Chapter 5 discusses the security threats imposed by these features and how you can mitigate them.

Windows 10 Security

Windows 10 comes equipped with sophisticated security capabilities to deter current and future cyber-attacks. As you already saw, being able to implement these modern Windows 10 security features depends on the hardware available in your computer. In this section, we will talk about the new Windows 10 security features and how you can harden Windows 10 to become more privacy friendly.

Windows Biometric Authentication

Windows Hello is a new feature/app introduced in Windows 10; it allows a user to log in to his or her Windows machine without entering a password; instead, he or she can use biometric characteristics such as a fingerprint, face, or iris. Microsoft claims that it will not store your biometric information on its servers; it will store the data only locally on each user's machine.

As we already said, Windows Hello is not supported on all computers. To check whether your PC supports Windows Hello, go to Windows Settings (press Windows Key+I), select Accounts, and then click "Sign-in options." If your PC does not support the Hello feature, you can simply buy an external fingerprint scanner or 3D camera for face recognition and attach it to your PC so that you can activate this feature.

▓ **Note**   You can find more information about the Windows 10 Hello feature in addition to PC accessories such as third-party fingerprint scanners and 3D cameras to activate this feature on nonsupported devices at https://www.microsoft.com/en-us/windows/windows-hello.

Windows Hello integrates with many apps and online services, allowing you to synchronize your data across different Windows 10 devices, make purchases, and access your Dropbox and OneDrive accounts without entering any password.

Despite the enhanced security and ease of use that Windows Hello offers for Windows users, we still recommend using a local account to authenticate a user upon signing in. No one can guarantee the security of your personal data if an attacker succeeds in compromising this feature, but perhaps the situation will change when this technology becomes more mature.

Use Local Account

Always use a local account on your Windows PC. Local accounts are like all the old-school accounts that you have used in the past to secure your Windows machines. They do not require an Internet connection to work. Beginning from Windows 8, Microsoft offers the possibility for its users to log in to their PCs using Microsoft account login credentials (Hotmail, Outlook, Live, or another Microsoft e-mail to log in). This creates security risks for the following reasons:

- You need to use your e-mail account to log in to your machine. If your password gets compromised, the attacker will have full access to your e-mail (and all Microsoft online services like OneDrive) in addition to all your computer's local files.

- Sending credentials across untrusted channels like the Internet should be minimized as much as possible because no one can guarantee what happens to your sensitive information when traveling online.

- Your personal habits and PC usage will be sent to Microsoft servers on a regular basis, and everything will get linked to your e-mail account. That is a lot of information stored in one place!

- The damage from a malware attack will double when using a Microsoft account; an attacker can reveal a great number of details about you if he or she successfully cracks your Microsoft account password.

For these reasons and more, it is highly advisable to use a local account when logging into Windows. Of course, there are some instances when you want to buy something from Windows Store or you want to install Windows apps. In those cases, you need to log in using your Microsoft account. However, make sure to return to your local account after finishing such tasks.

To switch from the local account to the Microsoft account or vice versa, press Windows Key+I to open Windows Settings. Click Accounts, then click the appropriate link near the top ("Sign in with a Microsoft account instead" or "Sign in with a Local account instead"), and finally follow the wizard to update your selection.

Windows Update

Windows 10 installs updates automatically without any user intervention. Keeping your system up-to-date is an excellent way to protect your data.

You can access Windows 10 updates and configure advanced settings by going to Settings ➤ Update & Security.

Windows Defender

Windows Defender offers basic antivirus capabilities for Windows 10. When you install a dedicated antivirus solution, Windows Defender will disable itself automatically. If you select to uninstall your current antivirus solution, Windows Defender will return and activate itself to protect your machine. Installing a dedicated antivirus solution, preferably with a built-in firewall, is important to protect your computer and data before going online.

Windows Backup

Windows offers a dedicated built-in utility to back up your data into an external drive, so there is no excuse for not backing up your data and system on regular basis. To access the backup utility under Windows 10, go to Settings ➤ Update & Security ➤ Backup. From here you can either use File History to back up your important folders, such as Desktop, Contacts, and Favorites (or any folder you select), or use the old Backup and Restore (Windows 7) to create a full system image of your Windows drive. This allows you to perform a full system restore from this image if your system becomes unstable.

Recovery

If a disaster happens and you want to recover your system or data, Windows 10 offers you these three options (you can access these options from Settings ➤ Update & Security ➤ Recovery):

- *Reset this PC*: In this case you can reinstall Windows while keeping your personal files intact, or you can reinstall Windows and remove them entirely with a clean installation.

- *Advanced startup*: This option allows you to restore Windows from a system image taken previously (stored on a network drive, USB flash drive, or CD/DVD). This helps you to restore Windows and all programs/configurations and personal data from a previous stable state (when the backup was taken).

- *Go back to an earlier build*: This option will be available only if you upgrade Windows and the current upgraded build does not work for you. This will revert the upgrade.

■ **Note**   You can find more information about the recovery options at the Microsoft web site: https://support.microsoft.com/en-us/help/12415/windows-10-recovery-options.

Find My Device

This is a new feature introduced in Windows 10–capable devices that already have GPS or a similar sensor to know the device's current location. It works by tracking your Windows computer, tablet, or smartphone periodically and stores the geolocation data in your Microsoft online account.

This feature allows Microsoft to record your location, so it is advisable to use full disk encryption (covered in Chapter 5) instead. If you lose your device, you can depend on the honesty of the person who finds it to hand it over to authorities or to you (provided you put your name or e-mail somewhere on the outside cover). If your device gets stolen, you can forget the device while being assured that your data will not get exposed because it is encrypted!

Privacy Settings

When Windows 10 was released to market, it fueled a heated discussion about the default privacy settings of Windows 10; many accused Microsoft of collecting information via the default Windows 10 Express installation settings to invade end users' privacy. Many famous security experts and privacy advocates explained that Windows 10 could collect vast amounts of data about the usage habits and online browsing of each user in addition to the user's calendar, location data, previous searches, and more. Windows sends this data to Microsoft for analysis to personalize the user experience and target him or her with customized advertisements.

Microsoft responded and assured people that the collected data would be used only to customize the user experience when using Windows, in addition to customizing certain services according to user location.

This book discusses the issue of privacy when going online, so we will not stop to discuss whether Microsoft is really respecting user privacy and to which extent. Users should always consider themselves working in a hostile environment when going online and must take all the precautionary measures mentioned in this book to safeguard their confidential data and personal information, without relying much on privacy promises offered by giant tech providers.

■ **Warning**   Security-conscious people working in extremely hostile environments who need to protect their confidential data shouldn't use the Windows OS. The Tails OS is recommended; you'll learn more about this in Chapter 4.

For now, let's return to the security issue of Windows 10. A good start for any user who wants to use this OS is to read the following two agreements to understand what data Microsoft collects about them and for any purpose:

- *Microsoft software license terms*: `https://www.microsoft.com/en-us/Useterms/Retail/Windows/10/UseTerms_Retail_Windows_10_English.htm`

- *Microsoft Privacy statement*: `https://privacy.microsoft.com/en-us/privacystatement`

Reading the Microsoft Windows usage term agreement and privacy agreement is a good start. However, Windows 10 allows its users to browse and update major settings that affect their privacy. Privacy settings in Windows 10 are bundled together in one place to simplify privacy management. You can access the privacy dashboard from Settings ➤ Privacy (see Figure 3-4).

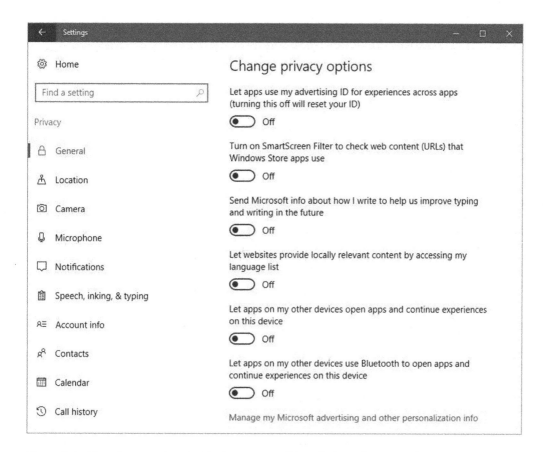

Figure 3-4. The privacy settings in Windows 10 are all bundled together in one location.

In the privacy dashboard, you can disable any setting that you think affects your privacy and customize other settings according to your privacy expectations. For example, if you are using Skype regularly to make Internet calls, you should allow the Skype app to use the camera and microphone in order to work, but if you are not making voice calls, you can prevent all apps from accessing your microphone by turning the microphone setting to Off for all apps. The majority of privacy settings can be disabled safely without affecting the Windows main functions.

■ **Warning** Do not use automated privacy tools targeted to Windows 10 to adjust Windows privacy settings. These tools are not reliable and can cause different problems in both Windows functions and apps. Always use the normal Windows privacy dashboard to adjust your Windows 10 privacy settings.

Additional Security Measures

Here are additional measures to better secure your privacy when using the Windows OS.

Use a Virtual Keyboard

Keyloggers are malicious programs that monitor your computer silently (screen captures, browsing history keystrokes, and anything you do on your PC). They come in two major types: hardware keyloggers, which are physical devices attached to your computer and covered thoroughly in Chapter 5), and software keyloggers, which work like any other malicious software.

Installing antivirus and anti-malware solutions should be enough to stop the majority of software keyloggers. However, if you are using a public PC (e.g., an Internet café PC) and you need to enter your password to access your online account, it is highly advisable to use a virtual keyboard (this is a simulation for the physical keyboard) to avoid exposing your credentials—just in case the computer you are using has a software keylogger installed. A virtual keyboard offers a good protective measure, and it simply works by encrypting your keystroke so the keylogger cannot see anything in clear.

A virtual keylogger does not offer 100 percent protection against all types of software keyloggers. However, using it is better than nothing. Table 3-4 shows some free virtual keyboards.

Table 3-4. *Free Virtual Keyboard to Protect Against Software Keylogger*

Keyboard Name	URL
Neo's SafeKeys	www.aplin.com.au
Oxynger KeyShield	www.oxynger.com (offers more protection)

Please note that many antivirus solutions offer an on-screen keyboard that you can use to protect your sensitive login information.

Automatic Program Updates

Installed applications must be updated regularly to avoid leaving any vulnerable application that can be exploited by attackers to invade your system. Different programs exist to remind you to update your currently installed programs to their latest version. However, using a software updater is a good option to help them secure all programs installed on your PC in one click without the hassle of manually updating them.

Table 3-5 lists some free tools to update Windows programs automatically.

Table 3-5. *Windows Updater Tools*

Program Name	URL
Secunia Personal Software Inspector	http://learn.flexerasoftware.com/SVM-EVAL-Personal-Software-Inspector
FileHippo App Manager	http://filehippo.com/download_app_manager/59899/
Patch My PC Updater	https://patchmypc.net/download

■ **Note** In this book, we recommend always using open source programs from a reputable source. The previously mentioned updater programs do not follow this criteria. Nevertheless, you can still check for new versions of each installed program and then download and update them manually. This is preferable to avoid using programs that aren't open source. This warning is applicable to security-conscious people; the majority of end users can safely go with any updater program. (But always remember to read the end-user agreement and privacy policy of the tool before installing it to know what type of information it collects about you.)

Virtual Machines and Portable Apps

Use virtualization technology to enhance your privacy and protect your host machine from malware and other security threats. A virtual machine allows you to execute programs, open e-mail attachments, test programs, and visit dangerous web sites safely without being afraid of malware affecting your operating system, as the virtual machine will run in a sandbox isolated entirely from its host machine's operating system. Popular virtual machines include VirtualBox (`https://www.virtualbox.org`) and VMware Workstation Player (`www.vmware.com/products/player/playerpro-evaluation.html`).

Virtual machines offer what is called a *virtual* hardware device that is independent of the host machine. However, there are some programs that offer virtualizing for separate programs running on your machine without creating a complete virtual device. Sandboxie (`https://www.sandboxie.com`) allows programs to run isolated from the host machine, thus preventing unwanted changes from affecting your operating system. This program is especially useful for the Firefox browser, which until now lacked the support of a full sandbox model compared to Google Chrome and Microsoft Internet Edge (and Edge).

■ **Note** The majority of web browsers and some desktop applications already have the sandbox feature. The sandboxing concept means anything executed within the sandboxed application web browser, for example, will remain within it and will not affect the underlying operating system.

Use portable applications that can run without the need to install them into the system. This will effectively reduce your digital footprint online, although some traces will remain on the host machine after executing such tools (e.g., in the Windows Prefetch folder and maybe in the registry). Here are some popular portable app suites:

- *PortableApps.com*: `http://portableapps.com/suite`

- *Liberkey, 295 Apps*: `www.liberkey.com/en`

- *Pendriveapps*: `https://www.pendriveapps.com`

■ **Note** Use a bootable USB token or live CD/DVD when working on sensitive documents. Running the Tails OS (https://tails.boum.org) in offline mode is a great practice. There are many tools can help you to create a bootable USB/CD drive. The following are some of them:

Windows USB/DVD download tool: https://wudt.codeplex.com

Rufus: https://rufus.akeo.ie

WinBuilder: http://winbuilder.net

Windows To Go (Windows 10)

Windows To Go is a new feature available in Windows 10. It allows you to run the complete Windows 10 Live feature from a USB drive without needing to install it on your computer's hard drive. This feature is available in both Enterprise and Education editions and can be accessed from Control Panel ➤ Windows To Go.

■ **Note** Some third-party tools allow you to install and boot Windows 10 from any Windows 10 edition.

These are some tools to help you create a Windows To Go drive of Windows 10:

Rufus: https://rufus.akeo.ie

AOMEI Partition Assistant Standard: www.disk-partition.com/download-home.html

Do not forget to configure your computer's BOIS or UEFI to boot from USB drives.

Please note that not all the usual Windows 10 features will be available when using the Windows To Go operating system. For instance, you cannot use TPM while encrypting using BitLocker. Hibernations and recovery options are also not available. For more information about Windows To Go features, go to the Microsoft web site (https://docs.microsoft.com/en-us/windows/deployment/planning/windows-to-go-overview).

Summary

Windows is an easy-to-use operating system. It also is still the most prevalent one across the globe. Despite all the rumors about default configurations set by Microsoft that may somehow invade your privacy, this operating system still is considered a secure and reliable one that can handle both personal and mission-critical tasks. Windows is not hardened by default to be an anonymous OS; it was not built for this role. Productivity and ease of use are what distinguish Windows from its rivals, not to mention its robust build and security features.

Windows, especially Windows 10, can be hardened to become more privacy friendly by updating its settings. Different security software is also available to install on this OS to make it more secure and anonymous, which is what we will cover in the rest of this book.

CHAPTER 4

▉ ▉ ▉

Online Anonymity

How to Anonymize Everything You Do Online

You do not have to be a spy to care about your anonymity. Regular Internet users have many reasons to conceal their identity and digital tracks online. Nearly anything we do online is logged, analyzed, and used for different reasons without a user's explicit consent. Internet users think that there is no way to stop this privacy invasion because they are not well educated about Internet security, and many of them find this topic hard to understand or scary. This is not always true; there are ways to anonymize what you do online. Although most Internet users are *not* specifically targeted by big intelligence agencies that have access to substantial resources and the ability to monitor communications using different online and offline methods, a percentage of these users may indeed be targeted by such mass surveillance programs utilized by nation-states and superpower intelligence agencies that work to harvest and acquire online traffic as intelligence. Giant companies also capture user activities online for various marketing purposes. This type of online monitoring constitutes the largest percentage of online monitoring and can be mitigated using simple protective steps.

As we already said, it is difficult to protect yourself if you are a target of a big intelligence agency like the National Security Agency (NSA) because it will find a way to capture your data. However, the guidance in this chapter, and in the rest of the book, will ensure that you understand how to defend against online risks and the potential of hacking attempts against your online profile.

Almost every week, the press announces various hacking attacks that have taken place against different companies. For example, on September 22, 2016, Yahoo announced that a security breach had resulted in exposing the personal details of 500 million user accounts in one of the largest cybersecurity breaches ever to have occurred.[1] The Yahoo case shows clearly that the Internet is a hostile environment and privacy violations are not limited to giant companies that record user activities to sell to various advertisement companies. Giant companies themselves are targets because they have confidential and sensitive data concerning end users.

In this chapter, you will learn how to conceal your identity online. As you already saw in Chapter 1, there are two types of data that prospective attackers are concerned with: personal identifying information and nonidentifying information. This chapter will teach you practically how to conceal both to mitigate or to reduce the potential of someone tracking your activities online.

Anonymous Networks

When working online (for example, surfing the Web, sending e-mails, conducting online banking, and posting data to blog), everything you do *could* be traced back to your machine. In Chapter 1 we described the concept of an Internet Protocol (IP) address, which is the main identifier of all online users. To anonymize your location online, you are mainly concerned with concealing your IP address. There are different techniques you can employ to conceal an IP address, some of which are more secure than others.

© Nihad A. Hassan and Rami Hijazi 2017
N. A. Hassan and R. Hijazi, *Digital Privacy and Security Using Windows*, DOI 10.1007/978-1-4842-2799-2_4

In this section, we will cover anonymous networks, which offer the maximum protection and anonymity in today's digital age. In addition to being used by casual users, anonymous networks are used by military personal, law enforcement, criminals, hacking groups, terrorists, pedophiles, whistle-blowers, journalists, and of course anyone else who wants to disappear when entering the online world.

Tor Network

Tor is the most popular anonymous network currently used online. The name is derived from an acronym for the original software project name, The Onion Router. Tor was originally developed by the U.S. Naval Research Laboratory to protect U.S. intelligence communications online. However, in December 2006, a nonprofit organization called the Tor Project took over Tor.[2]

Currently, the number of users using Tor is about 1700,000,[3] but of course the number of users changes daily.

Tor is mainly composed of two parts.

- The piece of software you run on your machine to access the Internet anonymously

- The Tor network of volunteer computers that direct your online traffic

How Tor Works

To fully appreciate how Tor works, it is vital to appreciate how the superhighway of the Internet functions. In a nutshell, the Internet comprises 13 route servers that sustain its entire backbone and that support massive numbers of computers that store and process data. These computers are known as *servers*. The devices, such as PCs, laptops, smartphones, and tablets, that retrieve information from these servers are called *clients*. For example, when you want to read an article on the CNN web site, you use your client device (an iPad, for example) to connect to the CNN server that hosts the article. The connection between servers and clients is made in a variety of ways, such as through wireless signals, fiber-optic cables, or copper cables.

The online information travels in two directions. In the earlier example, you initiate the connection to the CNN server, and your client device will send your request in multiple packets. These packets contain information about your client device (such as the source IP address among other data) and the destination address. When the CNN server receives this data, it will act upon it and send the article you requested to your local machine through the established connection.

During this connection, you must remember that the traffic initiated between devices and servers can be monitored by various third-party bodies or even intruders. Government agencies, Internet service providers (ISPs), and giant companies are willing to sell your web browsing habits to advertisement companies. Hacker groups are another example of entities that might be interested in capturing and analyzing the traffic for various purposes. This applies when sending e-mails too. There is great danger in working online without the appropriate defenses in place.

Tor helps end users maintain a level of online anonymity by encrypting both the data and the destination IP addresses prior to sending them through a virtual circuit, which consists of many nodes (no fewer than three nodes in any given time). Each node then decrypts part of the data to reveal only the next node in the circuit to direct the remaining encrypted data to it. The next node performs the same function until the message reaches the final node, called the *exit relay*. The exit relay decrypts the data without revealing the source IP address, sending it on to its final destination (see Figure 4-1).

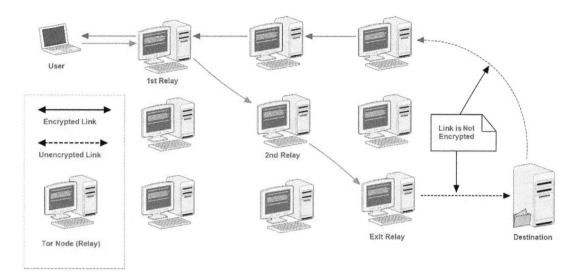

Figure 4-1. *How the Tor network works*

The term *node* is used to describe any server working as part of the Tor network of relays. Sometimes people use different terms for the node such as *server*, *relay*, or *router*. Bear in mind that all these names are interchangeable.

When using Tor to anonymize your location, it will use the exit relay IP address instead of your real IP address as the source IP address. This will effectively conceal your identity online.

The number of relays is increasing steadily. As of November 2016, there were about 7,166 relays available in the Tor network; 958 of them work as exit relays.[4] As the number of relays increases, the Tor network becomes faster and more stable.

Any user can become a volunteer in the Tor network and operate a relay using his or her PC; however, it is necessary first to know about Tor relay types and how each one works.

- Middle relays

- Exit relays

- Bridges

Tor assures that your Internet traffic will run through at least three relays before reaching its destination. The first two relays are the middle relays. They receive traffic and forward it to another relay. Middle relays show their presence to the rest of the Tor network so Tor users can connect to them. Individual volunteers usually run this kind of relay because they are not liable for any illegal activities that may pass through them because the traffic between middle relays is internal within the Tor network. Remember that the middle relay's IP address will not show publicly outside of the Tor network.

Tor exit relays are the gateways where encrypted Tor traffic will hit the Internet. Individuals are encouraged *not* to run an exit relay at home or use a home Internet connection. The exit relay's IP address will appear as the source IP address publicly.

Warning   If a malicious user conducts illegal activities and the traffic passed through an exit relay operated by you, law enforcement may consider you a criminal, and your PC can become part of the law enforcement investigation.

Bridges are the final type of Tor relay; these relays are not publicly listed as part of the Tor network. A bridge is used as a censorship circumvention in countries where the Tor's public IP address is regularly blocked, such as China and in other places with fewer freedoms. A bridge is generally safe to run in your home, in conjunction with other services, or on a computer with your personal files.[5]

As with all the techniques mentioned in this book, Tor is intended to be used by honest people seeking to maintain their privacy and to protect journalists and human rights activists living in countries controlled by oppressive regimes. However, it has been abused by criminals, black hat hackers, and terrorist organizations to conceal their incriminating communications. Tor is also used to access the underground Internet, also known as the *dark web,* as you will see later in this chapter.

Tor Browser

To use the Tor network to conceal your online identity, all you need to do is download the Tor Browser bundle, which works on all major operating systems. You can find it at `https://www.torproject.org/projects/torbrowser.html.en`. It is portable software, which means it requires no installation to work. You can safely run it from a USB drive.

The Tor Browser is a security-hardened Mozilla Firefox implementation and comes with Tor software associated with it. It helps a user access the Tor network transparently without making any complex configuration changes.

Download the Tor Browser and extract it to a specific folder on your drive; you can also extract it to a USB drive. Launch the Tor Browser by clicking the Start Tor Browser icon. Once Tor is ready, the Tor Browser will automatically open (see Figure 4-2).

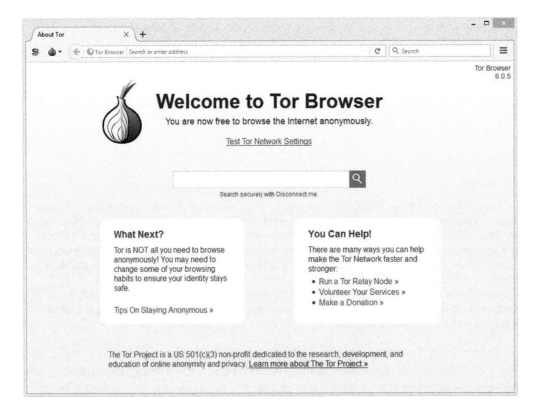

Figure 4-2. *Successful launch of Tor Browser*

Please note only web sites visited through the Tor Browser are anonymous and directed through the Tor network; other browsers already installed on your machine such as Opera and Microsoft Edge are not affected, and their traffic will not pass through the Tor Browser.

When you're done using the Tor Browser, make sure to close it properly by clicking the *X* in the top-right corner. Tor is preconfigured to forget and delete all your browsing history upon closing.

How to Hide Your Tor Usage from Your ISP

In some countries, Tor may be blocked because of censorship. In this case, you will not be able to launch the Tor Browser as described. In addition, in some countries using Tor could be prohibited by law, so using it could be considered suspicious or even dangerous and might land you in serious trouble with the local authorities.

ISPs can detect you are using the Tor network using a variety of ways, and hiding this fact is difficult and is still undergoing much research. However, you can still try to conceal your Tor usage to a great level using the following techniques.

Using a VPN

You can hide Tor from your ISP by using a virtual private network (VPN) service. A VPN allows you to mask your IP address and to establish a secure encrypted connection between your machine and the VPN service, which will act as your entry point to the Internet. Once the VPN is active, you can start the Tor Browser as described earlier, and the Tor usage will be hidden from your ISP to a large extent. (We will cover VPNs thoroughly later in this chapter.)

Using Tor Bridges

Bridge relays (or *bridges* for short) are Tor relays that aren't listed in the main Tor directory. Bridges are considered entry points to the Tor network. Since there is no complete public list of them, even if your ISP is filtering connections to all the known Tor relays, it probably won't be able to block *all* the bridges.[6]

Please remember that this method may *not* fully guarantee that your ISP will not detect your Tor usage, but it will make discovering this fact difficult and will require sophisticated techniques to uncover. To use Tor bridges, follow these steps:

1. Go to `https://bridges.torproject.org/bridges` and enter the captcha to access the secure area, where you will find three bridges (see Figure 4-3).

Figure 4-3. *Entering the captcha information to access the bridges*

2. You can also request the bridges to arrive in your e-mail by sending an e-mail to bridges@bridges.torproject.org with the line "get bridges" by itself in the body of the mail. You'll need to send this request from a Gmail, Riseup, or Yahoo account exclusively (see Figure 4-4).

Figure 4-4. *Getting Tor bridges by sending e-mail to bridges@bridges.torproject.org*

■ **Warning** Do not use your primary e-mail address to receive Tor bridges if you live in a country where Tor usage is illegal or prohibited. Automatic monitoring machines deployed by many nation-states can investigate e-mail contents and discover that you're trying to connect to the Tor network using customized bridges.

3. To enter bridges into the Tor Browser, launch Tor Browser, and before the Tor Browser connects, click the Open Settings button (see Figure 4-5).

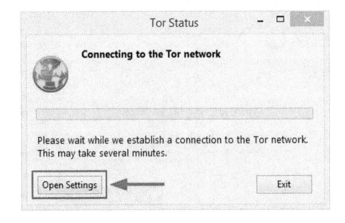

Figure 4-5. *Accessing Tor network settings through the Tor Browser*

4. A Tor Network Settings window appears; click the Configure button (see Figure 4-6).

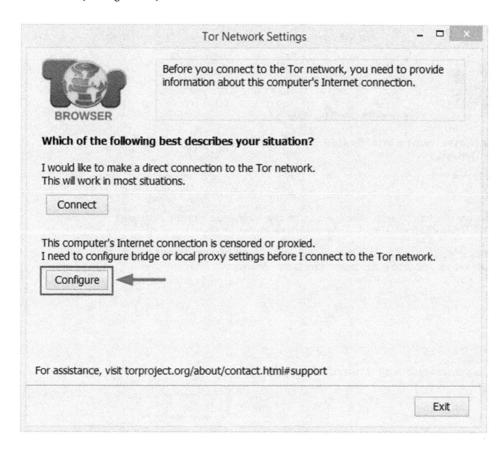

Figure 4-6. *Tor Network Settings window*

5.   Tor asks you whether your ISP is blocking or otherwise censoring connections to the Tor network; select Yes (see Figure 4-7) and click Next to continue.

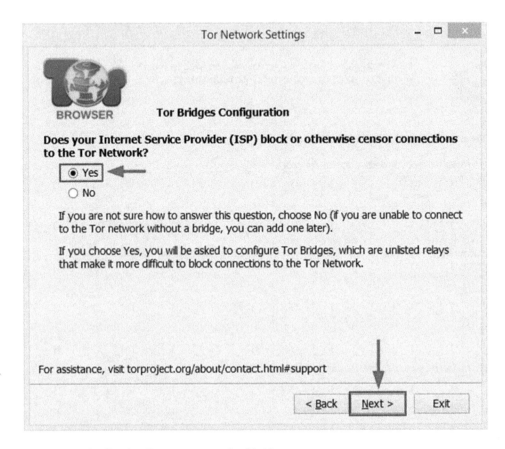

Figure 4-7. *Configuring Tor to use customized bridges*

6. In the next wizard window, select the option "Enter custom bridges." Copy the bridges you have from step 1 or step 2 and paste them in the box; click Next to continue (see Figure 4-8).

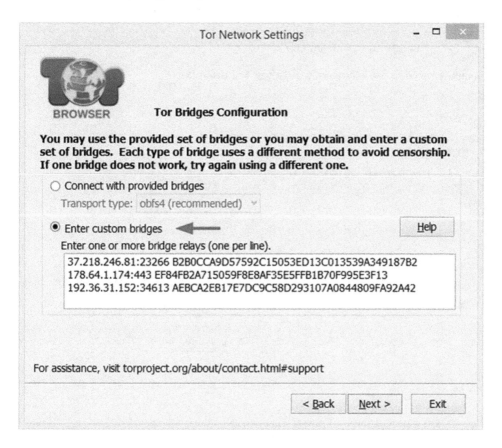

Figure 4-8. Entering custom bridges into Tor Browser

7. The next wizard asks you whether your computer sits behind a proxy server; in our case, we don't need one (which is most comment). Select No and click the Connect button to continue (see Figure 4-9). If you are sitting behind a proxy server, select Yes, then enter your proxy settings, and finally click Connect.

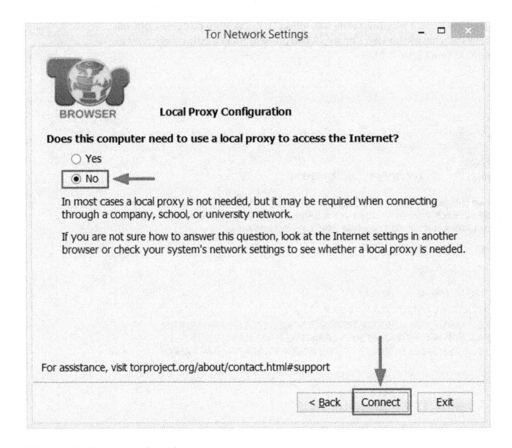

Figure 4-9. *Final wizard window*

If everything works as expected, the Tor Browser will open using the customized bridges.

As we have already introduced, using customized Tor bridges may not fully mask your entry to the Tor network. Some countries use a deep packet inspection (DPI) technique to analyze Internet traffic flows by protocol to examine whether they contain Tor traffic. China, Uzbekistan, and Iran are examples of countries that have used this technique to try to block Tor traffic.

NOTE! WHAT IS THE DPI TECHNIQUE AND ITS IMPACT ON PRIVACY?

When using the Internet, computers exchange data in the form of packets. Each packet of data contains a label, and this label will be read by routers to determine where to send it. This is how most Internet traffic works. Firewalls use the same principle of investigating packets to identify traffic passing through them.

In most cases, the contents of the packets go unmonitored; however, some governments and ISPs can deploy DPI equipment (firewall boxes) or simply install a DPI software solution on border routers. This way, they can investigate the source and destination of each packet flowing through the networks they control.

DPI has many advantages in terms of stopping spam e-mails, measuring network response time, determining the amount of time required for a packet to travel across a network path from sender to receiver, categorizing traffic into types based on destination server IP addresses and ports used, and measuring the total and relative volumes of traffic for each type.

DPI techniques can be abused to monitor the online traffic of honest people. By investigating each packet source and destination, the DPI operator can effectively monitor traffic closely for eavesdropping and censorship purposes. DPI can also be used to scan for more specific information like keywords.

SolarWinds and Procera both provide DPI solutions.

Using Pluggable Transports

To work around the DPI censorship technique, Tor has introduced the pluggable transport (PT). This will transform the Tor traffic flow between the client and the bridge into ordinary Internet traffic. This way, censors that monitor traffic between the client and the bridge will see innocent-looking transformed traffic instead of the actual Tor traffic.[7]

To use a Tor pluggable transport, follow these steps:

1. Launch the Tor Browser and click the Open Settings button before Tor starts.

2. Click the Configure button, select the Yes option when asked whether your ISP blocks or censors connections to the Tor Network, and click Next to continue.

3. Select the option "Connect with provided bridges" and select a bridge from the Transport Type drop-down menu (see Figure 4-10).

   Tor has many pluggable transports. Currently, the following are the most common ones:

   - obts4

   - meek-amazon

   - meek-azure

   - obfs3

   - scramblesuit

   Select one from the drop-down menu and then click the Next button to continue.

Warning The pluggable transports currently deployed in the Tor Browser may change with future releases of the Tor Browser. You can always select a different one from the drop-down menu, but you should begin by selecting the "recommended" one, as we did in Figure 4-10.

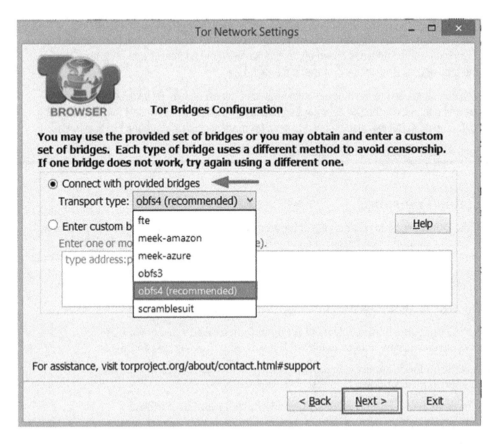

Figure 4-10. *Connecting to Tor network using a pluggable transport to conceal your Tor usage*

4. The final wizard window will ask you whether this computer sits behind a proxy server. In our case, it does not, so we select the No option and click the Connect button. If you are sitting behind a proxy server, select Yes, enter your proxy settings, and click Connect button.

If everything goes well, the Tor Browser should now be able to load successfully, and the browser window should appear using the new bridges.

Precautionary Steps to Stay Anonymous When Using the Tor Browser

To stay anonymous when using the Tor Browser, you must consider the following warnings to avoid revealing your true IP address:

- Do not install add-ons in your Tor Browser. Some extensions such as Flash Player and QuickTime tend to open connection outside your Tor network. This will reveal your true IP address. The Tor Browser is configured for anonymity, so you cannot use it as your regular browser.

- Don't open PDF files or view Flash video in your Tor Browser. As we already said, such an application may open its own connection outside the Tor network resulting in revealing your real identity.

- A Tor exit relay can be abused to monitor your Tor traffic. As we already mentioned, the exit relay establishes the actual connection to the destination server and is not encrypted (Tor does not encrypt the link between the exit relay and the final destination), so if an intruder captures your traffic at this location, the intruder can read everything unless you have encrypted your data before sending to the Tor network.

- Beware of a man-in-the-middle (MITM) attack (see Figure 4-11). This attack is a kind of active cyber-attack where an intruder inserts his or her device in the middle of the connection between the two communicating parties (these parties can be humans or systems). By doing so, an attacker has the ability to intercept the entire conversation of the victims in addition to gaining full access to all the sensitive information they are currently exchanging. An attacker can also impersonate the communicating parties by relaying information between them as if legitimate.[8] The main protective steps against this type of attack are to use end-to-end encryption and to pay extra care when verifying the server authenticity. Checking server authenticity can be done automatically by using SSL certificates checked by your browser through a set of recognized certificate authorities. If you receive a security exception similar to the one in Figure 4-12, you may be a victim of an MITM attack. Do not bypass this warning unless you have another method to verify the authenticity of the server.

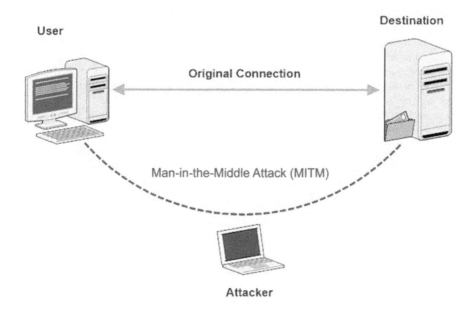

Figure 4-11. *Man-in-the-middle attack*

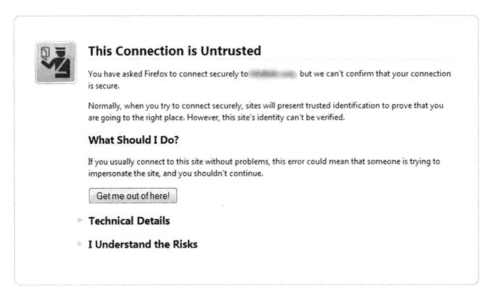

Figure 4-12. *Error message when trying to access a web site with an unverified identity (insecure certificate)*

- This last warning is related to the human security aspect and people's habits when using computers and surfing the Internet. For example, when you want to use a Tor Browser to conceal your online identity, you must not reveal your name or register with your real name and primary e-mail address on any web site that requires registration. In the same way, some users may use Tor while using Google to search. Such bad practices can ultimately reveal the user's identity even though when using Tor. The Tor network is designed to help you conceal your IP address and can do nothing to protect you if you spread your personal details everywhere. In this book, we will cover best practices and suggestions to keep your personal information private when working online with or without using the Tor Browser.

In this section, we introduced the Tor network and how you can access it via the Tor Browser. Using the Tor Browser is more than enough for the casual Internet user seeking privacy online. However, users who live in extremely hostile environments who need a way to communicate privately must access the Tor network using a security-hardened operating system. The Tails operating system is a Linux security-hardened OS that uses Tor as its default networking application. Later in this chapter we will cover this sophisticated operating system and give warnings and tips when using it.

I2P Network

I2P is an alternative anonymity network to Tor, and it supports common Internet activities such as web browsing, e-mail web site hosting, file sharing, and real-time chat.

Unlike Tor, whose focus is to access web sites from the normal Internet, I2P is more directed toward accessing a closed, anonymous Internet, also known as a *darknet*, separated from the normal Internet. I2P protects communications from dragnet surveillance and monitoring by different third parties (governments, ISPs, etc.). Anyone running I2P can run an anonymous server through a so-called eepsite, which is accessible only within I2P network using the `.i2p` top-level domain (similar to `.Onion` for Tor hidden services, as you are going to see in the next section).[9]

You can get I2P from its official web site (`https://geti2p.net/en/`). However, you may find that the description of I2P on its official web site is somehow difficult to understand, so in this section we will introduce in simple detail how to set up your browser to use the I2P anonymous network.

Warning I2P doesn't go through Tor.

To run I2P on your PC (we are using Windows for this experiment), you must have Java already installed on your machine because I2P is written using the Java programming language. You can download Java from `https://www.java.com/en/download/index.jsp`.

1. Download I2P from `https://geti2p.net/en/download` and install it like you would any ordinary Windows program.

2. Start I2P by clicking the "Start I2P (restartable)" program icon, as shown in Figure 4-13).

Figure 4-13. *Starting the I2P anonymous network*

3. The I2P service console will appear. Wait some seconds for it to connect. A browser window will also open to announce a successful connection to the I2P network.

4. After I2P starts, you need to configure your browser to access the normal Internet. In our case, we will use Mozilla Firefox to configure it for I2P usage. Go to the Firefox menu, select Tools ➤ Options, go to the Advanced tab and then the Network tab, and click the Settings button. In the Connection Settings window, select the option "Manual proxy configuration" and enter **127.0.0.1** in the HTTP Proxy field and **4444** in the Port field. Make sure the "No Proxy for" text box contains "localhost, 127.0.0.1." Finally, click the OK button to accept the new settings (see Figure 4-14).

Note We prefer and encourage you to use the Firefox browser over other popular counterparts such as Chrome and Microsoft Edge. Later in this chapter we will discuss why we prefer using Firefox over other browsers.

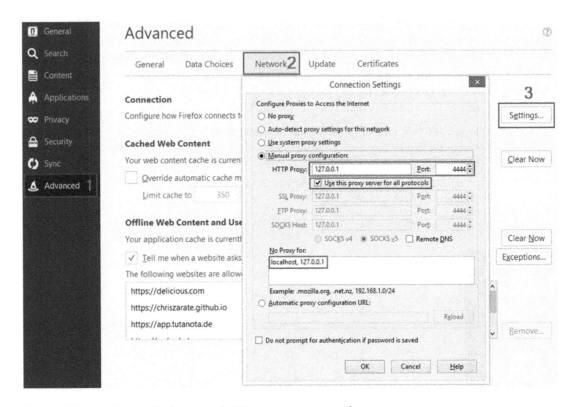

Figure 4-14. *Configuring Firefox to use the I2P anonymous network*

Now your Firefox browser is ready to use the I2P network. To make sure the configuration is working, use Firefox to visit any web site that can show you your current IP address, such as `https://www.iplocation.net` (see Figure 4-15).

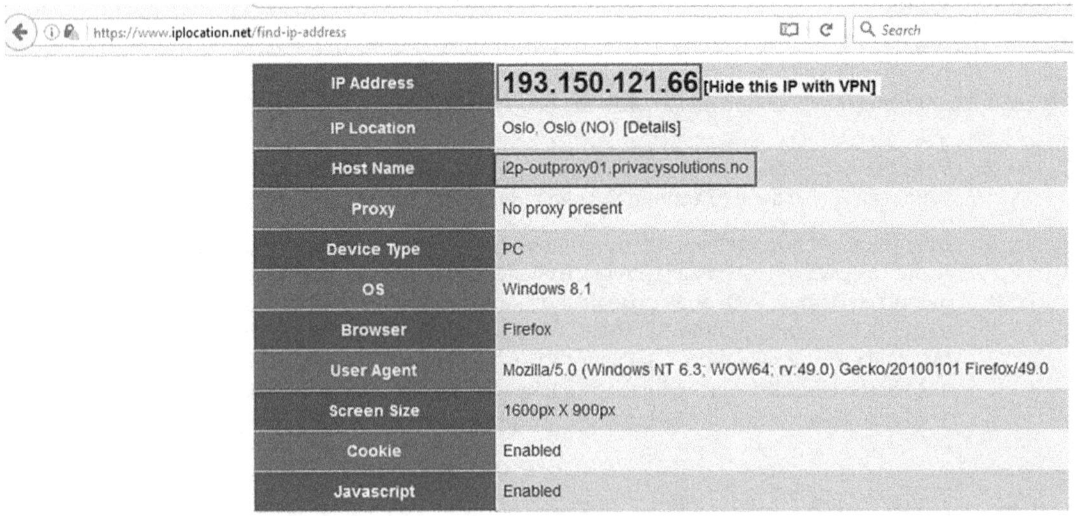

IP Address	**193.150.121.66**[Hide this IP with VPN]
IP Location	Oslo, Oslo (NO) [Details]
Host Name	i2p-outproxy01.privacysolutions.no
Proxy	No proxy present
Device Type	PC
OS	Windows 8.1
Browser	Firefox
User Agent	Mozilla/5.0 (Windows NT 6.3; WOW64; rv:49.0) Gecko/20100101 Firefox/49.0
Screen Size	1600px X 900px
Cookie	Enabled
Javascript	Enabled

Figure 4-15. *Making sure that I2P successfully masked your real IP address*

The previous configuration of Firefox allows you to use the normal Internet anonymously. In the same way, you can access any web site hosted on the I2P anonymous network (such web sites have an .i2p extension instead of .com or .org). To access a web site within the I2P network, follow these steps:

1. Point your browser to the I2P web site you want to access; you will receive an error message stating "Website Not Found in Addressbook." To solve this problem, you need to click one of the jump service links at the end of the page (see Figure 4-16).

Figure 4-16. *Adding an I2P web site to the address book*

2. Try to click each jump service link (boxed in red in Figure 4-16) until you find one that takes you to the page that allows you to add this web site to the I2P router address book (see Figure 4-17).

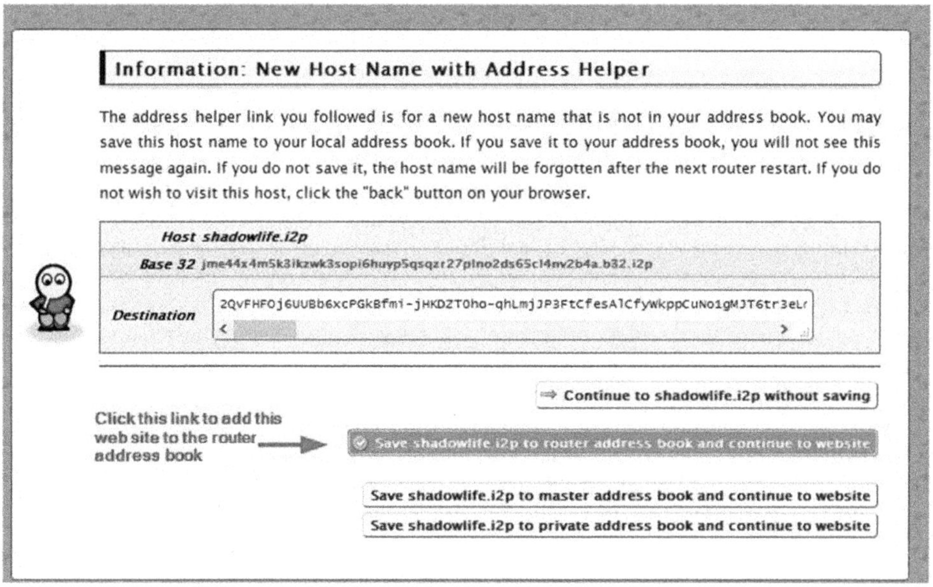

Figure 4-17. *Adding your newly I2P web site to router address book*

3. After clicking "Save *X* to router address book and continue to website," the page shown in Figure 4-18 will redirect you to the intended web site (`shadowlife.i2p` in this example).

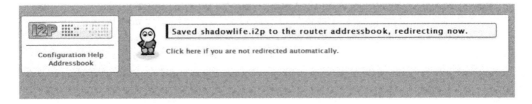

Figure 4-18. *Redirecting you automatically to the requested web site*

I2P is not suitable for casual Internet users. As we already said, it is for accessing web sites hosted on the darknet under the `.i2p` top-level domain name. Although it is a little daunting for beginners to use this network (and I2P is somewhat slow compared with Tor), we wanted to mention it in this book because we are going to talk about the darknet later in this chapter, and I2P is considered one of the darknet's major anonymous networks.

Freenet

This is another anonymous network. It is a fully distributed, peer-to-peer anonymous publishing network. We will not cover how to use this network like we did with the previous ones. However, you can check out `http://freesocial.draketo.de` for a complete tutorial on how to use this anonymous network.

Tor, I2P, and Freenet are the most popular anonymous networks currently available. Tor surpasses the other two in being more widely used and more mature. We recommend using the Tor network for all your work that requires online anonymity. Later in this chapter, we will introduce Tails, which is hardened specifically to stay anonymous and to protect users' confidential and sensitive online communications.

Darknet

In the previous discussion of anonymity networks, we introduced the term *darknet*, also known as the *deep web, deep net,* or *invisible web.* All these terms are interchangeable and point to the hidden underground of an unindexed Internet. It is hidden because regular search engines like Google and Yahoo cannot index its contents and thus it remains hidden from the general public. The deep web refers to anything that cannot be indexed. For example, many government web sites have millions of documents in databases that cannot be retrieved using ordinary search engines; thus, such documents are considered part of the deep web.

When we discuss the darknet in this book, we are considering web sites that are hosted by anonymous networks, such as I2P or Tor. There are no rules or regulations that govern the web sites hosted on the darknet. This makes this subnetwork an ideal location for criminals and other miscreants and malicious individuals to conduct their illegal activities with more assured levels of invisibility. Buying and selling guns, drugs, and people; sharing child abuse images and extreme pornography; selling false government documents (such as national IDs and passports); and selling hacked bank account and credit card numbers are but a few areas of illicit interests that thrive on the darknet. This makes the darknet an attractive place to visit but also a dangerous place to make deals or to talk with people who are using its resource.

After reading this short introduction to the darknet, you may think that this hidden Internet is only intended for criminal organizations and other groups such as terrorist groups. However, this is not always true because there are many web sites that are hosted within this environment to prevent some nation-state authorities from knowing the associated operators. For example, many human rights activists and political opposition groups in developing countries use the darknet as a sort of resistance movement to promote their ideas or to exchange information away from their governments' gaze.

■ **Warning**   Everything mentioned in this section is to educate regular Internet users about the darknet and its dangers. We strongly encourage you not to access the darknet or browse any of its contents. The only exception is for researchers, journalists, and human rights activists around the world who need to protect their active profile.

How to Access the Darknet

Web sites hosted on the darknet cannot be accessed from the regular Internet. To access these resources, you must use either the Tor or I2P network.

In previous sections, we briefly covered how to access the darknet using both Tor and I2P. All web sites hosted on the Tor network are accessible only through the Tor Browser, and all these web sites must end with the `.onion` top-level domain name. In the same way, all I2P web sites must be accessed from within the I2P network and have an `.i2p` extension.

A popular search engine to browse and search the darknet is Grams. It works on the Tor network only and can be found at `http://grams7enufi7jmdl.onion` (see Figure 4-19).

These are other dark web search engines:

- Onion.link (`http://onion.link`)

- Tor2Web (`https://hss3uro2hsxfogfq.onion.to`)

- SurfWax (`http://lookahead.surfwax.com`)

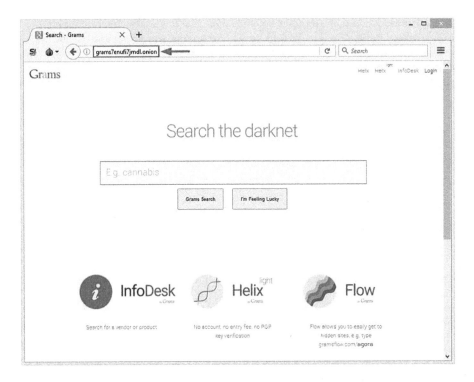

Figure 4-19. Grams search engine to search the darknet

Anonymous OS

Most ordinary computer users worldwide use the Windows OS for their daily tasks, but of course there are others who prefer the macOS, Google Desktop, or a Linux distribution.

Out of the box, most OS implementations are not configured to be robust, secure, or anonymous, although you can configure them it to be more secure. However, by design they are not built with consideration of users who seek anonymity and security by design.

In this section, we will cover how to use the Tails operating system from an end user's perspective. Tails is considered the best anonymous OS currently available, and for the record, this is the OS that Edward Snowden used to help stay anonymous during the initial NSA spying leaks. You can use Tails to communicate privately with confidence in extremely hostile environments. At the end of this section, you will find a list of security procedures that should be considered when using the Tails OS to assure that your work is 100 percent secure. For now, let's begin using this unique OS.

Tails

Tails stands for "the amnesic incognito live system." It is a Linux-based operating system built to provide the maximum security and anonymity possible for its users. It is a portable live OS, meaning that it can be launched from within your USB stick drive without installation, and it is completely independent from the host machine's current operating system.

Tails runs using the host machine's RAM and does not copy any files to the resident host machine's hard disk.

Tails achieves its anonymity by forcing all network connections to go through the Tor network. If an application tries to connect to the Internet directly, the connection is automatically blocked. Tails leaves no traces on the host machine's hard disk. Upon shutdown, Tails will delete all user files, unless explicitly asked not to (persistent storage). Tails also come with several built-in applications preconfigured with security in mind: web browser, instant messaging client, e-mail client, office suite, and image and sound editors, in addition to a plethora of cryptographic tools such as LUKS for disk encryption (Linux only), HTTPS Everywhere, OpenPGP, and OTR for secure IM chat.

To run Tails from within your USB drive, follow these steps. However, before you begin, prepare a USB zip drive with at least 4GB capacity. All data on the target USB drive will be lost, so make a backup copy first.

1. Download the Tails ISO image from `https://tails.boum.org/install/index.en.html`.

2. Download the Universal USB Installer program from `https://www.pendrivelinux.com/universal-usb-installer-easy-as-1-2-3/`. This is a portable tool used to burn Tails onto your USB drive.

3. Execute the Universal USB Installer, click "I agree" in the pop-up window, and supply the requested information, as shown in Figure 4-20. In step 1 in Figure 4-21, you can select Tails from the drop-down menu. In step 2 you select the location of the ISO image of the Tails OS. In step 3 you select the USB drive that will hold Tails. Remember to select the Format check box to format the drive before installing Tails.

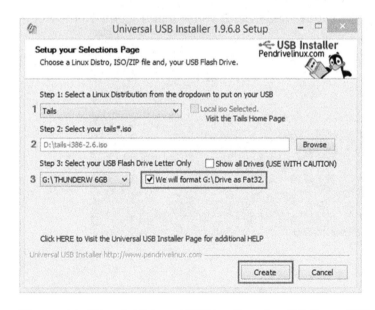

Figure 4-20. *Using the Universal USB Installer to install Tails on a USB disk drive*

4. Click the Create button to begin the process. A warning appears. Click Yes to start the installation. The installation takes a few minutes.

5. After the installation is finished, a pop-up window appears stating this. Click Close to close the wizard.

Now you have Tails ready on your USB disk drive. To boot from Tails, you need first to change the boot sequence of the host computer to start from the USB zip drive. You can apply this change to the boot sequence from within the BIOS settings. Each computer manufacturer has its own key to access the BIOS settings, the most common of which are F9 on HP; F10 on Sony; F11 on MSI; F12 on Lenovo, Dell, and Acer; and Esc on ASUS.

Note Please note that Tails can also be installed on CD/DVD by burning the Tails ISO image onto a CD/DVD using any burning utility. CDBurnerXP offers such a facility and is free: `https://cdburnerxp.se/en/home`.

If Tails start successfully, the Tails boot menu appears. Select Live and press Enter. You need to wait for less than one minute for the Tails welcome screen to appear (see Figure 4-21).

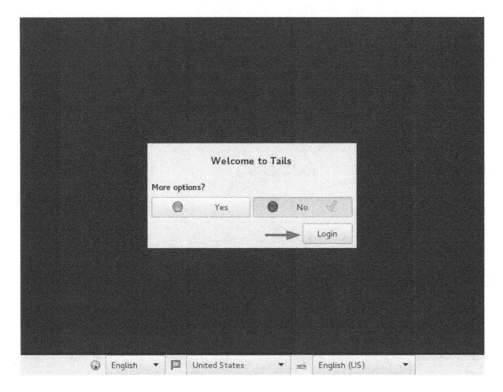

Figure 4-21. *Tails welcome screen*

Leave No selected and then click Login to continue. The Tails desktop will appear shortly.

Now you need to configure Tails to connect to the Internet. If you are using a wireless network connection, you need to configure Tails first to connect. From the top-right corner of the Tails screen, click the small arrow (near the battery indicator if you are using Tails on a laptop) and select Wi-Fi ➤ Select Network. A list of available wireless networks appears. Select one and click the Connect button. Enter a password for the selected Wi-Fi connection and click the Connect button.

To launch the Tor Browser, go to the upper-left corner of the Tails desktop; you will find a menu bar that contains two submenus. Click the Applications menu and select Internet ➤ Tor Browser.

Since you have started Tails and launched the Tor Browser successfully, you can begin your secure work online. When you're done using Tails, go to the upper-right corner, click the drop-down menu, and click the power button symbol. Tails will shut down immediately and wipe the host PC's RAM completely.

The previous configuration and installation of Tails is called *intermediary* Tails because you will not benefit from important features such as automatic security upgrades or the ability to store some of your documents and configurations in encrypted storage.

If you want to have Tails save user preferences, program configuration settings, and user data (persistent storage) when turned off, you need to install Tails as a final. Follow these steps to achieve this:

1. Launch Tails like you already did, prepare a USB drive with adequate storage capacity (we recommend at least 8GB), and plug it to your PC.

2. Go to the Application menu and select Tails ➤ Tails Installer to start the installer (see Figure 4-22).

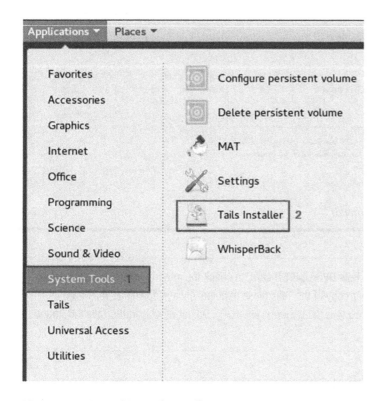

Figure 4-22. *Launching Tails installer*

3. Click the "Select by cloning" button and choose the USB stick that will hold your Tails from the Target Device drop-down menu (of course, select the second USB stick, not the one already used to launch Tails).

4. Finally, click the Install Tails button. A warning message appears; click Yes to continue.

You are done! Now you can use Tails from your new USB stick (final Tails), as you did the first time, but it will remember your preferences and program configuration on the next start.

TIP! USING TAILS IN OFFLINE MODE

You can use Tails without an Internet connection if you want to read or create sensitive documents. To start Tails in offline mode, launch Tails. When you reach the welcome screen, in the Welcome to Tails window, click the Yes button. Then click the Forward button to enter advanced startup.

The advanced startup window appears. Go to the bottom of the window and click the "Disable all networking" button. Then click the Login button (see Figure 4-23).

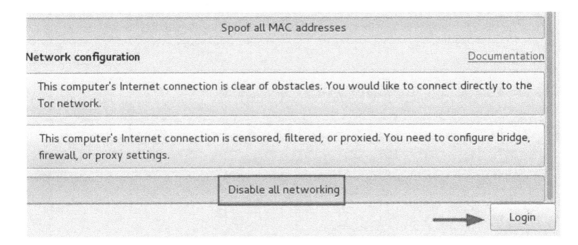

Figure 4-23. *Launching Tails in offline mode*

■ **Warning**   Before you create the live Tails DVD/USB/SD card, to check the integrity of the ISO image you have downloaded, you want to ensure your copy of the Tails file is genuine. Always download Tails from its official web site (`https://tails.boum.org/install/index.en.html`). Do not download the Tails ISO image from any other mirrored location.

Warning When Using the Tails OS

Tails is an excellent anonymous OS that uses the Tor anonymity network by default, but to stay completely anonymous when using this OS, you must be aware of some threats or attacks against the Tails OS that may result in your privacy being invaded while using it.

Tails is using Tor to anonymize Internet traffic, so all the earlier warnings for using Tor (in the section "Precautionary Steps to Stay Anonymous When Using the Tor Browser") also apply to the Tails OS. Here are some other warnings for and possible attacks against Tails:

- *Tails does not protect you against hardware-based attacks*: A hardware keylogger attached to a host machine can intercept your communications stealthily. In addition, some sophisticated attacks come from abusing BIOS or firmware to embed malicious software that can monitor all your Tails usage on the host machine. Tails cannot protect you against such attacks.

- *Encrypt everything before sending it through Tor*: As we mentioned previously, Tor is an anonymous network and not for encryption. Tails is the same; it cannot encrypt your data by default, but it still offers ready tools for encrypting files before sending them through the Tor network. In the coming chapter, we will cover encryption in detail.

- *Tails does not clear a digital file's metadata by default*: When creating files using Tails or any operating system, the software used to create these files usually stores details about the computer user's profile as well as technical details about the computer itself. Tails does not clear this metadata by default, so you must clear it yourself before sending such files online to avoid revealing your identity (deleting a digital file's metadata has been covered thoroughly in Chapter 2).

- *If you are using Tails and live in an extremely hostile environment, you should take extra care when working online by separating your online identity into many identities*: For example, use separate identities when you want to perform multiple actions online such as uploading a post to your blog, checking your e-mail, and replying to comments on a specific blog or web site. To remain anonymous in such cases, you should restart Tails after doing each task previously mentioned. This will effectively make tracking you by a global adversary with great resources almost impossible.

Tails and Tor are great projects for protecting user privacy online. However, keep in mind that both projects are works in progress. Computing technology is rapidly changing, and the attacks against user privacy are becoming much more complex and sophisticated. We advise you to always check the Tails official web site (`https://tails.boum.org`) and the Tor project official web site (`https://www.torproject.org`) for the latest news and updates. You can also check out `http://www.DarknessGate.com` where we will post information about all major updates to the tools contained in this book.

Secure File Sharing

Numerous providers offer file-sharing online services, many of which are free (although usually free accounts limit the file sizes you can upload). Almost all these providers store information about each online transaction that takes place through their servers. This is not the kind of service that security-conscious people should use. In this section, we will introduce two sharing providers that offer security and anonymity for their users.

OnionShare

OnionShare is a tool based on the Tor anonymous network dedicated to sharing files across the Internet in complete anonymity. OnionShare allows you to share files of any size anonymously using the Tor hidden network. It works by launching a temporary web site (similar to the Tor Onion service used in the dark web) that hosts your shared files. OnionShare will then produce an unguessable URL so the person you are corresponding with can access and download the shared files. What makes this program unique is that your shared files will not leave your computer and get uploaded to some location online; instead, they will remain on your local machine, and your correspondent will download them directly using the Tor Browser.

To share a file using OnionShare, follow these steps:

1. Download OnionShare from https://onionshare.org/ and install the application like you do with any Windows program.

2. Launch OnionShare and select the files you want to share by clicking Add Files (see Figure 4-24). You can also add entire folders by clicking the Add Folder button instead.

Figure 4-24. *Adding files to OnionShare, in the same way you can add files by dragging and dropping them in the empty panel*

3. Launch your Tor Browser. When your Tor Browser successfully connects to the Internet, click the Start Sharing button in the OnionShare program (see Figure 4-24).

4. When OnionShare successfully creates a hidden Tor service for your shared file (or files), also known as a temporary web site hosted on a Tor network, it will give you a URL to this file (see Figure 4-25). The shared file (or files) will remain on your PC.

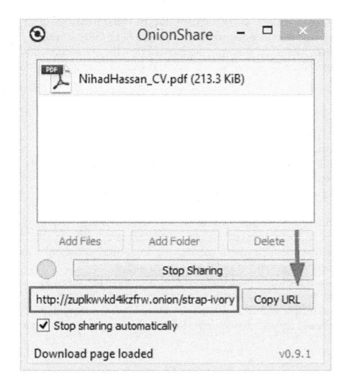

Figure 4-25. OnionShare provides a URL for your shared files, sends it to the recipient, and keeps it private.

5. Finally, all you need to do is to give the recipient the URL to that web site so he or she can download your shared file.

Bear in mind that you must leave your Tor Browser and OnionShare programs open until the transaction ends. Your computer is playing the role of a hosting server for the shared file. When the recipient receives your file successfully, OnionShare will stop the sharing process automatically (to stop sharing automatically after recipient receives the file, you must enable the option "Stop sharing automatically" in the OnionShare program before sharing files).

OnionShare is not vulnerable to sniffing attacks (when an eavesdropper monitors traffic on a Tor exit node) because connections between Tor hidden services and the Tor Browser are end-to-end encrypted. No network attackers can eavesdrop on the shared files while the recipient is downloading them. Despite this, we advise you to encrypt files before sharing them using the OnionShare program for maximum security.

A shared file URL (and its password if you decide to encrypt the file before sharing it) must be sent using safe routes. In the next chapter, we will introduce many techniques to encrypt and secure online communications.

For security-conscious people who want to share sensitive files, we advise you to use the Tails OS when sharing files through the OnionShare program.

▒ **Note**   It's advisable to disable any third-party tools that you may use to download files from the Internet (for example, Internet Download Manager) because they may cause problems when downloading from the Tor Browser.

Some providers do not offer the same level of anonymity as OnionShare, but you can still trust them for your daily needs. As we already said, Tor is preferred over all other services when you need the maximum security and anonymity, but there are many cases where you just want to send a normal file in a secure and anonymous way without attracting attention by using a Tor-based service, and this what you are going to learn next.

FileTea

FileTea is a new sharing provider that offers an anonymous and volatile file-sharing service. According to its privacy policy, FileTea does not store any information about its users; it also does not cache the contents of files shared through its server, and it stores only limited information about each file (name, size, and MIME type) in the processing server's volatile memory (RAM). The IP address of the user also is not recorded anywhere.

We've used this service many times and find it quite reliable; however, we advise you to encrypt any file you want to share through this service (Chapter 5 will cover encryption thoroughly). You can also encrypt the file name or simply change its name to anything that doesn't reveal its contents. Again, security-conscious users can launch the Tor Browser and use it to access this web site and share files through it.

Sharing files is easy; all you need to do is go to the home page (`https://filetea.me`), click the "Add files" button, and select the file or files you want to share. FileTea will generate a link for each file (see Figure 4-26), copy it, and send it to the intended recipient. Bear in mind that your browser should remain open until the recipient receives the file (FileTea will only process your file for delivery; it will not upload it to its server).

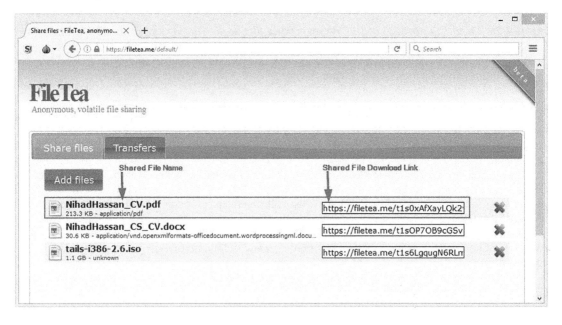

Figure 4-26. *Using FileTea service to share files anonymously. We used the Tor Browser in this experiment to achieve maximum security.*

VPN

A VPN works to establish a secure tunnel between two or more devices. Using a VPN helps users to add an extra layer of security and privacy to private and public networks such as Wi-Fi connections and the Internet. Enterprises use VPN services regularly to secure their sensitive and business-related traffic. However, its use by ordinary end users has become more popular of late because of the huge increase in digital communications along with the increase of cyber-attacks, making more people aware of the security dangers when utilizing online services.

When using a VPN (see Figure 4-27), an organization can secure private network traffic over an unsecured network such as the Internet. Thus, users feel safe connecting their personal devices to the Internet, ensuring their banking details, credit card numbers, passwords, and any other sensitive data is not intercepted by an unauthorized party. The VPN also gives the user an anonymous IP address, making them appear as if in another location so they can avoid censorship, share files with other people anonymously, and more. In today's digital world, using a VPN service is no longer considered as a security luxury.

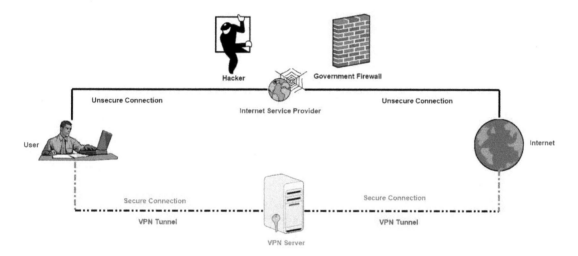

Figure 4-27. *How a VPN works (source. www.darknessgate.com)*

■ **Warning**   We advise you not to access the Internet at all (either from home or using public Wi-Fi hotspots) without a reliable VPN connection.

Criteria to Select the Best VPN

There are numerous VPN service providers worldwide. Many of them are reliable and offer distinct features. The prices usually are in the range of $5 to $10 for a monthly subscription (you can expect to get a discount for yearly subscription). There are also many providers that offer free VPN services in exchange for showing advertisements during the browsing session. For most users, any paid VPN providers will provision an adequate service to protect their online communications. However, if you want to approach your online security correctly, then you need to select your VPN provider carefully because the provider could intercept all your online communications passing through its service if it so wanted.

Note   Read the VPN provider's terms and conditions carefully.

In this section, we do not intend to describe how to use a specific VPN service provider to secure your connection, as each VPN provider may differ. Installing a VPN client is generally easy and requires a set of steps like when installing any other Windows software. We will focus on providing general advice to aid you when selecting a VPN provider.

Here are the criteria that must be met when selecting a VPN provider:

- Do not subscribe to VPN service providers that are based in one of the following countries: the United States, United Kingdom, Australia, New Zealand, Canada, Denmark, France, Netherlands, Norway, Belgium, Germany, Italy, Spain, Israel, Sweden, and of course countries such as Russia, China, Iran, and all Arab states.

- At the time of writing this book, the best secure providers are based in Swaziland and follow its jurisdiction.

- The VPN provider must support the OpenVPN software; this is an open source program that can be audited by anyone to make sure it is clean and does not contain backdoors.

- It is preferable that it have its own private DNS servers to avoid leaking users' DNS requests (web browsing history); you'll learn more about this in the next section).

- It should have integrated DNS leak protection technology built into the client VPN software.

- The VPN provider must separate Internet traffic according to the protocol used. For example, it should separate web browsing from file sharing, meaning that each one has a dedicated server.

- The VPN client software must support the ability to disconnect the Internet from your computer if the VPN fails for any reason (to avoid leaking your current activities to your ISP).

- It is better to support multiple devices at the same time, so you can protect your tablet and smartphone data in addition to your laptop or PC.

- It should accept anonymous payments such as bitcoin, gift cards, debit cards, and cash, if possible without showing any IDs (more on anonymous payments in the next section).

- It should not require many details to set up; a username and a password should be enough.

- It should not store any information about its users. This policy is also known as a *zero-knowledge policy*.

- Read the VPN provider's privacy policy and terms of service well. These two documents contain company policies and state the amount of data they are going to be logging about you and for how long. The privacy policy also declares the circumstances under which your VPN provider may turn your data over to governments or law enforcement.

- Do not use a free VPN service for mission-critical tasks online.

- If your ultimate purpose is anonymity and plausible deniability, use the Tor Browser instead of a VPN.

Opera Browser's Built-in VPN Service

The Opera browser has a built-in VPN function. This feature is completely free and unlimited (in terms of monthly bandwidth usage).[10]

You can activate the built-in VPN in your Opera browser by going to the Opera menu and selecting Settings. Go to the Privacy & Security tab, find the VPN section, and select the Enable VPN check box (see Figure 4-28).

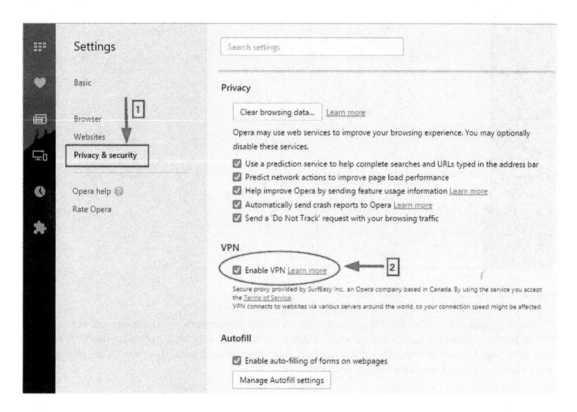

Figure 4-28. *Enabling VPN in the Opera browser*

After successfully enabling VPN in the Opera browser, you will see a blue VPN icon in the Opera address bar. You can further configure Opera VPN settings by clicking this icon (see Figure 4-29).

Figure 4-29. *Customizing Opera VPN settings*

Bear in mind that the Opera VPN is based on its dedicated VPN provider company named SurfEasy. This company is based in Canada and thus will follow its jurisdiction policies. You can use this VPN for your daily tasks to conceal your online tracks and unblock censored web sites. However, do not rely on it for mission-critical tasks, as we have already described.

Combine Tor with VPN

Using Tor with VPN will hide the fact that you are using Tor to surf online. As we already discussed, a VPN does not guarantee to mask your entry to the Tor network 100 percent. If your ISP or government uses advanced filtering techniques on Internet traffic, they can still discover indications that you are using the Tor Browser.

To use Tor with a VPN, first run your VPN client software. Once the VPN is turned on, you can start your Tor Browser. Please note that you cannot use a VPN when using the Tails OS.

Proxy Servers

A *proxy* or *proxy server* is basically another computer that serves as a hub through which Internet requests are processed. Your computer will connect to a proxy server requesting some services like a web page, a file, or other resources available from another server. The proxy server will fetch the required resources and send them to your computer. Today, most proxies are web proxies. Their major job is to facilitate access to content on the Internet and provide anonymity by changing the real IP address of the user's computer into the IP address of the proxy server (see Figure 4-30). There are many types of proxy servers. In this book, we advise exercising care with web proxies that anonymize and encrypt Internet traffic used to secure any online activities. In our opinion, using a proxy server is not necessary and should be replaced by a VPN provider. In the previous section, we talked about how to select a secure, reliable VPN provider. The same criteria will apply to selecting a proxy server provider if you want to utilize such a service.

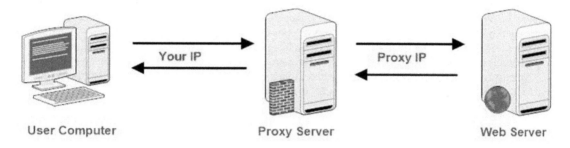

Figure 4-30. *How a proxy server works (source: www.darknessgate.com)*

Numerous free proxy servers are available online. However, we strongly recommend that such services are not used. A free proxy usually shows advertisements in your browser, which may introduce malicious software or other tracking scripts that could infect or compromise your machine if you click a malicious link. In addition, most free proxies are not secure enough to trust to process and communicate your critical data, such as credit card details and account passwords.

Connection Leak Testing

Sometimes even though you are protecting your connection using a VPN, a connection leak can occur and reveal the real IP address without you being aware. In this section, we will talk about how you can discover and handle this risk.

Check for DNS Leak

To understand what a DNS leak is, you must first understand the technical mechanism used to access web sites when you enter the web site URL in the browser address bar.

The Domain Name System (DNS) is one of the fundamental building blocks of the Internet and is utilized when you visit a web site, send an e-mail, have an IM conversation, or do anything else online. It can be considered the Internet's equivalent of a phone book. The system maintains a directory of domain names and translates them to IP addresses. This is necessary because although domain names are easy for humans to remember, computers and machines access web sites based on numeric IP addresses.[11]

For example, when you want to access the Google.com web site, you need to type its name in the address bar of your web browser. The request must then go to your ISP's DNS server (or to any DNS server that your computer is configured to use) and translate Google.com into its equivalent IP address, which is 216.58.198.46. (This IP could be different according to your geographic location as Google has many IP addresses assigned to the same site.)

■ **Tip**   If your connection is not functioning normally and you suspect that your DNS server is down, you can type the IP address of the web site you want to visit directly in your browser address bar and it should open normally.

Most Internet users worldwide connect via the default DNS server assigned by their ISP, which means that these ISPs can monitor and record a user's online activities whenever they send a request to the server. When using a VPN to encrypt your traffic, the VPN software should not use your default DNS server to resolve web site names to avoid revealing your web browsing history.

A DNS leak occurs anytime a DNS request is sent on your behalf to a DNS server other than the one you or your VPN provider intended. This happens most often when your DNS requests are routed outside of the encrypted VPN tunnel (because of the way operating systems handle DNS requests, especially in Windows OS). These unencrypted requests will then be forwarded to your ISP's DNS servers, allowing them to potentially monitor and log the complete web browsing history, even though you're using a VPN.

To ensure that your VPN provider is not vulnerable to this risk, you are strongly advised to test your connection directly after connecting to your VPN provider, as follows:

1. Go to `https://www.dnsleaktest.com`.

2. You will see two buttons along with your current IP address. The first button is labeled "Standard test," and the second is "Extended test." Click the second button for detailed results (see Figure 4-31).

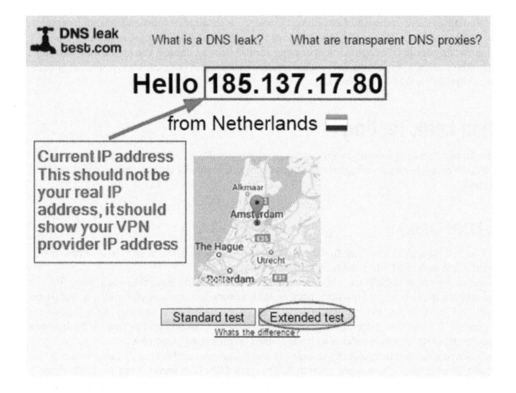

Figure 4-31. *Testing current VPN connection for DNS leak*

The detailed test report (see Figure 4-32) will show you all the DNS servers (along with their locations) that are used to resolve your typed web site URLs into IP addresses. If any of these servers (or the location of these servers) are not related to your VPN provider company, this means your connection is leaking information about you, and you should contact your VPN provider to solve this issue before using it to browse the Internet.

IP	Hostname	ISP	Country
74.125.47.141	none	Google	Netherlands
74.125.181.215	none	Google	Belgium
74.125.47.10	none	Google	Netherlands
74.125.47.7	none	Google	Netherlands
74.125.47.9	none	Google	Netherlands
74.125.181.212	none	Google	Belgium
74.125.47.5	none	Google	Netherlands
74.125.181.11	none	Google	Belgium
74.125.73.81	none	Google	Netherlands
74.125.47.148	none	Google	Netherlands
74.125.47.13	none	Google	Netherlands
74.125.73.72	none	Google	Netherlands
74.125.73.68	none	Google	Netherlands
74.125.73.87	none	Google	Netherlands
74.125.47.144	none	Google	Netherlands
74.125.181.4	none	Google	Belgium
74.125.73.89	none	Google	Netherlands
74.125.73.78	none	Google	Netherlands

Figure 4-32. *A partial report (extended test) generated by dnsleaktest.com showing DNS servers used by our current VPN connection*

Fix DNS Leak

There are many ways to fix DNS leaks. The following recommendations should do the job.

Use a VPN with DNS Leak Protection

We will not endorse any VPN provider in this book. We already covered the security criteria that must be met by a VPN provider. Before procuring a VPN service, ensure it explicitly supports DNS leak prevention. This option should also exist within the VPN client software installed on your machine. To further secure yourself, make sure to do DNS leak testing, as explained, to assure that your DNS traffic is tunneled through your VPN-encrypted tunnel and not through your ISP.

157

Stop DNS Leak in Windows 8 and 10

Newer versions of Windows (8 and 10) attempt to optimize DNS queries to improve web performance by sending DNS requests in parallel to all the available network interfaces. Even if you are using a VPN connection, Windows 8 and 10 may still leak some of your DNS requests without your knowledge (sending some requests to your ISP DNS server). This problem is more dangerous on Windows 10.

The Windows feature that causes a DNS leak connection is called *smart multihomed name resolution*. This feature is enabled by default; it must be disabled to avoid leaking your browsing history.

To disable this feature in Windows 8 and 10, follow these steps:

1. Open the Start menu and type **gpedit.msc** in the search bar. Click to open the Local Group Policy Editor (see Figure 4-33).

Figure 4-33. *Accessing Local Group Policy Editor under Windows*

2. Under Computer Configuration (see Figure 4-34), select Administrative Templates ➤ Network ➤ DNS Client and select "Turn off smart multi-homed name resolution." Double-click to access the properties, select Enabled to turn off the service, and then click Apply (see Figure 4-35).

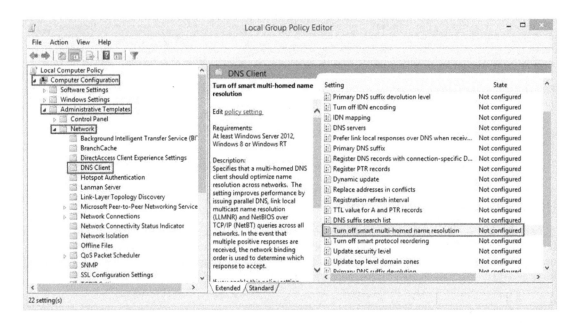

Figure 4-34. *Configuring smart multihomed name resolution to stop DNS leaking*

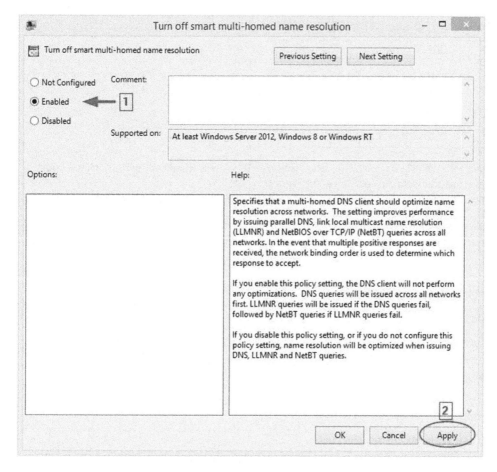

Figure 4-35. *Disabling smart multihomed name resolution feature in Windows 8 and 10*

    3.   Finally, reboot your computer and you are done.

Disable WebRTC

Web Real-Time Communication (WebRTC) is a standard that relies on JavaScript and provides browsers and mobile applications with real-time communication (RTC) capabilities via simple APIs.

    A good real-world example of WebRTC was the HELLO client integrated into Mozilla Firefox. This tool enabled Firefox users to conduct audio and video chat with another user who is using Firefox, Chrome, or the Opera browser without installing any additional add-ons or making any specific configurations.

    Firefox HELLO has been discontinued and was removed from Firefox starting with version 49. This happened automatically when you updated Firefox; no extra steps were needed.[12]

    There are many alternatives to the HELLO program that are using the WebRTC standard. Table 4-1 shows the most popular ones.

Table 4-1. *Chat Clients That Support WebRTC Standard*

Service Name	URL
Talky	`https://talky.io`
Cisco Spark	`https://web.ciscospark.com`
Appear.in	`https://appear.in`
Jitsi Meet	`https://meet.jit.si`

The problem with WebRTC is that it will reveal your true IP address when conducting a chat session with another user, regardless if you are using a VPN or not.

Any browser that supports the WebRTC standard will be vulnerable to this problem. For now, WebRTC is supported on Chrome, Firefox, Opera, Android, and iOS.

To avoid the risk, disable the WebRTC standard in your browser. We encourage users to use the Firefox browser (we discussed why in Chapter 2), so we will mention the ways to disable WebRTC using the Firefox browser only.

Method 1: Using an Extension

Use one of the following extensions:

- *Disable WebRTC*: `https://addons.mozilla.org/en-US/firefox/addon/happy-bonobo-disable-webrtc/?src=api`

- *uBlock Origin*: `https://addons.mozilla.org/en-US/firefox/addon/ublock-origin/`

Method 2: Disable WebRTC in Firefox

To disable Web RTC in Firefox, do the following:

1. Enter **about:config** in the Firefox address bar and press Enter. A warning message appears. Click "I accept the risk!" to continue (see Figure 4-36).

Figure 4-36. *Accessing the Firefox config file to modify its internal settings*

2. Search for *media.peerconnection.enabled*.

3. Double-click the entry to change its value; the column Value should now be false (see Figure 4-37).

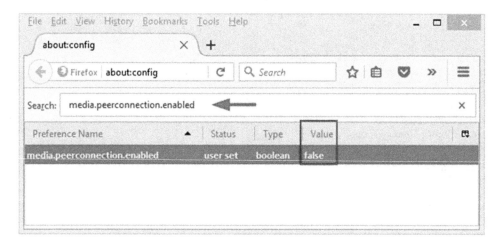

Figure 4-37. *Changing the media.peerconnection.enabled setting to false*

Fix IPv6 DNS Leak

IPv4 is the current Internet protocol; however, because the number of available IP addresses is dwindling, IPv6 will eventually become the standard protocol.

Some web sites have begun to use IPv6 to serve their users; however, the adoption of IPv6 is still at the beginnings because most web sites still use IPv4.

The problem with IPv6 in relation to using a VPN is that most VPN providers still do not support tunneling IPv6 requests through their encrypted tunnel. As a result, if a user connects to a web site that uses IPv6, the DNS request will go to his or her ISP DNS server, resulting in leaking the user's web history visits.

VPN providers that support DNS leak protection handle this IPv6 issue by disabling the IPv6 protocol in the operating system, so there's no need to worry about this issue.

If you want to disable IPv6 on your Windows PC manually, follow these steps:

1. Select Control Panel ➤ Network and Sharing Center. On the upper-left side select "Change adapter settings" (in Vista it is "Manage network connections"). Right-click the connection you want to disable IPv6 for and select Properties.

2. Uncheck the setting named Internet Protocol Version 6 (TCP/IPv6), as shown in Figure 4-38.

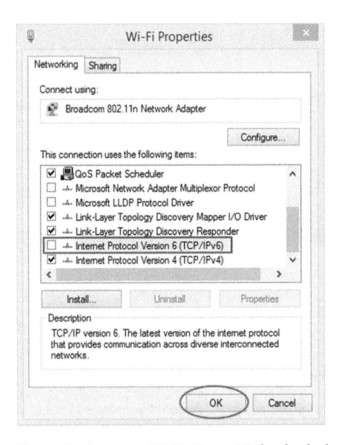

Figure 4-38. *Deactivating TCP/IPv6 in your Windows box for the selected connection*

By following the recommendations in this section, you can assure that no leak will happen while using a VPN connection. Nevertheless, periodically check your current connection at `https://ipleak.net` and `http://dnsleaktest.com` to make sure that everything is working well.

Secure Search Engine

Almost all Internet users have used a search engine in one way or another. Google is the largest search engine; it has a reputation for being easy to use and able to offer the best search results relevant to the user's search criteria. However, Google is a privacy nightmare for its users because it records everything done online, with many of its subscribers being unaware of this fact. This means there is constant potential for compromising online activities.

With Google Voice Search (which allows users to search using their voice instead of typing a search keyword), Google records all your voice searches in your Google account (of course you need to be signed in to your Google account when using it). Google also records all your typed search keyword history; the same history is kept for YouTube.com searches. The search history can reveal a great number of details about any user, such as current health condition, sexual habits, buying habits, political opinions, geographic location, and more.

Most users now use GPS-capable devices for accessing the Internet, such as smartphones and tablets, and if a user "check ins" at some locations while signed in to a Google account, Google will record this also (this service is known as *location reporting*). A timeline of all places the user has used his or her mobile phone or tablet will be recorded and linked to the user account.

What enables Google to perform these tracking issues in a simple and automatic way is the popular free e-mail service Gmail (note that Google can track your online activity even though you are not logged into your Google account). Users usually sign in to check their e-mail accounts and then remain signed in and use the Internet as usual. This allows Google to record their activities while using its services and link it back to each user account. The same thing happens with smartphone devices running Android OS (developed by Google): a user may remain signed in to his or her Google Play account (which is used to download/update apps and needs a Google ID to work) and use the phone as usual to send e-mails or to conduct online searches, resulting in tracking and recording much of his or her online activities.

In addition to all the tracking issues conducted by major search engine providers, they tend to perform a kind of censorship of user-returned search results. Major search engines try to anticipate what sorts of results their users like and display them accordingly. This means users receive fewer or unexpected search results filtered to suit their saved browsing habits without their knowledge!

The advance of computing technology allows Google—and other giant IT providers—to track user activities online even when they are not logged in to their accounts. For example, when a user checks an e-mail address and then signs out from his or her account, if the user continues the Internet usage session and uses one of the Google services (that does not require the user to sign in), Google is still able to link the current activities to the original account through the IP address or browser fingerprinting.

This invasion of user privacy is not limited only to giant IT providers like Google but includes many other software companies. These companies develop browser extensions and offer related free services to simplify Internet browsing for end users but are also involved in recording user activities to sell the data to advertisement companies. A recent report that appeared on German national TV shows stated nearly 3 million German Internet users' browsing history data has been collected by many companies that develop browser extensions for different popular browsers such as Firefox and Chrome. The report mentions only one popular add-on, which is Web of Trust (WoT). The report said that Internet users' data (nonanonymous data that includes user IP address, web history, and e-mail and Skype IDs) had already been sold to different third-party advertisement companies without users' consent.[13]

This clearly shows that despite all legislation that is promoted by different nation-states to protect user privacy, the Internet remains a hostile environment where users with limited IT skills (the majority) can become easy targets online.

In this section and the next, we will cover how you can stay anonymous online when conducting searches and how to harden your browser to avoid leaking private information about your online activities.

To stay anonymous online, it is vital to stop using regular search engines without proper defenses. In this section, we will introduce secure search engines in addition to showing how you can configure your Google account to prevent it from saving your online activities.

Configure Your Google Account to Stop Saving Your Activity

As mentioned, Google has the largest market share among all other search engine providers, so we will focus on it.

To configure Google to stop saving your private data (search history, location history, etc.) on any device you are using to access Google services, do the following:

1. Go to https://myaccount.google.com/activitycontrols (you must be signed into your Google account first).

2. Beginning at the top with the Web & App Activity section, move the slider to the left to turn off this feature (see Figure 4-39). A warning message will appear; click PAUSE to confirm your action (see Figure 4-40). Finally, the word *Paused* will appear next to the section title.

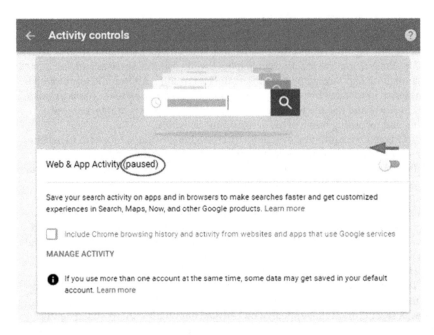

Figure 4-39. *Turning off Web & App Activity in a Google account*

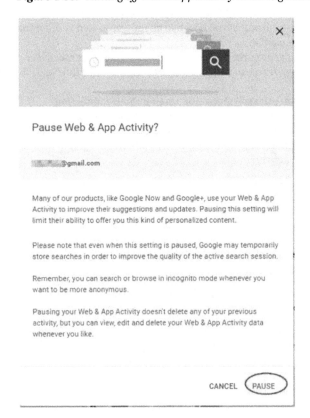

Figure 4-40. *Confirming you want to pause your Google account activity*

Repeat the same process with the rest of the sections on the page. Currently, the following sections are included in the Google account activity page: Device Information, Video & Audio Activity, YouTube Search History, YouTube Watch History.

To delete all your previous Google account activities, follow these steps:

1. Go to http://myactivity.google.com (you must be signed into your Google account first).

   - On the My Activity banner, click More (click the vertical dots) and then "Delete activity by" (see Figure 4-41).

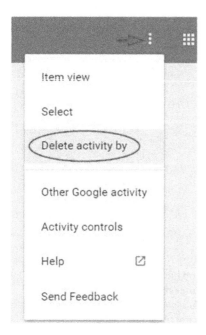

Figure 4-41. *Deleting previous Google account activities*

   - Below "Delete by date," select the down arrow and then select the option "All time" (see Figure 4-42).

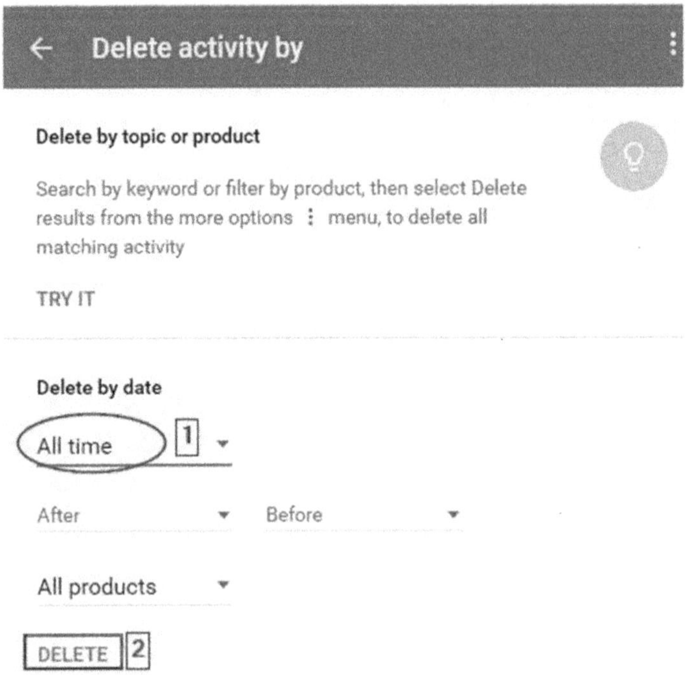

Figure 4-42. *Deleting all previous account history (All time)*

- Finally, click DELETE and confirm your action.

After turning off all these features, you can somewhat assure that you have more privacy when using Google services. However, from a privacy perspective, we cannot guarantee that Google will really stop tracking you completely even after turning off all its tracking features. To assure the maximum privacy possible, we encourage users to use anonymous search engines that do not track their users.

Privacy at Microsoft

If you are a Microsoft fan (in other words, you prefer to use the online services offered by Microsoft), then you will be happy to know that Microsoft has launched a privacy dashboard for its users. All you need to do is log in to your Microsoft account (`https://account.microsoft.com/account/privacy?destrt=privacy-dashboard`) to manage all the data that Microsoft uses to personalize your experience online.

Microsoft collects vast amounts of data about its users' online activities, covered next.

Web Browsing and Online Searches

You can choose whether your browsing history is collected for page prediction in your Microsoft browser settings by opening the Edge browser, clicking the dots in the top-right corner, and selecting Settings (see Figure 4-43). Go to the bottom of the window and click "View advanced settings. Disable the following options: "Show search and site suggestions as I type" and "Use page predication to speed up browsing, improve reading, and make my overall experience better." It is also preferable to select the following option "Block only third party cookies." from the drop down menu in the Cookies section.

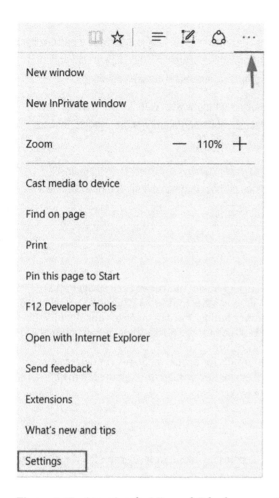

Figure 4-43. Accessing the Microsoft Edge browser settings area

Location Information

You can turn on or off location services for your device in Settings ➤ Privacy ➤ Location; in Windows 10 you can disable location services by clicking the Windows 10 Start menu and selecting Settings ➤ Privacy ➤ Location. Change the setting "Location for this device" to Off. From here, you can also choose which Windows Store apps have access to your location, and you can manage the location history stored on your device.

Data That Helps Them Assist You, Personally

This includes collecting other personal data related to users to predict future actions, such as checking a user's event calendar and user speech and handwriting patterns to predict what the user is aiming to do next and provide personalized recommendations. You can disable this online by going to `https://account.microsoft.com/privacy/cortana`.

> **Note** Cortana is the personal digital assistant for Windows 10 users. Its main task is to provide a personalized experience for Windows 10 users by offering suggestions when conducting searches in addition to remembering events, sending e-mails on the user's behalf (when configured properly), and many more useful things.

Cortana works through cumulative learning. Hence, when the user communicates with it more (through the PC microphone or by typing), it will understand the user's personal habits and attitude more, leading to more accurate results in future interactions.

To control Cortana's collection and use of your data, check `https://privacy.microsoft.com/en-us/windows-10-cortana-and-privacy`, which contains instructions on how to disable it on different Windows devices.

Fitness and Health

Health data help users to live healthier by monitoring their current health indicators such as heart rate, calorie burn, diet quality, blood pressure, and sleep quality, among other indicators. This data can be stored in your HealthVault, allowing you to share it with your doctors or family. You can manage your HealthVault account online at `https://account.healthvault.com` and can manage the Microsoft health dashboard at `https://dashboard.microsofthealth.com`.

Other data settings include "Data to show more interesting ads for the user," "Sign-in and payment data," and "information from device sensors." All these services can be disabled through the Microsoft privacy dashboard at `https://account.microsoft.com/privacy`.

Anonymous Search Engines

Anonymous search engines should have a number of criteria to be considered privacy friendly. Here are the main ones:

- They should not record the IP addresses of users.
- They should not record the browser fingerprint or plant cookies on the user's computer.
- They should use SSL to deliver data to users.
- They should allow access via the Tor anonymous network.
- They should have a zero-knowledge log policy about their users.

StartPage

StartPage (`http://startpage.com`) introduces itself as the world's most private search engine. This search engine intelligently connects the user securely to its portal through SSL, allowing the user to search as if he or she is using Google. StartPage will take user queries, fetch the results from Google, and present them to the user. This process is transparent and fast. StartPage also integrates a proxy server so that you can open any link anonymously from the search result pages and yet keep your IP address hidden from the destination server.

DuckDuckGo

DuckDuckGo (https://duckduckgo.com) is an Internet search engine that emphasizes protecting searchers' privacy and avoid personalizing search results according to each user's previous Internet browsing history.

DuckDuckGo emphasizes getting information from the best sources rather than the most sources (from more than 400 sources), generating its search results from key crowdsourced sites such as Wikipedia and from partnerships with other search engines such as Yandex, Yahoo, Bing, and Yummly (note that it does not fetch results from Google).[14]

DuckDuckGo does not record any information about its users (such as IP address) or log visits and does not plant cookies on your computer.

The following are other search engine providers that are worth mentioning for their privacy-enhanced techniques:

- *Disconnect* (https://search.disconnect.me): This fetches its results from major search engine providers anonymously.

- *MetaGer* (https://metager.de/en): This supports user privacy by not logging users' data (like IP address, browser fingerprint, and cookies). It provides secure access through HTTPS to all its search results in addition to a proxy server to anonymize your access to these results. It also allows access via the anonymous Tor network.

These secure search engines have a proven record in protecting user privacy. Nevertheless, you should always check the privacy policy of any search engine you use regularly to make sure that no updates take place that affect your privacy.

Web Browser Privacy Configuration

There are many browsers in the market. The market share is dominated by five of them: Firefox, Chrome, Internet Explorer, Opera, and Apple Safari.[15]

Of course, there are some lesser-known browsers such as UC Browser & SRWare Iron that have proven their presence in the market lately. However, these browsers are either an implementation of one of the major browsers already mentioned or were developed in countries where users' privacy is not respected. For example, Iron is an implementation of the Chromium project. Both Google Chrome and Iron share much of code and features from the same project but with different licensing agreements. The UC browser was developed by a Chinese company.

Firefox is the first truly open source browser. Chrome, on the other hand, was developed by Google, which has a long record of logging users' activities to target them with specific ads, so we do not encourage using it. Internet Explorer (and its successor Microsoft Edge) was developed by Windows and suffers from the same privacy concerns as Chrome. Opera was recently acquired by a Chinese company.[16] As a result, we discourage using it for mission-critical tasks.

Mozilla Firefox (or simply Firefox) is a free and open source web browser developed by the Mozilla Foundation. It has a great reputation for protecting users' privacy since its launch. In fact, the Tor project uses Firefox as the preferred engine for its Tor Browser bundle.

Firefox for Android is also open source software, and its code is available to anyone who wants to audit it.

In this section, we will cover how you can harden Firefox to become more privacy friendly. Then we will cover some security add-ons that can enhance Firefox security. But first, let's check what information current browsers are revealing about your identity!

Check the Browser Fingerprint

A browser fingerprint is any information that is used to identify your machine online. It can be used to fully or partially identify individual users or devices even when cookies are turned off. Browser fingerprinting is used to identify individual users online and is considered, relatively, a new technique for tracking and recording the online activities of users stealthily.

Browser fingerprinting can reveal a great amount of information about your computer. It works by loading a script (generally JavaScript or Flash) into your browser. Once it has loaded successfully, it will detect a wide array of technical information about your computer, such as screen resolution, OS type, supported fonts, browser type and version, add-ons installed, and even your PC hardware components. A hash is then made based on the information the script has collected. That hash can help identify and track your computer like an IP address would. A digital fingerprint can draw a comprehensive unique picture about each user, allowing different outside parties to easily profile people without using traditional tracking techniques like computer IP addresses and cookies.

Fingerprinting is currently considered the greatest risk that faces users when surfing online. Let's begin by seeing what your current digital fingerprint shows to the public. The following are two web sites that offer such services for free.

Browserleaks

At BrowserLeaks.com you will find the gallery of web browser security testing tools that tell you what exactly personal identifiable data may be leaked without any permissions when you surf the Internet.

Go to `https://www.browserleaks.com`. On the bottom-left side of the screen you will find the set of tools that can be used to reveal your digital fingerprint divided into groups; click each one to see a detailed report (see Figure 4-44).

Figure 4-44. BrowserLeaks.com offers different security testing tools to access your web browser digital fingerprint

Panopticlick

Panopticlick (https://panopticlick.eff.org/) is a research project created by the Electronic Frontier Foundation (https://www.eff.org/). It will analyze how well your browser and add-ons protect you against online tracking techniques (see Figure 4-45).

Figure 4-45. *Panopticlick home page*

Hardening Firefox for Privacy

In this section, we will give technical advice on how to modify the Firefox settings to assure your online privacy and lower the amount of data leaking from your browser.

Let's start with basic Firefox settings.

1. Access the Firefox options by clicking the menu in the upper-right corner of your browser and selecting Options (see Figure 4-46).

Figure 4-46. *Accessing the Firefox Options menu*

2. The Firefox Options page appears; let's begin with the Search tab. You need to configure Firefox to use only secure and anonymous search engines. To do so, uncheck all currently used search engines and keep only DuckDuckGo and StartPage. Also, make the first one your default search engine (see Figure 4-47).

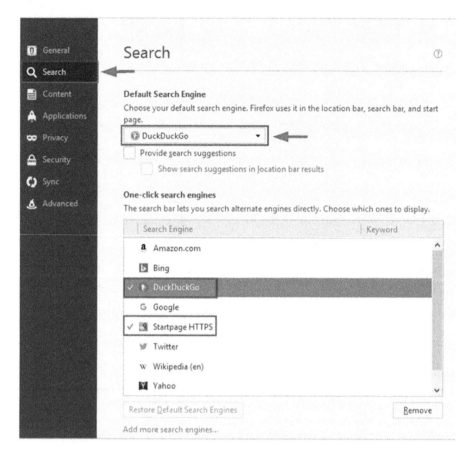

Figure 4-47. *Keep only secure, privacy-enabled search engines to avoid using other public search engines accidentally.*

NOTE!

To add StartPage.com to your list of supported search engines in Firefox, follow these steps:

1. Go to `https://www.startpage.com/` (you must access this page using Firefox).

2. On the home page, click Add to Firefox.

3. There is another way that performs the same thing; it's shown as Option 2 in Figure 4-48.

Figure 4-48. *Adding StartPage to Firefox search engine list of providers*

- Move to the Privacy tab. You need to turn on the option Use Tracking Protection in Private Windows. When this option is enabled, each time you visit a web site, Firefox will send a signal that you do not want to be tracked. Of course, this is a voluntary action because some web sites may not obey your request. Still, it's a good choice to enable it. Now go to the History section on the same page and select the option "Never remember history" so that Firefox will delete all your history every time you close it. Finally, go to the Location Bar section and disable all the suggestions in the search bar because the suggestion process can leak excessive data about you. Your Privacy tab should look like what appears in Figure 4-49.

Figure 4-49. Configuring the Privacy tab in Firefox browser for better privacy

- Move to the Security tab. Please configure it like in Figure 4-50 to prevent loading dangerous web sites and to prevent web sites from installing add-ons. Also, you need to configure Firefox not to store user passwords.

Figure 4-50. Configuring the Security tab to stop phishing and dangerous web sites

- Go to the Advanced tab. Here you will find multiple subtabs; select Data Choices. Disable the three available options named Enable Firefox Health Report, Share additional data (i.e., Telemetry), and Enable Crash Reporter (see Figure 4-51). Crash reports can contain valuable data about your computer status. If such data should fall into the wrong hands when traveling online from your PC to Firefox servers, this can reveal the type of vulnerability/error you are facing and enable an outside attacker to exploit your machine.

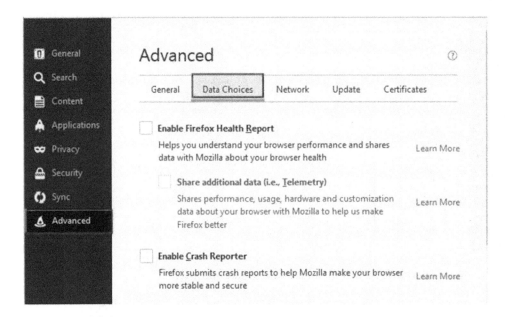

Figure 4-51. *Configuring the Advanced tab via the Data Choices subtab*

- While you are still in the Advanced tab, go to the Network subtab, and make sure that the option "Tell me when a website asks to store data for offline use" is selected. This prevents web sites from planting a tracking code on your computer.

- While you are still on the Advanced tab, go to the Certificates subtab and make sure that the options in this window are selected, as shown in Figure 4-52.

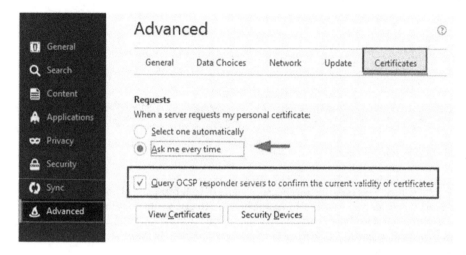

Figure 4-52. *Configuring the Certificates subtab to protect your personal certificate that identifies you online*

After configuring the basic settings of Firefox to become more privacy friendly, you need to access its advanced options menu to make it more robust against cyber-attacks and user profiling.

To access the Firefox advanced settings, type **about:config** in the URL address bar of your browser (see Figure 4-53). A warning message will appear; hit the button "I accept the risk!" to access the advanced settings panel.

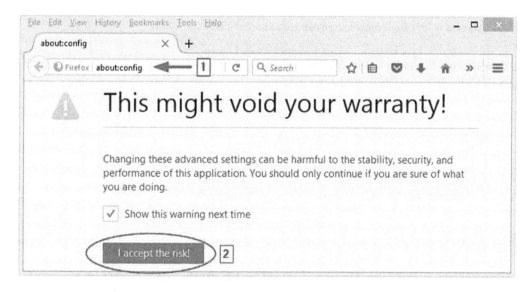

Figure 4-53. *Accessing Firefox advanced settings panel*

To access a specific setting, you need to type its name in the Search box that appears at the top of the page. Let's begin by searching for *browser.formfill.enable* to force Firefox to forget form information; double-click to change this setting to false (see Figure 4-54).

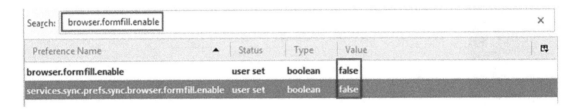

Figure 4-54. *Disabling form history in Firefox*

Firefox can cache data to disk. This is dangerous because some of your browsing history may reside on your disk even after you delete all your previous browsing history. To disable this feature, type **browser. cache.disk.enable** and double-click to change the setting to false (see Figure 4-55). You need to do the same with the setting browser.cache.disk_cache_ssl because Firefox has two setting for the content cache, one for normal web sites and the second for secure web sites (has SSL in its name).

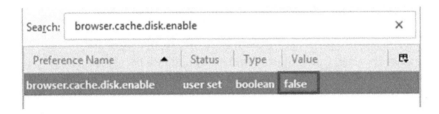

Figure 4-55. *Prevents Firefox from caching web content to the hard disk*

You must also prevent Firefox from caching web contents for offline use by changing the setting browser.cache.offline.enable to false (see Figure 4-56).

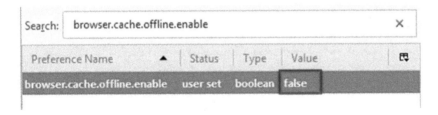

Figure 4-56. *Prevents Firefox from caching web contents for offline use*

You can prevent Firefox from accessing your clipboard by changing the setting dom.event. clipboardevents.enabled to false. This feature has some privacy implications because it can allow web sites to manipulate clipboard events in your web browser.

Now you need to disable geolocation services. This prevents Firefox from sending information about your network and location to third parties (the default party is Google). Change geo.enabled to false (see Figure 4-57).

Figure 4-57. *Disabling geolocation services in Firefox*

It is a good idea to ask Firefox to throw away all cookies automatically every time you close your browser. To do this, change the setting network.cookie.lifetimePolicy to 2. To change its value, double-click and enter **2** at the prompt (see Figure 4-58).

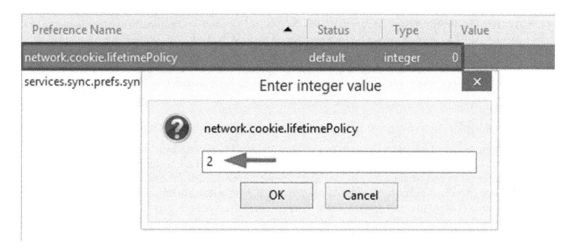

Figure 4-58. *Instructing Firefox to delete all stored cookies automatically upon closing*

The most interesting setting that can reveal your list of installed plug-ins is plugin.scan.plid.all. It is essential to disable this setting so visited web sites will not be able to distinguish your browser from the add-on already installed (to minimize browser footprinting). In addition, some web sites may ask you to disable an ad blocker to view their web site because they can detect if you have an ad blocker already activated in your browser. Change this setting to false (see Figure 4-59).

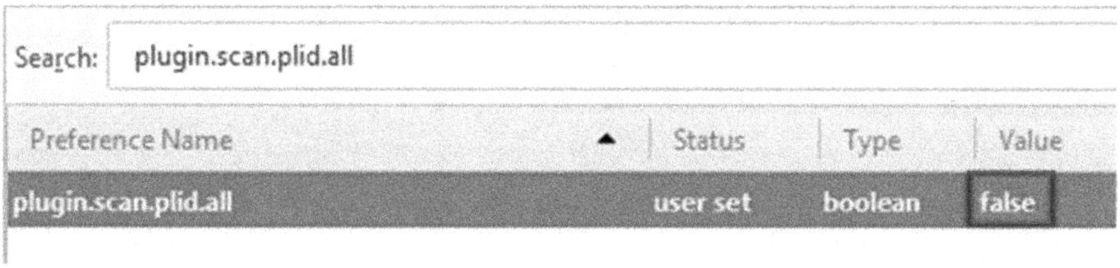

Figure 4-59. *Prevents Firefox from revealing your installed add-ons*

These advanced configurations will harden Firefox and make it more difficult for outside parties to track your activities. In the next section, we will cover privacy add-ons that can further secure Firefox and fight against online tracking and user profiling.

Browser Extensions for Privacy

In this section, we will cover Firefox browser add-ons that can further secure your browsing. To choose which add-ons to cover, we considered the developer behind the add-on, the estimated number of active users, and its overall reputation.

As we mentioned previously, some add-on providers may fool the user and collect personal identifying data about browsing habits and even personal information without his or her consent, so it is advisable to avoid installing any add-on except the ones mentioned in this section, and if a new reliable add-on appears later (maybe after publishing this book), ensure that it comes from a reputable trusted developer and install it from `https://addons.mozilla.org` exclusively.

HTTPS Everywhere

HTTPS Everywhere (`https://www.eff.org/HTTPS-EVERYWHERE`) is produced as a collaboration between the Tor Project and the Electronic Frontier Foundation. Many sites on the Web offer some limited support for encryption over HTTPS but make it difficult to use. For instance, they may default to unencrypted HTTP or fill encrypted pages with links that go back to the unencrypted site. The HTTPS Everywhere extension fixes these problems by using clever technology to rewrite requests to these sites to HTTPS.

Privacy Badger

Another great extension created by EFF is called Privacy Badger (`https://www.eff.org/privacybadger`). Privacy Badger is a browser add-on that stops advertisers and other third-party trackers from secretly tracking where you go and what pages you look at on the Web. If an advertiser seems to be tracking you across multiple web sites without your permission, Privacy Badger automatically blocks that advertiser from loading any more content in your browser. To the advertiser, it's like you suddenly disappeared.

Disconnect

Disconnect (`https://addons.mozilla.org/en-US/firefox/addon/disconnect`) is an add-on that blocks web trackers from gathering your personal information. It claims it can load pages 44 percent faster in addition to stopping tracking that comes from more than 2,000 third-party sites. Disconnect receives *Popular Science*'s 26th annual Best of What's New award honoring breakthrough products and technologies.[17]

uBlock Origin

uBlock Origin (`https://addons.mozilla.org/en-US/firefox/addon/ublock-origin`) is a popular open source add-on with more than 2,000,000 downloads. It is efficient and easy on memory and CPU and yet can load and enforce thousands more filters than other popular blockers.

Random Agent Spoofer

Random Agent Spoofer (`https://addons.mozilla.org/nn-no/firefox/addon/random-agent-spoofer/`) rotates complete browser profiles (from real browsers/devices) at a user-defined time interval. It includes many extra privacy-enhancing options.

> ## NOTE! USING A VPN SERVICE AND MASKING YOUR REAL DEVICE/BROWSER TYPE (DIGITAL FINGERPRINT) CAN GIVE YOU LOWER PRICES ONLINE!

In Chapter 1, we covered the different ways companies track your online activities, including your location, and how they can easily know the specification of the device you are using to connect to the Internet.

By using a VPN service, you can change your device IP address to look as if you are connecting from another country. Many travel companies set different prices for its flight tickets according to customer country. For example, reserving a flight ticket while pretending you are from Brazil (by using a Brazilian IP address) costs less than reserving one while you are in the United States (when using a U.S. IP address).

Agent spoofing also helps you to cover the device you are using to access the Internet (but there's no guarantee it will works perfectly on all web sites). For example, buying goods online using your newest iPad device will give the impression to the online merchant that you are willing to pay more for the items than a customer who connects using an old Nokia device!

Disable Flash Cookies and Java Plug-In

Most computer users have Flash Player already installed on their machines. You should adjust your Flash Player settings to disallow third-party web sites from installing Flash cookies on your computer. Modifying the Flash Player settings will influence all installed browsers on your computer (except the browsers that are Chromium based, including Google Chrome). To configure Flash Player for better security, go to the Control Panel and click Flash Player (see Figure 4-60) to access the Flash settings.

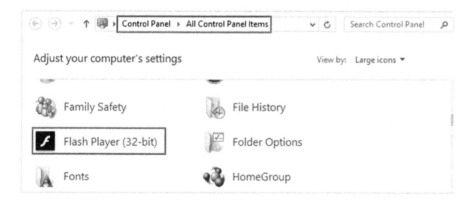

Figure 4-60. *Accessing Flash Player in the Windows Control Panel to update its settings*

On the Storage tab, make sure the option "Block all sites from storing information on this computer" is selected (see Figure 4-61).

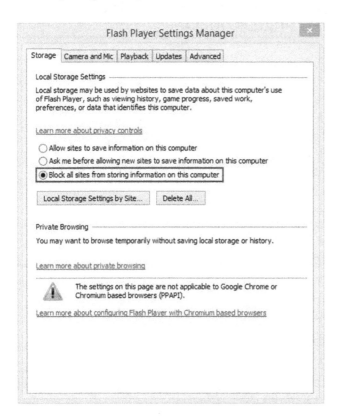

Figure 4-61. *Adjusting the Flash Player settings to disable third-party web sites from storing contents on your disk drive*

Another plug-in that could be exploited to invade your privacy or install malware on your computer is the Java plug-in. Today, few web sites still use the Java plug-in in order to function, so the advice is to disable it completely from your browser. However, if you want to keep the Java plug-in, it is necessary to harden its security settings by going to the Control Panel and clicking Java to open the Java panel. Ensure that you select the option Very High, as shown in Figure 4-62. Also, go to the Update tab and make sure the option Check for Updates Automatically is selected.

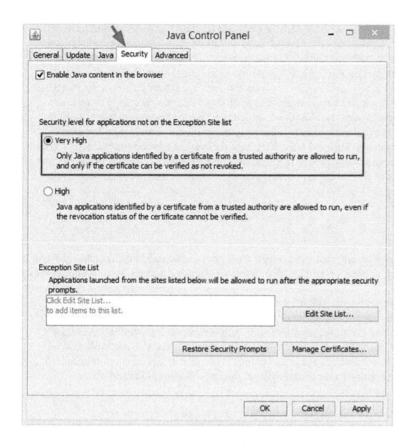

Figure 4-62. *Adjusting the Java settings to increase security*

Countermeasures for Browser Fingerprinting

Fighting against browser fingerprinting is difficult, and it doesn't seem there is a 100 percent guaranteed technical solution. Even after configuring Firefox for better privacy and installing many add-ons, outside adversaries can still recognize your digital fingerprint to a large extent.

The best technical solution to fight against browser fingerprinting is to make your browser look like most browsers' fingerprint! To achieve this, it is advisable to use a freshly installed copy of the Firefox browser configured manually with privacy-enhanced settings without installing any add-ons. This browser should run from a virtual machine that also freshly installed. By using this technique, your browser will look like most running browsers and thus effectively conceal your true digital footprint. Of course, you still need to use a VPN to encrypt your connection and conceal your IP address.

Anonymous Payment

To complete your endeavor to become completely anonymous online, you need to learn how to conduct online purchases without revealing your identity. Any time you make a purchase or send a payment, your name appears and may be stored along with other details about the transaction.

Anonymous payments are sometimes perceived by the public to be used by criminals and terrorist groups. However, in many instances, this is not the case as more and more ordinary users employ this to shield their identity and to prevent outside parties from knowing what they purchase. A user can have many reasons to conceal his or her purchase history. For example, some users may not feel safe to give their personal details to online merchants, others may not want to reveal what they buy (e.g., the purchase of sexual items could be embarrassing), and others want to hide their gambling, which may be against their religious beliefs. Security-conscious users who seek to maximize their online anonymity should use anonymous payment methods to conceal their identity when buying anonymity services online (e.g., paying for a VPN provider anonymously). This will effectively hide their usage to anonymity services. Other examples are journalists speaking against oppressive regimes, whistle-blowers, and free speech advocates.

In this section, we will introduce you to different anonymous payment methods that you can use to make anonymous purchase online.

Prepaid Gift Cards

Most credit card providers offer prepaid cards for their clients. This card can be used just like the ordinary one, and it does not require a client to have a credit check or bank account. In addition, most prepaid cards don't require a PIN to use.

There are different types of prepaid cards. What we care about for this book is the anonymous type, which is the "nonreloadable" card. Prepaid cards (the nonreloadable type) are available almost everywhere, from drug stores to supermarkets. You can purchase them with cash (untraceable) without revealing any personal information; even your e-mail address is not required. Prepaid cards are also available online; however, buying online will of course require you to reveal your real identity to facilitate a purchase electronically (e.g., you must use a regular credit card/PayPal to purchase the prepaid one).

Here are the other types of prepaid cards:

- *Open-loop prepaid card*: This belongs to a general credit card provider and carries its logo (e.g., Visa, Mastercard, American Express, Discover). You can use this card anywhere you can use the ordinary card type. However, this type is not anonymous because you need to supply your information to get one.

- *Closed-loop prepaid card:* This card can be used to make purchases from a single company. It will carry the initiated company logo (not the credit card provider company like Visa or Mastercard) and cannot be used for general purchases. Examples of this card are from Starbucks, telephone, fuel, stores.

- *Reloadable prepaid card*: This is a general-purpose card that consumers "load up" and spend almost anywhere. This type is usually issued by popular credit card providers like Visa, Mastercard, and American Express. Consumers can load it with cash using different methods like direct deposit and bank transfer. This type of cards is not anonymous as you need to supply your personal information to get one (almost the same procedure as an ordinary credit card).

- *Nonreloadable card*: This card doesn't require any personal information to have it. This type of card is widely available in major supermarkets and pharmacies, and you can buy it with cash to completely conceal your identity. Major credit card providers like Visa and Mastercard issue this type of card. This means you can use it anywhere you can use the ordinary card. However, unlike the reloadable card, when the balance of the card reaches zero, it will expire automatically and you cannot reuse or reload it with more funds. The maximum value that can be placed on this card is established by the card issuer (many issuers have a limit of $2,000).

■ **Warning**   Do not buy prepaid credit cards online. If you buy a prepaid credit card online, you need to pay for it using some form of nonanonymous payment like an ordinary credit card, a bank check, or PayPal. In addition, you need to supply your postal address to receive the card (if it is a physical plastic card). This will link the purchased credit card to your real identity.

- *Payroll card*: This is usually issued by employers to their employees who do not have a bank account to receive their salary. Employees can use this card to purchase items online and pay bills. Obviously, this is not an anonymous card.

- *Government benefits card*: This is issued by some government agencies to pay unemployment benefits, child support, and other government benefits.

- *Student prepaid cards*: These cards are offered by universities for their students to pay for things on campus.

Here are some prepaid credit card providers:

- Mastercard (https://www.mastercard.us/en-us/consumers/find-card-products/prepaid-cards/gift-card.html)

- American Express (https://www.americanexpress.com/gift-cards/)

- Discover (https://www.discover.com/gift-cards/)

■ **Warning**   It is advisable to buy the "nonreloadable" prepaid cards from a location that doesn't have security cameras to avoid revealing your identity.

Virtual Credit Card

This is an electronic card with no physical plastic presence. This type of card can be used for online transactions only. To get this type of card, you need to have a valid ordinary credit card or you can simply attach it directly to your charging bank account. The number on the virtual card will be randomly generated and will be associated with your actual credit card (if it is associated with an ordinary credit card). You can set the amount of money that this card will hold in addition to the expiration date and can deactivate it instantly if it is stolen. Whenever you buy something online, the actual bill will appear on your credit card account (or the charging bank account). However, the online merchant will see only your virtual card details, thus helping you secure your actual credit card number. Most of the largest credit card issuers offer virtual credit card services; other third-party companies also offer this service, including Entropay (https://www.entropay.com), which currently supports a Visa card only, and SpectroCard (https://spectrocard.com), which currently supports Mastercard only.

Virtual credit cards provide a type of anonymity to users (in terms of protecting the actual credit card details). However, we cannot consider this method of payment completely anonymous, as the virtual card is linked to either an actual credit card or an actual bank account. If you perform something illegal online, authorities can track your transaction back to you.

A virtual credit card allows people to buy products online while concealing their true identity against the merchant they deal with, in addition to protecting users from online fraud. This why we mention it here as a kind of anonymous payment method.

Cryptocurrency

This is a type of digital currency that is designed to work as a medium of exchange using cryptography to secure the transaction and to control the creation of additional units of currency.[18]

Bitcoin was the first decentralized crypto-currency, appearing in 2009, and remains the dominant currency in terms of use and capitalization, so it will be our focus in this section.

Note There are hundreds of crypto-currency types already in use. As we said, the most famous is still Bitcoin system. You can find a list of currently available crypto-currency at `https://coinmarketcap.com`.

Bitcoin

Bitcoin (`https://bitcoin.org`) is an innovative Internet protocol created by a software developer group called Satoshi Nakamoto. Bitcoin uses SHA-256, which is a set of cryptographic hash functions designed by the U.S. National Security Agency. It is a decentralized peer-to-peer payment network (similar to the Torrent network) that is powered by its users with no central authority or middleman. Bitcoin is a digital system; it is not printed like ordinary currency (dollars and euros) and is created by people and companies using a specialized open source software program called a *bitcoin wallet* (the wallet can be an online service; hence, it is called an *e-wallet*). Bitcoin does not charge fees on transactions, and it is nonrefundable (once you send bitcoin to a recipient, it will be gone forever unless the recipient returns them to you).

We will not delve deeply into the technical side of the bitcoin digital currency because it is out of the book's scope. What you should know about bitcoin is that you can make anonymous purchases using this currency. In the following sections, we will show you how to open a bitcoin account and fund it with cash to begin trading online.

Open Bitcoin Account

The following steps show you how to open a bitcoin account and how to fill it with bitcoin currency.

Step 1: Open Bitcoin Account

Like with a bank account, you first need to have a bitcoin account. In bitcoin naming, it called an *address*. A bitcoin address is a single-use token, which looks like this: 1MauqJEVKx7mohEAAaWYnn96RFvLEGnVjV.

Users can have as many addresses as they want (it is not limited); all these addresses are stored in a user's bitcoin wallet.

To get your new bitcoin address, you need to register for a wallet. There are many web sites that offer bitcoin wallets. At blockchain (`https://blockchain.info/wallet/#/signup`), you can sign up for a new wallet by entering your e-mail and password (this password is to access your bitcoin wallet); then click the Continue button to create your new bitcoin wallet. To see your bitcoin address, log in to your wallet account and click the Receive button (see Figure 4-63).

Figure 4-63. *Viewing your bitcoin address*

■ **Note**   Here are some other bitcoin online wallet web sites:

https://easywallet.org/

https://www.zenwallet.org/

https://www.instawallet.org/

Step 2: Buy Bitcoin

Bitcoin is a kind of currency, so to buy them, you need to pay real money to exchange for them. Here are some methods to fund your bitcoin wallet with cash.

If you followed along and created your wallet at Blockchain, you can get bitcoin currency by logging in to your bitcoin wallet and then going to Buy Bitcoin on the left side of the page. Blockchain works with exchange partners all around the world; select your country from the drop-down menu and click the Continue button.

Now you need to enter the amount of bitcoin you want to buy; in our case, we want 100 euro (see Figure 4-64); click the Buy Bitcoin button.

Figure 4-64. *Entering the amount of bitcoin currency you want to buy using your selected country currency*

The next screen will create an account for you on the bitcoin exchange partner that you select in the first step; just accept the terms of service and click Continue (see Figure 4-65).

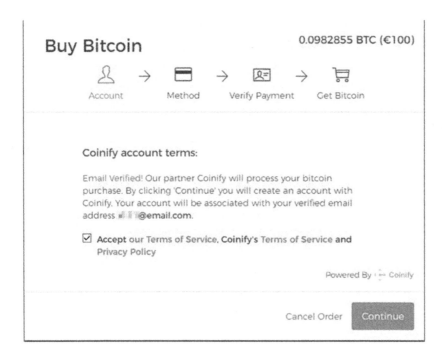

Figure 4-65. *Your current wallet account will be associated with the chosen bitcoin exchange partner*

Now, you need to select your payment method. You have two options (see Figure 4-66).

- Credit/debit card

- Bank transfer

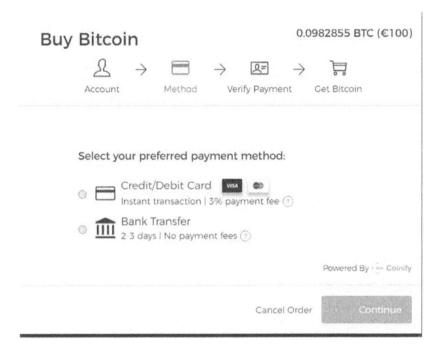

Figure 4-66. *Selecting how you will buy your new bitcoin currency*

Obviously, both payment methods will reveal your identity and link your purchased bitcoin with your real identity. In the next section, we will suggest other methods to buy bitcoin anonymously.

After selecting your payment method, click Continue to see the order details. If everything is OK, click the Confirm button to purchase the specified bitcoin amount (see Figure 4-67).

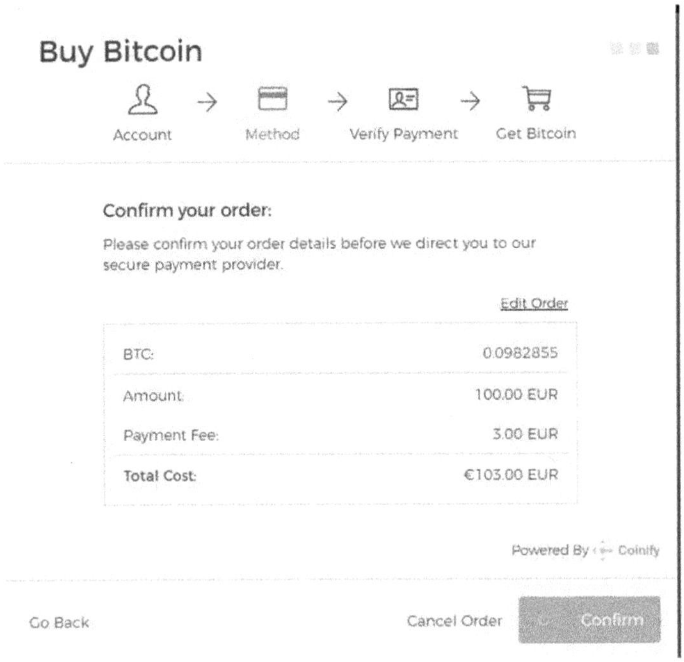

Figure 4-67. *Confirming your order details to purchase bitcoin*

░ **Note** At the end of this section we will show you different ways, including anonymous methods, to buy bitcoin.

Step 3: Make Payments

After you have currency in your bitcoin address, you are ready to make online purchases. Go to the site where you want to purchase the item/service and find out the merchant bitcoin address you need to pay your money to and the amount of money needed.

A simple example of a bitcoin transaction is to send 2 bitcoins to the address 16TxBiZSfUdkWPtU6htKzxnkxHXcxzpnPi.

Go to the web site you used to get your address from (in our example `https://blockchain.info`), find the location where you can input your recipient's address (in `https://blockchain.info` it is the Send button) and the amount, and send the payment. It should be straightforward (see Figure 4-68).

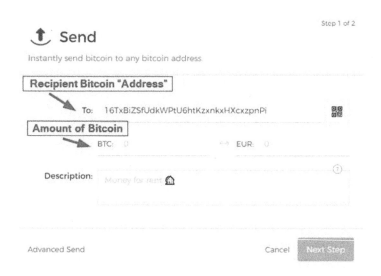

Figure 4-68. *Sending a payment to bitcoin Address*

This is how you use bitcoin to make online payments; as we noted, it is straightforward and easy to use.

Bitcoin Client Software

In the previous example of bitcoin usage, we showed you how to use bitcoin to make purchases using an online service called an *e-wallet*. There is another way to use bitcoin without third-party online wallets; it works by using independent client software that manages the bitcoin address creation and purchases.

There are different bitcoin wallet programs; you can find a list at https://en.bitcoin.it/wiki/Clients. However, we prefer to use the standard one developed by bitcoin.org (also known as Bitcoin-QT) at https://bitcoin.org/en/download.

Bitcoin core initial synchronization will take time and download a lot of data. You should make sure that you have enough bandwidth and storage for the full block chain size (more than 100GB).

Once that is done, the client will control your wallet file. Be sure to protect it with a password and back it up regularly. It is stored in a file called wallet.dat in your bitcoin data directory. If you lose it or it gets stolen, you lose your money.[19]

As we have mentioned, there are different ways to buy bitcoin currency; our focus in this book is to charge your bitcoin address with cash using anonymous methods. In the coming section, we will list anonymous ways to buy bitcoins.

Buying Bitcoin

There are different methods to buy bitcoin. However, most charging methods can be traced back to your real identity, which is what you do not want to happen.

For instance, the following buying methods are available: PayPal, credit cards, bank transfer, cash, personal checks, gift card (prepaid card), money order, MoneyGram, direct seller online, physical trading, and ATM (only the supported one).[20]

These are the anonymous methods to buy bitcoin:

- *Cash*: This is the best anonymous option. Find someone to sell your bitcoin to in person. You can find potential buyers by going to `https://localbitcoins.com` and see who is near your physical location. This service (called *local bitcoin*) requires you to register an account. To remain anonymous, do not use your primary e-mail address. Instead, create a new e-mail and use it for this purpose only (in the coming chapters we will cover anonymous secure e-mails). Also, be sure to take care to meet the person who will buy your bitcoin in a location where no security cameras exist.

- *ATM machines*: You can buy bitcoin anonymously with cash using ATM machines; however, such machines are not available everywhere. Bitcoin ATM machines allow you to generate a new bitcoin address, if you do not supply one, and this new address will be printed on paper. Then you can take this paper and import the private keys on it to your e-wallet online service/client. To find ATM machines that support bitcoin, go to `https://coinatmradar.com`. From here you can select your country/city and see a list of ATMs along their physical locations; you can buy the bitcoin from these machines using cash.

- *Prepaid cards*: This type of anonymous payment was already covered; you can use such cards to buy bitcoin online without submitting any personal details. Make sure to use Tor and a secure e-mail account to perform the buying transaction. `https://www.coinmama.com` accepts gift cards to buy bitcoin.

■ **Note**   Some services like `https://bitpay.com` allow people to accept bitcoin, store and spend bitcoin securely, or turn bitcoin into dollars with the BitPay Card.

Bitcoin payments are extremely anonymous; however, there is a bit of a learning curve for buying and exchanging bitcoin.

Registering for anonymity services, like a VPN, and even conducting some online purchases using an anonymous payment method may require users to supply their e-mail address as part of the transaction (e.g., you need to supply your e-mail address when buying a VPN service to receive the username and password). In this case, to stay anonymous, you should not supply your real e-mail; instead, use a temporary e-mail address. In the coming chapters, we will cover different secure, anonymous e-mail providers.

■ **Warning**   Encrypt your online connection before making an anonymous payment. When paying anonymously online, make sure to anonymize your connection using an anonymizing network like Tor or I2P. Paying anonymously without masking your IP address will expose your technical connection details to different parties, and this may lead to revealing your true identity.

Summary

In this chapter, you learned how you can conceal your identity online. As you already know, there are two types of information that can recognize you when surfing online. The first one includes your name, Social Security number, biometric records, or any other detail that uniquely belongs to you and is personally identifiable. The second type includes your digital footprint, which can include a variety of technical identifiers that cannot be related to your personality but can collectively distinguish you among millions of online users.

If anonymity is the goal, you must use the Tor Browser, which is the best one in the field. For people who live in extremely hostile environments, using the Tails OS is advisable.

We cannot guarantee a 100 percent technical solution to disappear completely online, but if you follow the instructions in this chapter along with other recommendations from the rest of this book, we can assure you that you can become invisible to an extent that is nearly impossible to discover. We say "nearly impossible" because in the computer security field, we cannot guarantee any technical solution to be completely perfect. For instance, if a big intelligence agency like the NSA targets you, it can use a set of elaborate and sophisticated online and offline techniques to break into your machine, whatever your defense.

Bibliography

Blockgeeks, "What is Cryptocurrency: Everything You Need to Know." http://blockgeeks.com/guides/what-is-cryptocurrency/.

Nihad Hassan and Rami Hijazi, *Data Hiding Techniques in Windows OS: A Practical Approach to Investigation and Defense* (Syngress, 2016).

Notes

1. Seth Fiegerman, "Yahoo says 500 million accounts stolen." CNN, September 23, 2016. http://money.cnn.com/2016/09/22/technology/yahoo-data-breach/.

2. The Tor Project, Inc. https://www.torproject.org/about/corepeople.

3. Tor Metrics. "Statistics about current status of Tor network," https://metrics.torproject.org.

4. Tor Network Status. https://torstatus.blutmagie.de.

5. EFF web site, "What is Tor?" https://www.eff.org/torchallenge/what-is-tor.html.

6. The Tor project, "Tor: Bridges." https://www.torproject.org/docs/bridges

7. The Tor project, "Tor: Pluggable Transports." https://www.torproject.org/docs/pluggable-transports.html.en.

8. Tails, Warnings. https://tails.boum.org/doc/about/warning/index.en.html.

9. Tails, Using I2P. https://tails.boum.org/doc/anonymous_internet/i2p/index.en.html.

10. Free VPN integrated in Opera for better online privacy. http://www.opera.com/blogs/desktop/2016/04/free-vpn-integrated-opera-for-windows-mac/.

11. Network solutions, "Managing Domain Name Servers." http://www.networksolutions.com/support/what-is-a-domain-name-server-dns-and-how-does-it-work/.

12. Mozilla Foundation, Support for Hello discontinued in Firefox 49, https://support.mozilla.org/en-US/kb/hello-status.

13. gHack, "Your browsing history may have been sold already." http://www.ghacks.net/2016/11/01/browsing-history-sold/.

14. DuckDuckGo search engine results source. `https://duck.co/help/results/sources`.

15. Desktop Browser Version Market Share. `https://www.netmarketshare.com/browser-market-share.aspx?qprid=2&qpcustomd=0`.

16. Steve Dent, "Opera browser sold to a Chinese consortium for $600 million." Engadget, July 18, 2016. `https://www.engadget.com/2016/07/18/opera-browser-sold-to-a-chinese-consortium-for-600-million/`.

17. Highland Capital Partners, Disconnect's Privacy and Security Software Named One of the Top 100 Innovations of 2013. `http://www.hcp.com/disconnect-wins-popular-science-best-of-whats-new-award-2013`.

18. Andy Greenberg, "Crypto Currency." *Forbes*, April 20, 2011. `https://www.forbes.com/forbes/2011/0509/technology-psilocybin-bitcoins-gavin-andresen-crypto-currency.html`.

19. Bitcoin.it, "First-time buyers guide." `https://en.bitcoin.it/wiki/First-time_buyers_guide`.

20. Bitcoin.it, "Buying Bitcoins (the newbie version)." `https://en.bitcoin.it/wiki/Buying_Bitcoins_(the_newbie_version)`.

CHAPTER 5

Cryptography and Secure Communication

How to Obscure Your Sensitive Data

We are living in a digital age. Various online threats exist that may compromise and steal your data, your money, and even your entire identity. Any systems that are connected to the Internet are exposed to a large number of potential cyber-attacks from different outside adversaries who are targeting the systems and open communication channels, either to steal the sensitive information or to disrupt the critical information system. It can be extremely difficult to create a system that is impregnable to outsiders unless you disconnect it from the Internet!

Modern cryptographic systems provide a robust set of techniques to ensure secure transactional sensitive data flows online, thus preventing hackers and cyber-criminals from accessing sensitive contents, even if they succeed in capturing the transmitted encrypted data. The mathematical formulas involved in today's cryptographic standards are enough to prevent the majority of attackers from decrypting stolen data.

The future of cryptography is brighter than ever before. With more companies becoming increasingly vulnerable to cyber-attacks, it's crucial that organizations strengthen their line of defense with strong encryption techniques and systems. Passwords, disk encryption, SSL certificates, electronic signatures, security access systems, simple end-user mobile solutions such as the InvizBox, and anything else that incorporates some form of security in the digital world must use some form of robust cryptographic techniques.

Individuals also need to use encryption to secure their personal data. Encryption is considered the last line of defense if an attacker successfully gains access to your confidential data. In other words, encryption will be your last hope to prevent the compromise, use, or disclosure of your sensitive information to the public or to your enemies.

In a world where everything is connected to everything else by the Internet, the demand to keep secrets has never been thus hard. In this chapter, we will give you thoughtful insight about some of the terms and concepts behind basic cryptographic methods. You will also learn how to use different cryptographic tools to encrypt data at rest and possible attacks against full disk encryption. We'll also cover protecting data in transit as well as steganography techniques (the science of hiding data in plain sight).

© Nihad A. Hassan and Rami Hijazi 2017
N. A. Hassan and R. Hijazi, *Digital Privacy and Security Using Windows*, DOI 10.1007/978-1-4842-2799-2_5

The Difference Between Encryption and Cryptography

The majority of computer users think the terms *cryptography* and *encryption* are interchangeable. This is not completely correct. *Cryptography* is the science of "secret writing." It can be looked at as an ancient art that has taken many forms over the years. It includes *steganography*, which is the science of hiding a secret message inside another, seemingly legitimate message that acts as the carrier so the hidden, unseen message will not appear during transit.

Encryption is considered a component of cryptography, and it is concerned with concealing secret messages by obscuring them. In other terms, encryption converts plaintext data into another obscured form called *ciphertext* using a specific cryptographic algorithm. This ciphertext can't be decrypted to its original state without owning or having access to the associated decryption key.

Encryption helps to ensure the confidentiality of the data stored on servers when at rest or when communicated through public networks such as the Internet.

Theoretically, we have distinguished between cryptography, steganography, and encryption. However, the majority of people still use the term *cryptography* to refer exclusively to encryption.

■ **Note** We will not delve into the history of cryptography and steganography as that is outside the book's scope. However, if you want to learn more about these topics, see *Data Hiding Techniques in Windows OS: A Practical Approach to Investigation and Defense* (Syngress, 2016).

Cryptographic Functions

Cryptography is an essential information security tool. It provides the four most basic services for information security.

Authentication

Authentication works by using a cryptographic system to ensure that a user (or system) is who they say they are. The process works technically by comparing the credentials provided by the remote entity against a list of authorized entities stored in a file system or database.

Authentication precedes authorization. Most people think both terms are interchangeable, but this is not completely correct. For example, when a user requests access to remote resources stored on a server, he or she needs to supply their credentials, for instance, a username and password. If the user credentials match, the system will grant the user access, or *authorize*, the access to the data or computing resources matching the associated access control tables; otherwise, access will be denied.

Nonrepudiation

The concept of *nonrepudiation* is important in the e-commerce world. To repudiate means to deny, and this concept is simple: when a user performs an action, he or she cannot later deny it.

As an example, think about when a bank client sends a money transfer from his or her account to another account using an electronic transfer. Later, this client may deny sending any transfer from his or her account and demand the money be returned. Here, there should be a technical mechanism in the bank to confirm that this client has legally authorized the transaction. Nonrepudiation can be technically guaranteed via digital signatures and/or encryption, as you are going to see later in this chapter.

Confidentiality

In simple terms, *confidentiality* ensures that data is not made available or disclosed to unauthorized parties. This has always been the main purpose of creating cryptographic systems. When the data is confidential, no one should be allowed access to it except the authorized people who possess the decryption key. Confidentiality can be achieved by using a strong encryption algorithm combined with a strong and complex passphrase.

Integrity

Integrity means that data is not viewed or manipulated by an unauthorized, or even an authorized, user during storage or transit. Technically, users can assure data integrity in transit by using hashing, which provides a mechanism to ensure that data has not been tempered with or changed during transmission. While the data is at rest, integrity can be achieved by physically controlling access to server/network device rooms, restricting access to data, and implementing strict authentication procedures in addition to storing sensitive data encrypted on company servers.

Cryptographic Types

There are different classifications of cryptographic algorithms. The most common one is classifying them according to the number of security keys used in the encryption/decryption process.

A cryptographic algorithm works in combination with a key (a number, word, or phrase) to encrypt and decrypt data. This key is composed of a string of bits. The larger the key (contains more bits), the greater the number of patterns that can be created, thus making it harder to break. A cryptographic key is the core part of modern cryptographic operations.

Symmetric Cryptography

Also known as secret key cryptography (SKC), in this type of encryption, both the sender and the receiver use the same key to encrypt and decrypt the data. The main disadvantage of this scheme is that the entire operation is dependent on the secrecy of the key. If the key is compromised by an unauthorized party, the whole system is breached. Figure 5-1 shows the process of symmetric cryptography.

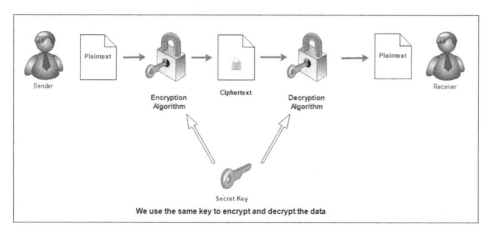

Figure 5-1. *Symmetric key cryptography system*

Symmetric encryption algorithms are split into stream ciphers and block ciphers. Stream ciphers encrypt plaintext bits individually, whereas block ciphers encrypt an entire block of plaintext bits at a time as a single unit. The majority of modern block ciphers have a block length of 128 bits (16 bytes).

Some of the popular symmetric encryption algorithms are AES/Rijndael, Blowfish, CAST5, DES, IDEA, RC2, RC4, RC6, Serpent, Triple DES, and Twofish.

Asymmetric Cryptography

Also known as public key cryptography (PKC), this cryptographic schema uses two different keys for encryption and decryption. The two keys are mathematically linked. However, no one can derive the decryption key (private key) from the encryption key (public key). Figure 5-2 illustrates the use of the two keys between the sender and the receiver.

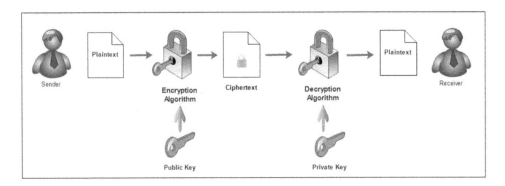

Figure 5-2. *Asymmetric encryption, public key cryptography*

In asymmetrical cryptography, the public key can be distributed freely; however, the private key should be kept secret to avoid collapsing the whole system. The public key is used to encrypt the secret message or to verify the digital signature of the sender, while the private key is used to decrypt the scrambled message or to create a digital signature. A message encrypted using this technique can only be decrypted back using the corresponding private key pair.

Some of the popular asymmetric encryption algorithms are the RSA encryption algorithm, Diffie-Hellman, Digital Signature Algorithm, ElGamal, ECDSA, and XTR.

▦ **Note**   Compared with symmetric cryptography, public-key encryption requires more computation power, which can make it inappropriate for encrypting large amounts of data (according to some studies, asymmetric encryption techniques are almost 1,000 times slower than symmetric techniques).

To counter this issue, some implementations suggest using public-key encryption to send a symmetric key, which can then be used to encrypt a large amount of data. This approach is used by the SSL protocol.

Cryptographic Hash

A cryptographic hash function (also called a *digest*) converts a digital file (input) and returns a fixed-size value, which is called the *hash value* (see Figure 5-3). You find the hash of any digital file (or piece of data) by running the data through a hash generator. Every time you hash the same data, you should get the same hash value as a result. This effectively helps you to create a digital fingerprint for any digital file.

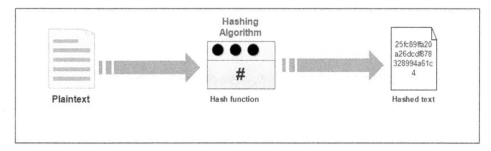

Figure 5-3. *How a hash function works*

To ensure the integrity of a file (or any piece of data), a hash of a file can be sent to accompany the file. The receiver may then compute a hash of the data received and compare it with the hash received. If the two outputs match, then you can assert that a message has not been tampered with.

There are different hash functions, the most popular of which are MD5, SHA-1, and SHA-256. The best secure hash algorithm is the one that has the best speed and is collision resistant. (*Collison* means producing the same hash from two different inputs. This is rare, especially when using hashing algorithms that create a higher bit hash of 256 bits and more.)

■ **Warning**   You should stop using SHA-1. Google just cracked it! The company's researchers declared that with enough computing power (110 years if using one computer for just one of the phases), a collision can occur. The new revelation renders SHA-1 obsolete.[1]

Hash values are used extensively during digital forensics investigations to examine, identify, and authenticate digital evidence. Hashing is also used to store user credentials (password) in management information systems (MISs) so that even the administrator of the MIS does not know a user's password. Hashing can also speed up the process of searching through a database because searching for hash values is faster than searching for long string names within databases.

■ **Note**   Encryption is a two-way operation; it converts input data from cleartext into ciphertext, and vice versa (from cipher to cleartext). Hashing is one-way encryption; it's never meant to be reversed.

How to Calculate File Hash?

There are many programs to calculate a digital file hash. Febooti Hash & CRC (www.febooti.com) is one of them that can integrate natively into Microsoft Windows file properties. After installing the program, right-click any file for which you want to calculate its hash, select Properties, and go to the Hash/CRC tab.

You can also calculate the hash of any file in a modern Windows version without using a third-party tool. To do this, go to the Windows Start menu and select Windows PowerShell. Run the command in Figure 5-4, replacing C:\Users\Nihad\Desktop\NihadHassan.txt with the path to the file you want to view the hash of.

Figure 5-4. *Using Windows PowerShell to calculate a digital file's hash*

Key Exchange Algorithms

A *key exchange* is any method in cryptography that allows a user to safely exchange encryption keys with an unknown party in order to use a cryptographic algorithm. For example, when two parties want to use symmetrical key cryptography to exchange secret data, they need first to share the "secret key." Public key cryptography can be used to share the secret key securely between authorized communication parties through an untrusted network like the Internet. The following are two of the most common key exchange algorithms currently used:

- Diffie-Hellman key agreement algorithm

- RSA key exchange process

In general, the Diffie-Hellman key exchange algorithm (used for SSL connection) provides better performance than the RSA key exchange algorithm. Figure 5-5 shows the basic Diffie-Hellman key agreement process.

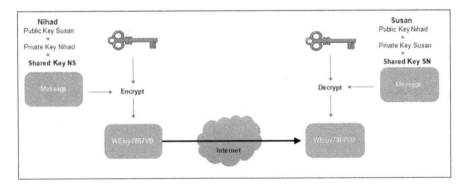

Figure 5-5. *Diffie-Hellman key agreement*

Digital Signature

A *digital signature* is a way to assure that an e-mail or digital file is authentic. Authentic means it is from the correct person who purports to be the authorized party and that the file content has not been tampered with after sending. A digital signature is considered the digital equivalent of a handwritten signature or a rubber stamp. The legal systems in most developed countries consider digital signatures to have the same legal significance as the more traditional forms of signed documents.

A digital signature is based on asymmetric cryptography (public key). For example, to have your e-mail signed, you need first to generate two keys (private and public keys). The signing software (such as an e-mail client like Thunderbird) creates a hash (also called a *message digest*) of the data that you are going to sign. The private key is used then to encrypt the hash. The result is the digital signature. Finally, the e-mail client appends the digital signature to the e-mail. Now all the data that was hashed has been signed (see Figure 5-6).

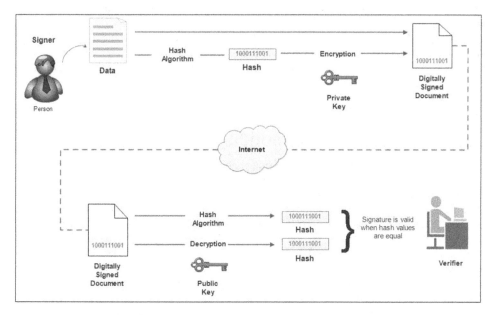

Figure 5-6. *How a digital signature works*

As you saw previously, hashing algorithms produce a fixed-length hash value that is unique for the hashed data (unless a collision occurred, which is practically near impossible to happen, especially when using modern hashing algorithms). Any change in the hashed data (even a single character) will produce a new hashing value. So, when a recipient wants to validate the integrity of the received message, all he or she needs to do is to use the signer's public key to decrypt the hash. If the decrypted hash matches the value of the hash generated by the recipient's software for the same data set, this means the message is authentic and has not been tampered with after sending. If the two hashes do not match, this means either the message has been tampered with during transit or the signature was created using a private key that does not correspond to the public key pair used to decrypt it.

■ **Note**   A digital signature can be used with any kind of message, whether it is encrypted or not, to authentic sending partners. Today, the majority of modern e-mail clients support the use of digital signatures.

In this chapter, we will show you practically how to send/receive digitally signed e-mails using the Mozilla Thunderbird e-mail client.

The Difference Between Digital Signatures and Electronic Signatures

You should not confuse the terms *digital signature* and *electronic signature* (*e-signature*) even though, again, both names are often used interchangeably. Both digital signatures and e-signature solutions allow you to sign documents and authenticate the signer. However, they differ in the purpose, technical implementation, and legal acceptance. For instance, most electronic signature solutions are easy to use; a user can just click to sign the document or can simply insert an image containing a handwritten signature on the document to sign it.

E-signatures aren't regulated like digital signatures, and each vendor has its own standards and technical implementation that cannot compare with the strict security standards implemented by the digital signature algorithms currently deployed. However, some more secure e-signature solutions protect the signed document with a cryptographic digital signature, thus making it have the same strict security standards as a digital signature in term of linking the signer's identity to his or her e-signature.

Cryptographic Systems Trust Models

Cryptographic systems are designed to form the basis of information security. However, despite their importance, you still need trust between communicating parties in order to securely exchange data online. For instance, in SKC, both the sender and the receiver must share the "secret key" in advance in order to encrypt/decrypt the data, but how can they assure safe transmission of this key in an untrusted channel (such as the Internet) if, for example, each one lives in a different country? PKC tries to solve the problem of sharing the secret key securely by introducing two keys for each party. The public key of the receiver is used to encrypt the data and can publish publicly, and the private key pair (of the receiver) is used to decrypt the data and must remain private. Nevertheless, you still have additional problems in PKC. For instance how you can assure that the sender of the encrypted data is actually the authorized party? For example, when Susan receives an encrypted message from Nihad, how she can assure that this message really originated from Nihad? What if a malicious person (Jim) is impersonating Nihad? How will Susan know this?

This section will answer these questions. In a cryptographic schema, there are a number of methods to assure that the person you are communicating with is really the authorized party. The following are the most popular trust models:

- The Web of Trust concept is used in Pretty Good Privacy (PGP) and other OpenPGP-compatible systems.

- Kerberos is a distributed authentication service designed to provide strong authentication for client-server applications by using secret key cryptography.

- A certification authority (CA) is a third-party entity that issues a digital certificate to authenticate a user's.ownership of a public key.

■ **Note**   An open source implementation of OpenPGP is called GNU Privacy Guard (GnuPG); see https://www.gnupg.org.

Web of Trust

The Web of Trust is used in Pretty Good Privacy and other compatible systems to establish a trust relationship between a public key and its owner. It is a decentralized security model in which participants authenticate the identities of other users. The Web of Trust is similar to social networking web sites. A user can add unknown people to his or her list of friends if they already have friends in common. You can see this clearly on Facebook and LinkedIn.

For example, if Susan trusts Nihad, then Susan could also trust the public key of Rita, who does not know if this key has been authenticated by Nihad.

Kerberos

Kerberos is a network authentication protocol developed by MIT. It works through a client-server architecture by using secret key cryptography. Kerberos provides secure authentication between the user and server rather than a host-to-host approach. The main component of a Kerberos schema is a central server (or a trusted third-party server) used for authenticating requests.

In a Kerberos network, each connected host has its own secret key, and one of these hosts is the central Kerberos server, also known as a *key distribution center* (KDC). All host secret keys will be stored on the KDC server. (In some networks, not all host keys will be stored in the central KDC; the group of systems that are under the same master KDC is called a *realm*.) Kerberos provides secure communication by checking each connected host's secret key with the one stored on it (the host can do the same with the Kerberos server). After a client and server have used Kerberos to assure their identities, they can begin to exchange encrypted data across an unsecured network such as the Internet.

■ **Note**   The main disadvantage of Kerberos is that user credentials are stored on a central KDC server. If a malicious hacker gains access to the central server, the entire Kerberos authentication system is at risk of being compromised.

Certificates and Certificate Authorities

Certificate authorities (CAs) issue digital certificates for web sites, online services, IoT devices, and individuals. These certificates contain their identity credential in order to be recognized and trusted online (trusted because CA has already verified the identity of each digital certificate holder). CAs play a critical role in today's digital age. They build trust relationships between different business partners online, encrypt business transactions, and secure the communications between different parties conducting e-commerce transactions.

A digital certificate is like your passport; you can use it within your country to verify your identity. If you are in the United States and your passport is issued from New York, you can safely use it in Washington. The local authorities in Washington will recognize and trust your personal information because your passport is issued by a government agency they trust (New York authorities). If you moved outside the United States, foreign countries that accept U.S. passports will also verify and trust your details, because they trust in the government papers issued by U.S. authorities. This analogy represents the certificate trust chain where your "certificate" is accepted so as long as it is issued from a recognized trusted party (the CA).

For online transactions, digital certificates are small data files that contain identifying information (certificate issuer, public key, holder name, expiration date, serial number, version, certificate issuer digital signature, and other information according to each CA provider). A certificate enables its holder to bind (or prove ownership) of a public key to him or her (or an organization, web site, or any other entity currently holding this certificate). A digital certificate encrypts the connections between communication parties, ensuring the secure exchange of confidential information online. It also lists what actions its holder can do and what actions the holder cannot.

A popular type of digital certificate is the SSL certificate issued for web sites. SSL binds the ownership details of a web server (and consequently web sites) to their cryptographic keys. These keys are used to establish a secure session between the client's browser and the web server (web site) hosting the SSL certificate. See Figure 5-7 for a sample digital certificate for LinkedIn.com issued by DigiCert Inc.

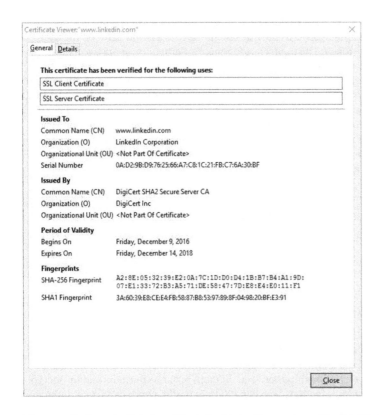

Figure 5-7. *Sample digital certificate for LinkedIn.com issued by DigiCert Inc*

Let's now return to the role of digital certificate with regard to the trust relationship between a sender and a receiver. For example, when Nihad wants to send an encrypted e-mail to Susan, he needs to get her public key from Susan's CA issuer. If both Nihad and Susan have their certificates from the same issuer, the process is clear, and the trust relationship is already established. However, if Susan's certificate is issued from a different CA other than the one that issued Nihad's certificate, how can Nihad trust Susan's certificate? When people face such a challenge, they can simply trust the receiver's public key certificate when it is issued by a global reputable CA company. CA providers like Comodo (`https://ssl.comodo.com`), Digicert (`https://www.digicert.com`), and Symantec (`https://www.symantec.com/ssl-certificates`) are known to be trusted on a global level (and, of course, there are others).

The most commonly used standard for issuing digital certificates for a public key schema is the X.509 format that is defined in International Telecommunication Union Telecommunication Standardization Sector (ITU-T) Recommendation X.509. The information in an X.509 certificate includes the following: version, serial number, algorithm information, issuer name, expire date, subject name, subject public key, and optional standard extensions. Many SSL certificates follow the X.509 standard format.

■ **Note** In Chapter 2, we covered the validation requirements for issuing a new SSL certificate for web sites and other entities.

Cryptographic Algorithm Selection Criteria

Many types of cryptographic algorithms are already in use. Some are considered more secure than others. Their strength depends on mathematics and the size of the encryption key. To achieve the maximum security possible when using encryption tools to protect your sensitive information, it is advisable to check the following criteria before selecting the algorithm you are going to use:

- Do not use proprietary encryption algorithms if you are on a top-secret mission. No one can guarantee they don't have a backdoor. The RSA encryption company has been accused of receiving $10 million to incorporate a weaker algorithm into an encryption product called BSafe, according to a Reuters report.[2]

- For security-conscious people, do not trust algorithms developed or sponsored by official government agencies. For example, Advanced Encryption Standard (AES) was developed by the U.S. National Institute of Standards and Technology (NIST). SHA and its family (SHA-224, SHA-256, SHA-384, SHA-512, SHA-512/224, SHA-512/256) were developed by the U.S. National Security Agency (NSA), which makes it unfavorable choice.

- Do not use algorithms that have been previously broken or are considered relatively insecure in today's computing standards. Examples include MD5, SHA-0, SHA-1, and DES.

- Open source cryptographic algorithms are considered safer than the closed alternatives; the public can audit them for trustworthiness, and their code can be rigorously tested and reviewed by global security experts and academics alike.

In cryptographic algorithms, the key length, which is the number of bits in a key used by a cryptographic algorithm, is an important parameter to measure the security of the encryption algorithm. Longer keys provide stronger encryption. The preferred key length differs between asymmetrical and symmetrical algorithms. For instance, to achieve the same level of encryption strength, a 1,024-bit RSA key (asymmetrical algorithm) is only considered equivalent to an 80-bit symmetric key.[3]

■ **Note** The site at `https://www.keylength.com/en/compare` gives advice on the minimum key size requirement for your cryptography system.

For security-conscious people, it is advisable to use the Twofish algorithm. It is a symmetric key block cipher with a block size of 128 bits and key sizes up to 256 bits developed by Bruce Schneier and other scientists. Twofish is unpatented, and the source code is uncopyrighted and license-free. According to Schneier, "Currently there is no successful cryptanalysis of Twofish."[4]

■ **Note**   As we already said, encrypting a large amount of data using asymmetrical key is not practical, so always exchange the symmetric encryption key using an asymmetrical algorithm and encrypt your data using a symmetrical algorithm like Twofish.

The Whirlpool hash algorithm is a hash function designed by Vincent Rijmen and Paulo S.L.M. Barreto that operates on messages less than 2,256 bits in length and produces a message digest of 512 bits. It has been adopted by the International Organization for Standardization (ISO) and other international bodies. Whirlpool is not patented, and it will not be according to its authors. Anyone can exploit its source code for any purpose freely.[5]

The previous selection criteria can be considered somehow rigorous by today's standards. However, remember that for the majority of Internet users, using encryption algorithms developed by the RSA or NIST is considered more than enough to protect their sensitive data. The strict selection criteria are best suited for government agencies and private-sector companies (such as banks and hospitals) dealing with sensitive, protectively marked, and of course top-secret information and the like. Such entities need to implement extreme security measures to protect their precious data. Closed cryptographic algorithms—unless developed by them (government-use AES)—may not be the best choice to go with.

Create a Cryptographic Key Pair Using Gpg4Win

In this section, you will begin your practical work on using cryptographic systems to secure your sensitive data. As you might guess, the first thing you need to do is to generate your cryptographic key pair (public and private key). There are different programs to create a cryptographic key pair; however, this book is directed to Windows users, so you will use the most popular encryption program that meets all the trustworthiness criteria in terms of security, open source, and reputation; this tool is Gpg4win.

Gpg4win enables users to securely transport e-mails and files with the help of encryption and digital signatures. It supports both relevant cryptography standards, OpenPGP and S/MIME (X.509), and is the official GnuPG distribution for Windows. It is maintained by the developers of GnuPG.

Gpg4win is not a program in itself; rather, it's a suite of five utilities bundled with a comprehensive manual and a powerful encryption engine. Gpg4Win contains the following:

- *GnuPG*: The core encryption tool

- *Kleopatra*: A certificate manager

- *GPA*: An alternate certificate manager (GNU) for OpenPGP and X.509

- *GpgOL*: A GnuPG extension for Microsoft Outlook to provide e-mail encryption (supports Microsoft Outlook 2003, 2007, 2010, 2013, or 2016—both 32-bit and 64-bit versions)

- *GpgEX*: A plug-in for Windows Explorer to provide file encryption

This section will walk you through the process of generating the keys on Windows. First, go to https://gpg4win.org/download.html and download the latest available version; currently, Gpg4win 2.3.3 is available.

■ **Note** Gpg4win is open source software; you can find its source code at `https://git.gnupg.org/cgi-bin/gitweb.cgi?p=gpg4win.git;a=summary`.

Second, install Gpg4win like you do with any Windows software; it is advisable to leave the default installation settings as they are.

Third, let's generate your key pair following these steps:

1. Launch the Kleopatra program; you should find it in the Windows Start menu in the Gpg4win folder.

2. Select File menu ➤ New Certificate.

3. The Certificate Creation Wizard appears; you have two options.

   a. Personal OpenPGP key pair

   b. Personal X.509 key pair and certification request

We have already described both options; select the first option for an OpenPGP key pair (see Figure 5-8).

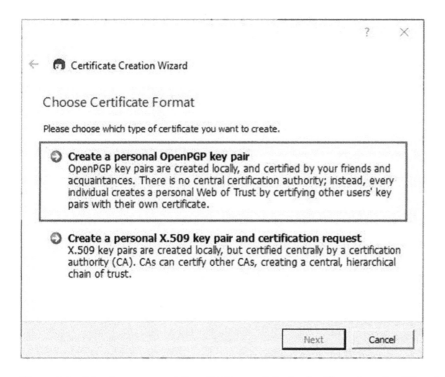

Figure 5-8. *Selecting a personal OpenPGP key pair in the Certificate Creation Wizard*

4. Now you need to enter your personal details. This includes your name, e-mail, and comments. Although the first two fields are required, you can fill out any information inside them. For instance, we will supply a name and an e-mail. Then click the Advanced Settings button at the bottom of this window to further customize the algorithm used to create the key pair (see Figure 5-9).

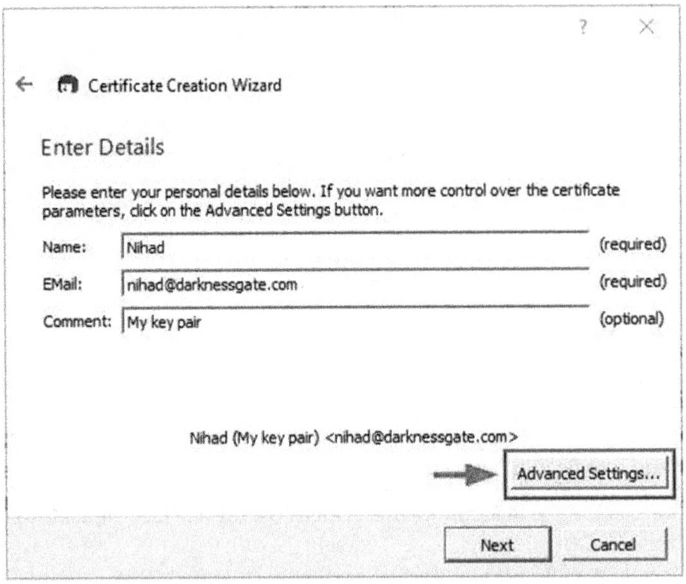

Figure 5-9. *Entering your name, e-mail, and comments for a new key pair*

5. After clicking the Advanced Settings button, the window shown in Figure 5-10 appears. In the Key Material panel, select RSA and 4,096 bits and make sure to select the +RSA box and give it the length of 4,096 bits as well. This offers the highest security measures. Once you're sure your information matches Figure 5-10, click OK to close the current window.

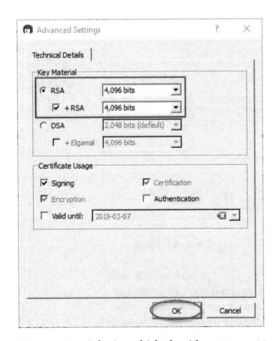

Figure 5-10. *Selecting which algorithm you want to use for creating your key pair*

■ **Note**   Please note that keeping the default key size of 2,048 bits is recommended unless security is the overriding concern. The longer the key size, the greater the strength of the encryption, but there is a corresponding decline in performance (if you are using an old PC) with a longer key length.

NOTE! WHAT IS THE DIFFERENCE BETWEEN THE RSA AND DSA ALGORITHMS?

Gpg4win offers two encryption algorithms to choose from when creating your cryptographic key pair. The cryptographic strengths of these two algorithms are just about the same; however, they differ in performance and ability to migrate to other applications.

Digital Signature Algorithm (DSA) was developed by the NIST. Originally, it supports key lengths between 512 and 1,024 bits. However, the 512 has been cracked recently. Now DSA is available in 1,024; 2,048; and 3,072 bit lengths. DSA can be used only for signing data, and it cannot be used for encryption.

The Rivest, Shamir, Adleman (RSA) algorithm can be used for asymmetric encrypting and signing data.

The major advantage of RSA over DSA is that an RSA certificate can be easily exported into other applications/services (e.g., smart cards) because it is widely supported by the overwhelming majority of the OpenPGP ecosystem. Many studies found that RSA-2048 is believed safe until at least 2020 (NIST claims until 2030).

RSA is the most widely used encryption algorithm in the business sector; however, DSA remains a favorable choice used by government contractors and subcontractors.

When using DSA, the process of creating a digital signature is faster than validating it, while with RSA, the process of validating the digital signature is faster than creating it.

Depending on the circumstances and the available computing resources, a choice will need to be made, but both DSA and RSA have equal encryption capabilities.

6. Click the Next button to move to the next wizard window (see Figure 5-11). This window will show you a summary of certificate parameters, so you can review them if you want to change something.

Figure 5-11. *Viewing a summary of the certificate (key pair) details before generating it*

7. If everything is OK, click the Create Key button.

8. Another window will pop up asking you to enter a passphrase. This is used to protect your secret key. Make sure to enter a complex password; refer to Chapter 2 for the best practices when creating and storing your passwords.

9. Kleopatra will generate your key pair now. It will ask you to make some random actions on your PC like pressing some keys and/or moving your mouse around to help the wizard create a more secure key.

10. Your key pair is now created. A success window appears that contains your certificate fingerprint in addition to more steps such as creating a backup for your certificate, uploading it to a directory service, and choosing to send the certificate by e-mail (see Figure 5-12). For instance, you will create a backup of your certificate and store it in a USB zip drive. To do this, click Make a Backup Of Your Key Pair and select where to store it. Finally, click the Finish button to close the window.

Figure 5-12. *Success message announcing that your key pair was created successfully*

After creating your cryptographic key pair, you need to find your public key in order to send it to the people you want to communicate with. Remember, anyone who wants to send you an encrypted message must have your public key first in order to encrypt the message with it. To extract your public key, follow these steps:

1. Open the Kleopatra program, go to the My Certificates tab, find your certificate (that you already created), and right-click it and select Export Certificates (see Figure 5-13). Select where you want to save this file (it will have an .asc extension).

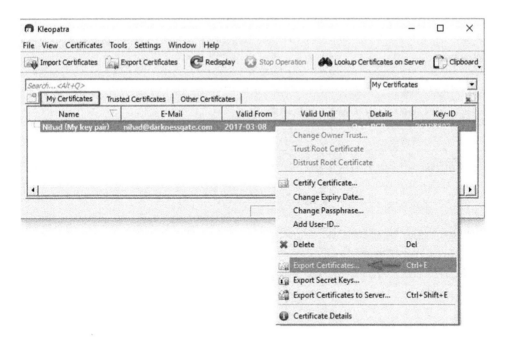

Figure 5-13. *Exporting your public key certificate using the Kleopatra program*

2. To open/view your public key, go to where you saved the file in the previous step.
    Right-click the file and select Open with ➤ Notepad.

You can advertise your public key as you want, put it as a signature in your e-mail, or publish it to your web site or blog so anyone can find it and send you encrypted messages.

Now how do you import other people's public key?

In the previous step, we demonstrated how to export your public key from the Kleopatra program in order to send it to other people so they can communicate with you privately. But how can you send encrypted messages to other people? For example, if Nihad wants to send an encrypted e-mail to Susan, he needs to have her public key first. To do this, Nihad can ask her to send him her public key (for example, through an e-mail attachment). When Susan responds and sends her public key to Nihad, he must import it into the Kleopatra program first (or any other compatible/similar program) before he can use it for encryption. You'll now learn how to import other people's public keys into Kleopatra.

If the person you are corresponding with sent you his or her public key as an e-mail attachment, follow these steps:

1. Open Kleopatra, select File ➤ Import Certificates, locate the public key file
    (it usually has an .asc extension), and open it.

2. Your newly imported certificate (public key) should appear in Kleopatra
    on the Other Certificates tab (see Figure 5-14).

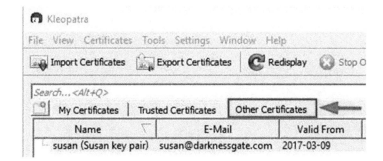

Figure 5-14. *Imported certificates (public keys) can be found on the Imported Certificates tab*

If your correspondent sent you his or her public key as a text in a message, follow these steps to import it into Kleopatra:

1. Copy everything from ----BEGIN PGP PUBLIC KEY BLOCK---- to ----END PGP
    PUBLIC KEY BLOCK---- (see Figure 5-15).

Figure 5-15. *Sample public key code opened using Notepad*

2. Open the Kleopatra program (if it is not already open), go to the Windows taskbar, right-click the Kleopatra icon, and select Clipboard ➤ Certificate Import (see Figure 5-16).

Figure 5-16. Importing the public key certificate for the Kleopatra program by copying its contents into the clipboard

3. If everything goes well, a success message should appear, and you will see your newly imported certificate in Kleopatra on the Other Certificates tab, as you saw in Figure 5-14.

What if you already have a digital certificate (cryptographic key pair) and you want to import it into your Kleopatra program?

We showed you how to export your public key, but in some cases you may need to have your private key (if you want to use it in another encryption program). To export your private key from the Kleopatra program, follow these steps:

1. Open Kleopatra, go to the My Certificates tab, right-click your certificate (or the one you want to export its private key), and select Export Secret Keys.

2. Select the location where you want to save the private key, make sure to select the "ASCII armor" option (see Figure 5-17), and then click OK. A success message should appear.

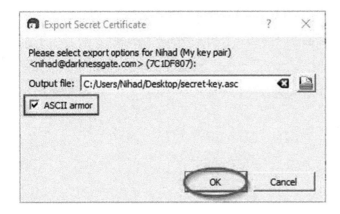

Figure 5-17. Saving a secret key after exporting it

■ **Warning** Do not share your private key with anyone. Make sure to store it in a safe location and keep it confidential.

Now, after you have your private key ready in a separate file, you can import it into any compatible program. For instance, we will assume that you want to move it to another Kleopatra instance on another device. To import your private key, open Kleopatra and select File ➤ Import Certificates. Browse to where your private key is located and open it. A pop-up message should appear to show your certificate import results. Click OK to close the window. If everything is correct, you should find your private key on the My Certificates tab.

In this section, we covered thoroughly how you can use Gpg4win to create a digital certificate and how to import/export your cryptographic key pair. In a later section, you will learn how to use Gpg4win with the Thunderbird e-mail client to encrypt and sign e-mails and other files.

Please note that once your key is created, you can export your cryptographic keys to a variety of encryption tools. Gpg4win is the most important free encryption project for Windows. It is vital to understand this section to understand how you are going to use cryptography later to protect your sensitive data and online communications from interception.

Disk Encryption Using Windows BitLocker

BitLocker Drive Encryption is a data protection feature offered by newer versions of Windows beginning with Vista. It allows you to encrypt your entire disk drive, including the Windows partition and removable USB drives, securely. BitLocker will protect your sensitive data if your computer gets stolen or lost; it also offers a secure way to dispose of your old computer because recovering encrypted data from a disk drive is extremely difficult and costly. In addition to this, BitLocker helps to secure your computer against sophisticated malware that targets the computer firmware level.

■ **Note** We already advised you not to use proprietary encryption solutions, especially from giant companies, because no one can guarantee their safety from security flaws and backdoors. BitLocker is offered freely as part of the Windows installation (some versions), and it offers excellent protection for Windows users with minimal configuration. BitLocker is more than enough for most Windows users and for the majority of private companies that want to protect their data, so it is advisable to use it unless you are in a working with high-level corporate government data assets that are protectively marked; in that case, it is better to use a more robust solution appropriate to the risk.

BitLocker is not available in all Windows versions. Currently, the following Windows editions are supported:

- Windows 10 Pro, Enterprise, and Education editions

- Window 8 and 8.1 Enterprise and Pro editions

- Windows Server 2008 R2, all editions

- Windows 7 Enterprise and Ultimate editions

- Windows Vista Enterprise and Ultimate editions

■ **Note**   Starting from Windows 7 and Windows Server 2008 R2, BitLocker adds a feature to encrypt removable drives. If you are still using an older Windows version such as Vista and XP and you have a removable drive encrypted using BitLocker that you want to read, you can do this through a program called BitLocker To Go Reader (https://www.microsoft.com/en-us/download/details.aspx?id=24303). It provides users with read-only access to BitLocker-protected, FAT-formatted drives.

■ **Warning**   Windows XP is not being supported with patches anymore.

BitLocker uses the AES encryption algorithm with a 128-bit key size by default, but you can change the key length to 256 bits for enhanced security.

A longer key size is more secure, but it also means more overhead when performing the encryption/decryption process. This should not be a problem for computers with good hardware. For individuals, it is more than enough to use the default 128-bit key size, but when it comes to companies dealing with sensitive data, it is preferable to increase the key size to 256 bits for maximum protection.

To change the default BitLocker key size to 256-bit AES, follow these steps:

1. Press Windows Key+R to open the Run dialog.

2. Enter **gpedit.msc** in the dialog; then press Enter to access Local Group Policy Editor.

3. Go to Computer Configuration ➤ Administrative Templates ➤ Windows Components ➤ BitLocker Drive Encryption. In the right pane, double-click "Choose drive encryption method and cipher strength" (Windows 10 [version 1511] and later). In this case, you are using Windows 10; if you are using Windows 7 or 8, select the corresponding setting (see Figure 5-18).

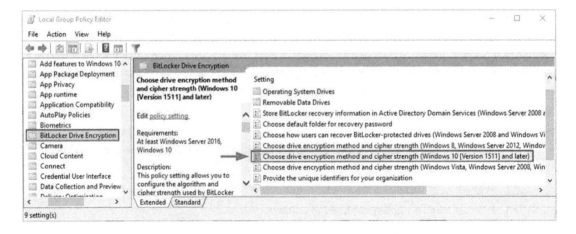

Figure 5-18. *Accessing Local Group Policy Editor to change BitLocker settings*

4. In the new window, select Enabled, click the drop-down box (operating system drives, fixed data drives, and removable data drives), and select AES-CBC 256-bit. (Of course you do not need to change the three values; change the encryption method for the drive type you want to encrypt only.) Click OK to save your changes (see Figure 5-19).

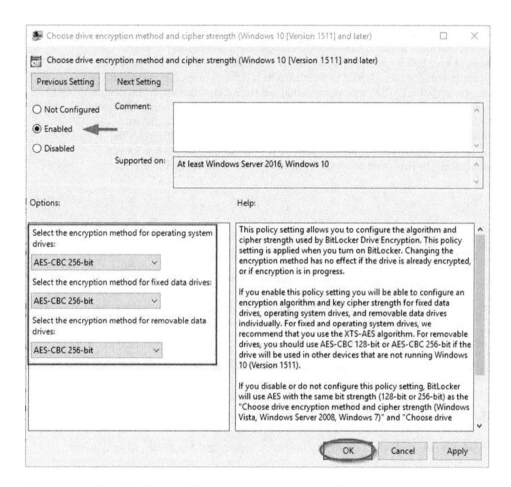

Figure 5-19. *Changing the BitLocker encryption settings to 256 bits*

BitLocker will use 256-bit AES-CBC encryption for any new drive you want to encrypt, but existing drives encrypted with BitLocker will continue to use the default 128-bit ASE encryption.

■ **Note**   If you want to change the encryption setting of the existing encrypted volumes from 128 bits to 256 bits, you must decrypt the drive first and then encrypt it again after changing the encryption settings to 256 bits like you already did.

Encrypting Windows/Fixed Data Drives

After you have the necessary information about the BitLocker feature, let's begin encrypting your first drive. BitLocker differentiates between three types of disks (although the encryption process is transparent to the user): Windows drive, fixed data drive, and removable data drive. To encrypt the Windows drive, your computer must meet the following three prerequisites:

- Your OS partition should be formatted using the NTFS file system.

- A system partition that is at least 350MB. This partition is necessary to store Windows boot files because Windows cannot recognize an encrypted boot loader at startup. This partition should be formatted as NTFS for computers that use BIOS firmware and with FAT32 for computers that use UEFI-based firmware. You can see this drive and its size by going to Control Panel ➤ Administrative Tools ➤ Computer Management ➤ Storage ➤ Disk Management (see Figure 5-20). The majority of modern laptops that come with Windows preinstalled contain this partition. However, if your current PC does not have one, BitLocker will create one for you automatically by shrinking the current Windows drive (usually the C:\ drive).

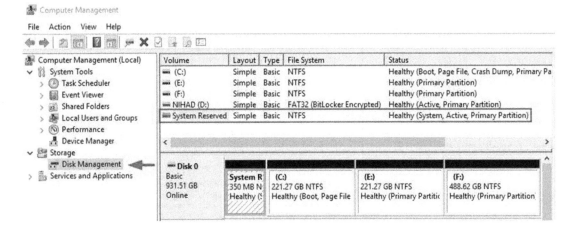

Figure 5-20. *Viewing all the computer's hard drive partitions including the one reserved by Windows*

- Administrative access.

To begin encrypting Windows disk drive, follow these steps (applicable to all supported editions of Windows 7, 8, 8.1, and 10):

■ **Warning** You should back up your personal data before encrypting the drive to prevent data loss.

---

1. Go to Control Panel ➤ BitLocker Drive Encryption, select the drive you want to encrypt, and click Turn on BitLocker on the right side (see Figure 5-21).

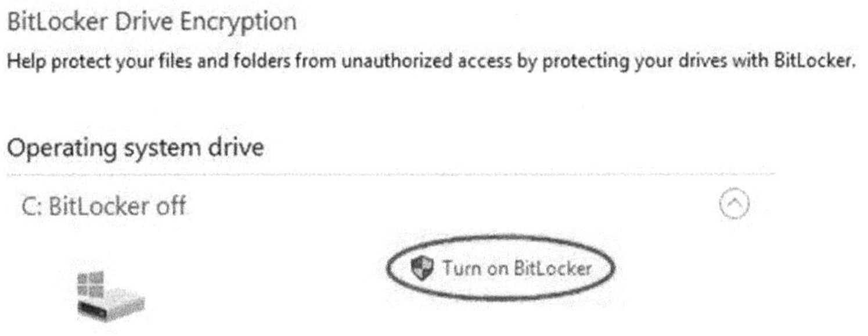

BitLocker Drive Encryption

Help protect your files and folders from unauthorized access by protecting your drives with BitLocker.

Operating system drive

C: BitLocker off   ⌄

🛡 Turn on BitLocker

Figure 5-21. *Turning on BitLocker on the C:\ drive (Windows partition)*

2. If your computer doesn't have a TPM chip, you will see the following error message: "This device can't use a Trusted Platform Module. Your administrator must set the 'Allow BitLocker without a compatible TPM' option in the 'Require additional authentication at startup' policy for OS volumes." In other words, BitLocker requires a computer with a Trusted Platform Module (TPM). This is a small microchip located on your computer mainboard. The majority of modern Windows devices come equipped with this chip; some motherboards manufacturers allow the addition of this chip separately. The main role of the TPM with regard to BitLocker encryption is to store BitLocker encryption keys. It also offers a mechanism to detect any attempt to change the host OS software or hardware used by attackers to crack your encrypted drive. Once TPM detected any changes, it will make your PC boot in a restricted mode, thus preventing attackers from gaining any information from you that can aid them to crack your encrypted drives (we will cover attacks against BitLocker and full disk encryption later in this chapter). Nevertheless, if your PC does not contain a TPM chip, you can continue to use BitLocker on your Windows device, but you need to change the Group Policy setting on your computer first.

3. Press Windows Key+R to open the Windows Run dialog.

4. Type **gpedit.msc** and then press the Enter key.

5. Go to Local Computer Policy ➤ Computer Configuration ➤ Administrative Templates ➤ Windows Components ➤ BitLocker Drive Encryption ➤ Operating System Drives.

6. Double-click the setting named "Require additional authentication at startup" in the right pane. Select Enabled and make sure the option "Allow BitLocker without a compatible TPM (requires a password or a startup key on a USB flash drive)" is selected (see Figure 5-22).

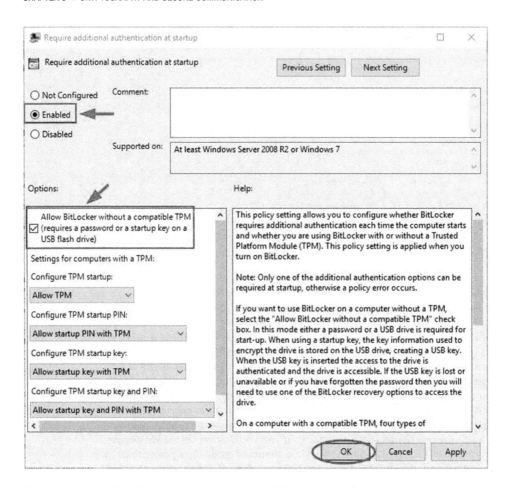

Figure 5-22. *Enabling BitLocker without a compatible TPM*

7. Click OK and close the Local Group Policy Editor. Now you can continue setting up your BitLocker on a device without a compatible TPM chip.

■ **Note** If you do not know whether your Windows PC has a TPM chip, do the following check (applicable to all Windows versions): press Windows Key+R to launch the Run dialog. Type **tpm.msc** and press Enter. If your PC has a TPM module, its version and type should appear; otherwise, the following message will show up: "Compatible Trusted Platform Module (TPM) cannot be found on this computer…."

In some devices, the TPM could exist; however, it is disabled in the motherboard settings. To reenable it, restart your PC into its UEFI or BIOS. Search for a setting named TPM or Trusted Platform Module and reenable it if it is already disabled.

8. After enabling BitLocker to run without a compatible TPM, return to the first step and click Turn on BitLocker next to the operating system drive (see Figure 5-20). Please note that in this experiment you are encrypting the Windows drive; encrypting a fixed data drive is almost identical.

9. The first window in the wizard appears. Click Next to continue.

10. The second window states that "You will no longer be able to use Windows Recovery Environment unless it is manually enabled and moved to the system drive." Click Next to continue.

11. Now, BitLocker will ask you to "Choose how to unlock your drive at startup." You have two options: enter a password each time your PC boot or insert a USB flash drive. In this case, select "Enter a password." Please note that if you select to use a USB drive, you must connect this USB to your computer each time you boot up in order to decrypt your drive.

12. We select to use a password, so you need to enter it twice in the new wizard window. Make sure to use a strong password according to our tips in Chapter 2. Click Next to continue.

13. The wizard will ask you "How do you want to back up your recovery key?" You have four choices (see Figure 5-23): save it to your Microsoft account, save it to a USB flash drive, save it to a file, and print the recovery key. In this case, you will store the recovery key to a USB drive. A list of connected USB drives will appear, so select the one that will hold your recovery key (you can also select to print the recovery key; the BitLocker wizard allows you to choose more than one recovery method).

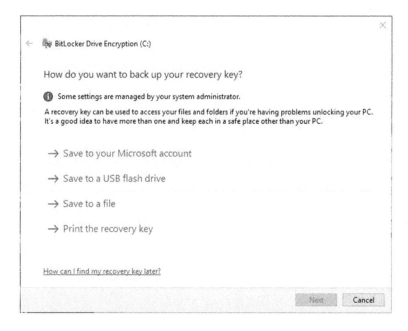

Figure 5-23. Selecting how you want to back up your BitLocker recovery key

---

■ **Warning**   Store the BitLocker recovery key in a safe location and make sure not to lose it. If you forget your password or your computer (with a TPM chip) gets damaged and you have to move your hard disk into another computer, the recovery key is your only way to decrypt your data. Otherwise, you will lose all your encrypted data for good.

---

14.   After saving the recovery key to a USB flash drive, click Next to continue. The next window will ask you to "Choose how much of your drive to encrypt." You have two options. You can encrypt used disk space only (which is fastest and best for new PCs and drives) or you can encrypt the entire dive (which is slower but better for PCs and drives already in use). Basically, you have been using your computer for some time, your disk drive will certainly contain different data and information other than the one appears (for example, deleted files and fragments of deleted files and folders). In this case, it is essential to enable BitLocker to encrypt the entire drive (including the free space area) to assure that an attacker cannot retrieve the remnants of deleted files from the unencrypted area. On the other hand, if your PC is new, there's no need to bother and encrypt the entire drive; only encrypt the area that contains data.

15.   After selecting how much drive you want to encrypt, click Next to continue. A new wizard window, which is dedicated to Windows 10 build 1511 or later, appears. It asks you "Which encryption mode to use." You have two options. The first is "New encryption mode," which is more suitable for fixed drives on devices with Windows 10 installed. This mode provides additional integrity support, but it is not compatible with older versions of Windows. The second option is "Compatible mode" and works on all previous Windows versions (Windows Vista and 7 and 8). This option should be used if you are encrypting a removable drive that can be used on older Windows versions (see Figure 5-24).

Choose which encryption mode to use

Windows 10 (Version 1511) introduces a new disk encryption mode (XTS-AES). This mode provides additional integrity support, but it is not compatible with older versions of Windows.

If this is a removable drive that you're going to use on older version of Windows, you should choose Compatible mode.

If this is a fixed drive or if this drive will only be used on devices running at least Windows 10 (Version 1511) or later, you should choose the new encryption mode

◉ New encryption mode (best for fixed drives on this device)

○ Compatible mode (best for drives that can be moved from this device)

Figure 5-24. *Choosing which encryption mode to use (applicable only to Windows 10)*

16. After selecting your encryption mode, click Next to continue. The final wizard window appears and asks you to run a BitLocker system check to ensure that BitLocker can read the recovery and encryption keys correctly. Windows will reboot, and the encryption will begin. It may take some time depending the size of the drive; you can check the encryption progress by checking the BitLocker Drive Encryption icon in the system tray. You can continue your work while the drive is being encrypted.

After finishing the encryption, whenever you boot into Windows, BitLocker will prompt you for a password (or a USB drive if you have already selected that) before unlocking your computer.

Encrypting a fixed data drive is similar. However, Windows will not prompt you for the decryption key upon bootup. Instead, you can double-click the encrypted disk drive after booting to Windows and then enter your password in the prompt to unlock the drive.

If you lost the unlock method you use to access BitLocker drive, you must press the Esc button upon booting to Windows. When BitLocker prompts you to enter the password or insert the USB, then you need to provide the recovery key in order to decrypt your drive.

Encrypting Removable Disk Drives

Using BitLocker to encrypt removable storage such as external HDDs, SD cards, and USB sticks is straightforward. BitLocker offers an effective method to protect your portable storage units that should be used by any Windows user who cares about his or her privacy. Follow these steps to encrypt removable storage devices:

1. Insert the USB drive you want to encrypt (the same applies to portable HDDs or any supported drive).

2. Right-click "USB drive" in Windows File Explorer and select Turn on BitLocker. Alternatively, you can go to Control Panel ➤ BitLocker Drive Encryption, and in the "Removable data drives" section (BitLocker To Go) click Turn on BitLocker next to the USB you want to encrypt.

3. The BitLocker wizard launches and asks you to "Choose how you want to unlock this drive." You have two choices, a password and a smart card. In this case, you will select the first option, a password. (You can select both options, a password and smart card, for additional security.)

4. After entering the password used to unlock the drive, click the Next button to move to the next screen. BitLocker will ask you how you want to back up your recovery key in the event that you forget your password (you have three options: upload to a Microsoft account, save to a file, and print on paper). Select your preferred method and click Next.

5. BitLocker will ask you how much data on your drive you want to encrypt. You can encrypt used space only or encrypt everything. Select your choice and click Next.

6. The next wizard screen asks you which encryption mode to use. Because you are encrypting a USB stick, leave the encryption mode set to "Compatible mode" and then click Next.

7. The final wizard asks if you are ready to encrypt the drive. When you are ready, click the Start Encrypting button.

BitLocker will start the encryption process, which can take some time depending on the amount of data you want to encrypt and the size of the USB drive.

When you open Windows File Explorer, you will notice that the encrypted USB drive icon has changed; it now contains a padlock (see Figure 5-25) that indicates this drive is encrypted using BitLocker.

Figure 5-25. A USB drive encrypted using BitLocker

To access the locked drive, double-click it in File Explorer. BitLocker will prompt you to enter the password to unlock the drive. In the same window, you can click "More options" to see additional options such as "Automatically unlock on this PC," which allows you to unlock the drive on this computer automatically without entering a password each time you insert it. The second option is to enter the recovery key if you forget your password (see Figure 5-26).

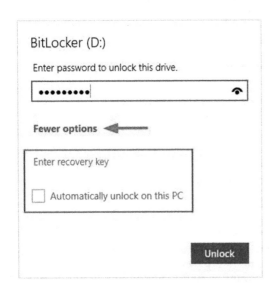

Figure 5-26. Accessing advanced options in the USB drive locked using BitLocker

Finally, to manage BitLocker locked drives and removable ones attached to this PC, go to Control Panel ➤ BitLocker Drive Encryption. On the right side of each BitLocker-enabled drive, you will see a list of options, such as backing up your recovery key, changing/removing the password, and turning off BitLocker (see Figure 5-27).

Removable data drives - BitLocker To Go

NIHAD (D:) BitLocker on

Back up your recovery key
Change password
Remove password
Add smart card
Turn on auto-unlock
Turn off BitLocker

Figure 5-27. *Managing options for a BitLocker-enabled drive*

NOTE! CHECK YOUR BITLOCKER VOLUME'S ENCRYPTION METHOD

To check whether your existing BitLocker volumes use AES-126 or AES-256, follow these steps:

1. Launch a command prompt elevated as the administrator (to do this, right-click the Command Prompt icon in the Windows Start menu and select Run as Administrator. In newer Windows versions such as 8 and 10, you can press Windows Key+X and then click Command Prompt (Admin).

2. Type **manage-bde -status** at the command prompt and press the Enter key.

3. A list of all BitLocker-encrypted volumes and nonencrypted ones will appear along with each encryption method (see Figure 5-28).

Figure 5-28. *Revealing the encryption type used by BitLocker to encrypt your drives*

Best Practices When Using BitLocker

When using BitLocker to encrypt your disk drives, it is essential that you heed the following tips to achieve the maximum security possible when using this feature:

- Use a strong and complex password to protect your BitLocker drive following our tips in Chapter 2. Keep your passwords safe in a secure, encrypted password manager.

- Keep your BitLocker recovery key in a safe location. It is better to store two copies of each key in two separate physical locations (for example, keep one in a USB flash drive and save the second one on paper in a secure cabinet).

- Make sure the name of each recovery key reflects the computer/tablet name or removable drive so you will not be confused when you have many recovery keys stored in one location.

- Use multifactor authentication for operating system drives for enhanced security. For example, store TPM and the startup key on a USB flash drive.

- If you select USB authentication, do not confuse it with the recovery key. A USB authentication key (also known as *startup key*) is a file with a .bek extension, while the recovery key is a text file. Make sure to back up the startup key to a safe location.

- Before upgrading your OS (for example, from Windows 8 to 10), make sure to suspend BitLocker protection. You can do this by going to the BitLocker Drive Encryption option in the Control Panel and suspending protection for the target drive. Please note that the suspension does not mean that BitLocker decrypts data on the volume; it will make this data unlocked for everyone. However, any new data written to the disk is still encrypted.

- Make sure to suspend and resume BitLocker protection after you perform a recovery to your locked drive, as the recovery key will be saved unencrypted on the disk drive, and the drive will remain unprotected until you suspend and resume the BitLocker protection.

- Make sure to turn off your Windows PC or put it in hibernation mode when you finish working. BitLocker is active in these states only. BitLocker is not active in Sleep mode.

- If you suspect that your BitLocker keys have been stolen, make sure to decrypt the drive and then encrypt it again to avoid leaving any traces related to BitLocker metadata that can help attackers to crack it.

- For people storing sensitive data on their machines, it is advisable to encrypt the drive first before moving sensitive files to it. Do this especially for SSDs and USB flash drives.

BitLocker is a great security feature available in most Windows versions. It is easy for novices to use and offers strong protection for your sensitive data. BitLocker adds minimal performance overhead on your machine and is highly recommend, especially on portable Windows computers such as laptops and tablets in addition to removable storage such as USB, SDs, and portal HDDs. Companies using Windows OS for their IT operations are highly encouraged to use BitLocker to protect business data at rest.

Disk Encryption Using Open Source Tools

As we've mentioned, open source encryption software is more trustworthy than proprietary (closed) solutions when it comes to protecting highly sensitive or classified information. The main advantage of open source solutions is that they don't have backdoors (although an audit should be performed before using any program). This does not mean all proprietary solutions have one, but the open source solutions can be reviewed by the public for possible backdoors or for any feature that might facilitate an attack against their cryptographic algorithm. Open source encryption software also has a reputation of being more stable and interoperable with other open source products and protocols and of supporting different hardware (many open source encryption tools support multiple platforms such as Windows, Mac, and Linux). Closed software is usually linked to one vendor, which can impose restrictions on its usage and the other system that can integrate with it. Finally, open source software, especially the popular programs, is used by millions of users and has hundreds of volunteer developers, making open source software more stable, more secure, and less prone to bugs than proprietary systems.

On the other hand, paid solutions usually surpass open source software in being easy to use. They have better user interfaces and offer technical support after the sale. (Most open source products rely on community support or offer paid support service.) Finally, closed software is usually less vulnerable to attacks compared with open ones because no one can view its source code to exploit any weakness.

To end this discussion, open source programs are better than closed counterparts in regard to cryptographic tools. However, you should select your open source encryption tool carefully. Do not consider a product safe just because it is open source. For instance, you need to check the following:

- Make sure to select an encryption tool that incorporates open source cryptographic algorithms like Twofish and Whirlpool.

- Check what current users of this software say about it. Do a search online for any problems, major bugs, or security flaws related to it.

- Check whether experts in the field have made any audit or review of this software and see what their opinion is.

- Use mature software. A program with millions of downloads is better than a new one just developed.

- It should be updated continuously and under active development; old releases with no continual updates are not a good sign.

The most popular open source encryption program (used for file and disk encryption) is the legendary program TrueCrypt. For years it has been the number-one choice by security professionals around the world. TrueCrypt can be installed on different platforms and supports wide arrays of the best secure cryptographic algorithms.

TrueCrypt development ended suddenly in 2014 through a message on its web site stating the following: "Using TrueCrypt is not secure as it may contain unfixed security issues." The TrueCrypt developers did not give any further details regarding the announced security flaws and advised Windows users to use the BitLocker Drive Encryption feature instead. The last version of TrueCrypt was the 7.1a version, released in 2012, and it is still used by millions according to some unofficial statistics.

Unconvinced of any security flaws, the Internet community made an independent audit of TrueCrypt's source code (version 7.1a). The final summary found that "TrueCrypt has no evidence of backdoors or otherwise intentionally malicious code. However, the code suffers from some vulnerabilities resulted from using some deprecated functions and inconsistent variable types which can be fixed by updating the current code."[6]

■ **Note** You can download the last version of TrueCrypt (7.1a) at `https://www.grc.com/misc/truecrypt/truecrypt.htm` along other information regarding this program.

The popularity of TrueCrypt and its reputation has encouraged developers to create other forks for this project. The following are the main projects based on this tool:

- VeraCrypt (`https://veracrypt.codeplex.com`): This is based on TrueCrypt 7.1a. It adds enhanced security to the algorithms used in encryption and fixes major security bugs found in the TrueCrypt security audit. VeraCrypt cannot open encrypted containers created in TrueCrypt.

- CipherShed (`https://www.ciphershed.org`): This is another fork based on TrueCrypt. It maintains backward compatibility with the previous TrueCrypt container format.

In this book, we will opt to use VeraCrypt as it is in active development more than CipherShed, and it already has fixed the main vulnerabilities raised by the TrueCrypt audit project. (The most current audit to the VeraCrypt source code was done in October 2016 and fixed a critical vulnerability related to cryptography.[7])

Encryption Using VeraCrypt

VeraCrypt offers similar functions as its ancestor TrueCrypt. It can encrypt the Windows partition, fixed drive data partitions, and removable media, and it can create encrypted containers to store sensitive information. VeraCrypt also supports plausible deniability through the following:

- It supports hidden volumes and hidden operating system.

- Encrypted VeraCrypt devices and volumes look as if they are full of random data; they contain no signature for being a VeraCrypt container.

■ **Note** Plausible deniability can also be achieved by using steganography techniques in which secret data can be concealed within an ordinary file (e.g., concealing a secret text file within an image).

In this section, we will demonstrate how to use this stable software to create an encrypted volume, and later we will demonstrate how to create a hidden volume in addition to encrypting removable USB devices.

Creating an Encrypted Container (Volume)

The following steps detail how to create an encrypted container to store your sensitive data securely.

1. Download and install VeraCrypt from `https://veracrypt.codeplex.com`. Make sure to download the latest version.

2. Launch the program and click the Create Volume button in the main program window.

3. The Volume Creation Wizard window will appear, allowing you to select which kind of encrypted volume you want to create. You have three options (see Figure 5-29): encrypt a file container, encrypt a nonsystem partition (fixed data drive or flash memory), and encrypt a system partition drive (Windows partition). In this case, select the first option and click Next to continue.

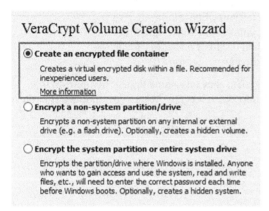

Figure 5-29. *VeraCrypt allows you to create three different types of encrypted volumes. This shows only the right side of the wizard window.*

4. The next wizard window asks you whether you want to create a standard or hidden volume. Select Standard VeraCrypt Volume and click Next to continue.

5. Now, you need to select the volume location and name. Bear in mind that VeraCrypt containers are like ordinary files. You can move them onto a USB drive or to another PC, rename them, and delete them. Do not select an existing file in this step. You need to supply a new file name to avoid overwriting any existing file (see Figure 5-30). After finishing this step successfully, click Next to continue.

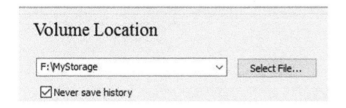

Figure 5-30. *Storing a volume in the F:\ drive with the name MyStorage*

6. The next wizard window asks you to select the encryption and hash algorithm for this volume. We already discussed the main criteria for selecting the best secure algorithm. In this case, select Twofish for the encryption and Whirlpool for the hash. Click Next to continue.

7. Here you need to specify the volume size. In this case, you will choose 500MB. Please note that you cannot increase the volume size after creating it. Click Next to continue.

8. The next wizard window asks you to enter a password to protect the volume. Select a complex and long password according to our tips in Chapter 2. However, it is strongly recommended that you use at least 20 characters. You can also further secure your volume by using a key file. After typing the password and confirming it, click Next to continue.

9. In this window, you need to move your mouse within it randomly for some time (at least one minute; a progress bar appears to tell you when it is enough) to increase the cryptographic strength of the encryption keys. Make sure to set the filesystem type to FAT as it is widely supported on different platforms and leave the cluster set to Default. After finishing, click the Format button.

VeraCrypt will begin creating your encrypted container. This may take some time depending on the size of the volume. After it finishes, a success message will pop up saying "The VeraCrypt volume has been successfully created." Click Exit to close the wizard.

Opening a VeraCrypt-Encrypted Volume

To open an encrypted container, follow these steps:

1. Launch VeraCrypt and select a drive letter from the list.

2. Click Select File to select your encrypted container file.

3. Click the Mount button (Figure 5-31). The password dialog will appear.

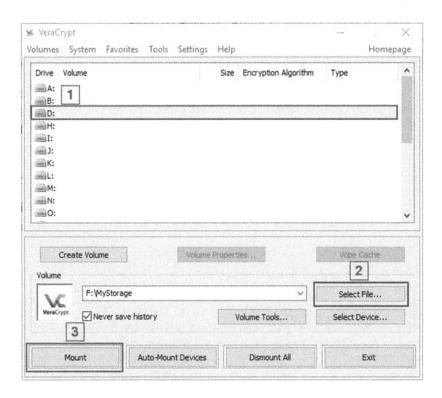

Figure 5-31. *Opening the VeraCrypt-encrypted container*

4. Enter your volume password in the prompt and click OK.

5. If the password was correct, the mounted container will appear as a virtual disk drive in Windows File Explorer. You can also access it by double-clicking the drive letter in the main program window.

VeraCrypt will encrypt any file or folder on the fly as it is being written to its volume. In a similar way, whenever you open a file stored in a VeraCrypt container, it will automatically decrypt it to computer RAM without writing anything to the host computer disk.

To close the opened VeraCrypt container and make your stored encrypted files inaccessible again, you can either turn off/restart your computer or select the mounted drive letter in the VeraCrypt main window and then click the Dismount button.

Creating Hidden VeraCrypt Volume

A VeraCrypt hidden volume allows users to protect their sensitive data if they are forced to disclose their VeraCrypt-encrypted volume password. A hidden volume can be created within another VeraCrypt volume (including a standard volume or a partition/device volume) by exploiting the available free space in the outer volume. To create a hidden volume, follow these steps (which are similar to creating a standard volume but with minor differences):

1. Launch VeraCrypt, click the Create Volume button, select the option "Create an encrypted file container," and then click Next.

2. The next window asks you about the volume type. Select "Hidden VeraCrypt volume" and click Next to continue.

3. The next wizard window asks you which mode creation you want to use. In this case you already have a standard volume, so use the "Direct mode" option and click Next to continue. If you do not have a ready encrypted volume, you should select the "Normal mode" option to create an encrypted volume first and then create the hidden one.

4. The next window asks you to select your existing encrypted VeraCrypt volume. Select the one you have created in the previous step (this volume will hold the hidden one inside it). Click Next to continue.

5. Now you need to enter the outer volume password (see Figure 5-32). Click Next to continue.

Figure 5-32. Enter the outer container password. This will hold the hidden volume inside it.

6. VeraCrypt will scan the outer volume cluster bitmap to determine the maximum possible size of the hidden volume. Click Next to move to the next steps to set the options for the hidden volume.

7. The next wizard window will ask you to select the encryption and hash algorithm for the hidden volume. Select them as you did previously and click Next to continue. In the next window, you need to set the hidden volume size. VeraCrypt will determine the maximum possible size of the hidden volume. In this case, the maximum size was 495.26MB (see Figure 5-33).

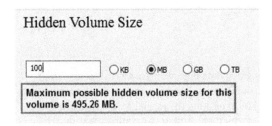

Figure 5-33. *Determining the hidden volume size*

8. After typing the hidden volume size, click Next to continue. The next wizard will ask you for a password for the hidden volume. Type one that is different from the outer volume password. Click Next to continue.

■ **Warning**   Do not use the same password for both the outer volume and the hidden volume. VeraCrypt uses the password to distinguish between both volumes when you want to mount any one of them.

---

9. Now you need to select the filesystem format as you did previously (select FAT and leave the cluster size to the default). Move your mouse within the wizard for one minute and click Format. If everything goes well, the hidden volume will be created, and VeraCrypt will launch the window shown in Figure 5-34.

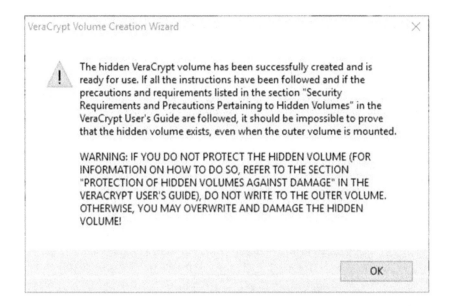

Figure 5-34. *VeraCrypt announcing the successful creation of the hidden volume*

10. Finally, click the Exit button to exit the wizard.

Opening the Hidden Volume

Opening a hidden volume is just like opening the standard volume, which you did previously (see the section "Opening a VeraCrypt-Encrypted Volume"). But instead of entering the outer volume password, you need to enter the hidden volume password. VeraCrypt will show the volume type as Hidden after mounting it (see Figure 5-35).

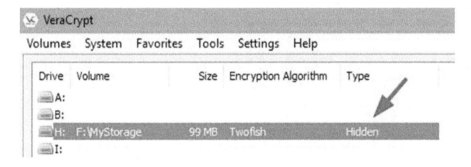

Figure 5-35. *VeraCrypt showing the type of volume mounted in its main program window*

Protecting Your Data in the Hidden Volume from Accidental Deletion

You may wonder what will happen to the data stored in the hidden volume if you write data to an outer volume that consumes its entire space. The answer is simple. The data in the hidden volume will get damaged. To avoid this, follow these steps:

1. When you want to mount (open) your outer volume to view its data, after typing your password for the outer volume, click the Mount Options button before clicking OK (see Figure 5-36).

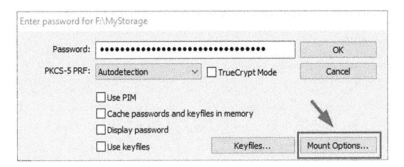

Figure 5-36. *Clicking Mount Options before accessing your outer volume*

2. Another window will pop up. Select the option "Protect hidden volume against damage caused by writing to outer volume." You also need to supply your hidden volume password, as shown in Figure 5-37.

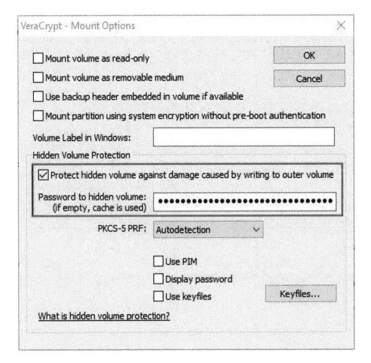

Figure 5-37. *Accessing the VeraCrypt container mount options to protect the hidden volume data*

3. Click OK to close the current window; then click OK again in the password dialog to mount your outer volume without damaging the data on the hidden volume stored within it. If there is no error and you have entered both passwords correctly for both volumes, you will see a pop-up message stating that "The hidden volume is now protected against damage until the outer volume is dismounted."

Please note that this procedure to protect the hidden volume does not mean that VeraCrypt has mounted it. It has only decrypted the portion of the hidden volume that contains its size. When you open your outer volume using the previous steps, both the outer and hidden volumes will open as read-only. Note that VeraCrypt decrypts the volume and displays it as Outer in the program main window. This is because you opened it in a protected mode. If security is an issue, do not mount your volume in this way, as it will give a clue that your outer volume contains within it a hidden one. When you decrypt a VeraCrypt container, it will mount as Normal in ordinary circumstances.

When you have a hidden volume, it is advisable to store some insensitive data in the outer volume and stop adding more data to the outer volume after creating your hidden volume. This will effectively save your important data and prevent accidental damage to the data stored within your hidden volume.

■ **Warning**   Using VeraCrypt could be dangerous in some circumstances. When using VeraCrypt to encrypt your data, there is no technical way, as far as we know, to know whether the encrypted container contains a hidden volume within it. For instance, if an honest foreigner traveler is visiting the United States and the U.S. border agency finds a VeraCrypt container on his or her PC, they may ask the traveler to hand over the decryption key (the password/and keyfile) to decrypt the container. This traveler could be in trouble if the encrypted container does not contain a hidden volume within it because the officers (or any adversary) may not believe the traveler that the encrypted container does not have another one hidden within it.

We advise you to use Windows BitLocker if you are not protecting sensitive/high-grade information. However, if you opt to use VeraCrypt and you want to protect yourself from such a scenario, you can simply create a hidden volume within each encrypted container you create. In this way, if an adversary forces you to decrypt your VeraCrypt volume, you can provide the passwords for both encrypted and hidden volumes to prove your innocence from hiding secret data.

Please note that each VeraCrypt container can contain one hidden volume within it.

Encrypting Fixed Data and USB Drive Using VeraCrypt

Encrypting USB drives and other fixed data drives (non-Windows partitions) is similar to creating standard volumes. To encrypt a removable drive, follow these steps (in brief):

1. Launch the VeraCrypt program. Click Create Volume in the main program window. The Volume Creation Wizard will appear.

2. Select "Encrypt a non-system partition drive/drive" and then click Next to continue.

3. In the next wizard window, select "Standard VeraCrypt volume" and then click Next to continue.

4. The next wizard window will ask you to select the device that you want to encrypt. Click Select Device and select the drive you want to encrypt. All connected devices and partitions on the current computer will appear; make sure to select either the fixed data or the USB drive only (this wizard is not applicable to Windows drives), as shown in Figure 5-38.

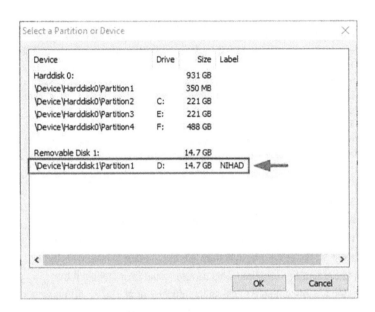

Figure 5-38. *Selecting the USB drive you want to encrypt*

5. After selecting your device, click Next to move to the next wizard window, which gives you two options (see Figure 5-39). The first is "Create encrypted volume and format it." Use this option if you want to encrypt a clean USB stick that contains no data (do not use this option if your device/USB holds data because everything will get lost). The second option is "Encrypt partition in place." Use this option if your current device/USB stick contains data that must be maintained and encrypted.

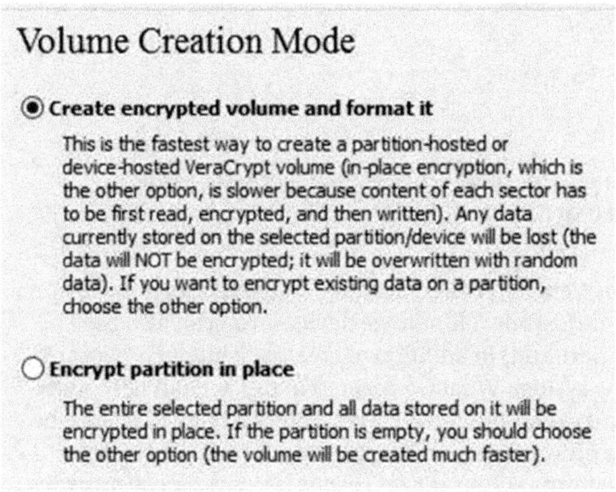

Volume Creation Mode

◉ **Create encrypted volume and format it**

This is the fastest way to create a partition-hosted or device-hosted VeraCrypt volume (in-place encryption, which is the other option, is slower because content of each sector has to be first read, encrypted, and then written). Any data currently stored on the selected partition/device will be lost (the data will NOT be encrypted; it will be overwritten with random data). If you want to encrypt existing data on a partition, choose the other option.

○ **Encrypt partition in place**

The entire selected partition and all data stored on it will be encrypted in place. If the partition is empty, you should choose the other option (the volume will be created much faster).

Figure 5-39. *The first option will format the drive and then encrypt the data, while the second option will encrypt the existing data in the drive without formatting it*

6. The next wizard window will ask you to select your encryption algorithm, set a volume password, and set whether you want to store large files (more than 4GB, and set the filesystem type. After setting all these parameters (like you did earlier), click the Format button.

If everything works as expected, VeraCrypt will launch a success message stating that the volume was created successfully. Click the Exit button to close the wizard.

To mount the encrypted device/USB volumes, follow these steps:

1. Click the Auto-Mount Devices button in the main program window. The password dialog will appear. Type your device/USB password and click OK. VeraCrypt will mount your device to one of the available drive letters (see Figure 5-40).

Figure 5-40. *Mounting a device/USB in VeraCrypt*

Alternatively, you can mount your device by selecting a drive letter (different from the current device/USB drive letter) and clicking the Select Device button in the main program window; then click the Mount button.

After successfully mounting your device/USB drive, two drives will appear in Windows File Explorer; these are the encrypted drive and the mounted (unlocked) container, which contains its data (see Figure 5-41).

Figure 5-41. *Each mounted device/USB will reserve two drive letters, one for the encrypted drive (inaccessible) and the second for the mounted version that contains its data*

In this section, we have thoroughly covered using VeraCrypt to create a standard container and a hidden container and to encrypt a fixed data drive and removable storage devices. You can also use VeraCrypt to encrypt the system drive (the Windows partition) in addition to creating a hidden operating system if someone forces you to decrypt the operating system. What we covered in this section is enough for all users with varying IT skills to begin using VeraCrypt for their daily tasks. For experienced users who may want to use it to encrypt the operating system partition or check out all its advanced features, we recommend reading the VeraCrypt documentation at `https://veracrypt.codeplex.com/documentation`.

Multitask Encryption Tools

Sometimes you may not want to use a dedicated tool for your encryption work. For instance, you don't need a VeraCrypt container if you want to send a small file to your friend via e-mail or you want to store some files on an unencrypted USB device. There are many programs already used by millions of Windows users that can offer encryption capabilities to safeguard your sensitive data with a few clicks. You can also find many open source security tools that do not need advanced configurations or cryptographic keys in order to encrypt files and folders. This section will introduce some of these tools; they have been selected specifically to meet our tools selection criteria of being open source, reputable, and easy to use.

7-Zip

7-Zip (`www.7-zip.org`) is open source archiver software that works on all Windows versions (beginning from NT). It allows you to compress and encrypt data using the AES-256 encryption algorithm for the 7ZIP format and uses AES-256/ZipCrypto for the ZIP file format. Using it is simple; just right-click the file or folder you want to compress and select Z-Zip ➤ Add to archive.

AES Crypt

AES Crypt (`https://www.aescrypt.com`) is a free, open source program that integrates with the Windows right-click context menu. It uses AES-256 encryption to do its job. To encrypt a file, right-click the file and select AES Encrypt. Then enter the password to lock the file; another file with the same name but with AES extension will appear in the same directory. To decrypt it, right-click the encrypted result and select AES Decrypt. Then enter its password. The encrypted file should appear unencrypted in the same directory with its original extension.

Protect Microsoft Office Files

All Microsoft Office documents beginning with Microsoft Office 2007 can be protected with a password to prevent others from opening or modifying your documents. This feature uses AES-128 by default. To password-protect a Microsoft Word document, follow these steps:

In Microsoft Office 2007, click the Microsoft Office button and select Prepare ➤ Encrypt Document. Type your password and confirm it. Then click OK. Finally, save the changes to your file.

For Microsoft Office 2013 and 2016, open the document you want to protect, select the File menu, go to the Info tab, click the Protect Document button, select Encrypt with Password, enter the password, and click OK. Finally, save changes to your document. In Excel, select File, go to the Info tab, select Protect Workbook, and select Encrypt with Password. In PowerPoint, select File, go to the Info tab, select Protect Presentation, and select Encrypt with Password.

Protect PDF Files

Like the Microsoft Office products, Adobe has a password protection feature for its documents. PDF documents are used widely for both personal and business use. To protect a PDF file with a password, open the file you want to protect, select File ➤ Properties, and go to the Security tab. From the Security Method drop-down menu, select Password Security. Another window will pop up where you should select the option "Require a password to open the document" and type the password in the corresponding field. Click the OK button, and another pop-up window will appear asking you to confirm your password. Type it again and click OK. Then close all open dialogs and save your document (you can save it by closing it and selecting Yes when Adobe asks you whether you want to save your changes to the file).

Attacking Cryptographic Systems

These types of attacks aim to find the secret key used to decrypt the confidential data in order to gain unauthorized access to it. As computing technology advances daily, you can expect to see more attacks against cryptographic systems. For instance, you should know that using full disk encryption to encrypt your entire disk drive does not ensure 100 percent safety of your data at rest. In the same way, encrypted data transmitted across untrusted networks like the Internet also suffer from many threats. Scrambling your data is a great protective method, but you still need to understand the different types of cryptographic cyber-attacks so you can take some precautionary steps to deter them successfully.

Disk encryption is able to protect you against one type of attack, which is the physical attack. Even though you have your PC encrypted, there are a large number of cyber-threats already traveling the Internet that can strike your machine. For instance, full disk encryption does not protect against an adversary who intercepts your communication online. Unpatched Windows, old software, an older OS (such as Windows XP), and some dangerous services can be exploited remotely to plant malware on your machine. This will effectively steal your decryption keys and make your disk encryption useless.

We already covered how to use BitLocker and VeraCrypt to encrypt entire drives. In Chapter 4, we advised you to use the Tails OS, which boots from a CD/DVD or USB stick to assure complete anonymity when going online in extremely hostile (in terms of censorship) environments. All encryption tools and techniques already covered in this book can suffer from similar attacks. Thus, we are dedicating a separate section for them. The following are the most popular and known attacks against cryptographic techniques.

Harvest-Then-Decrypt Attack

With advances in computing technology, you can expect that currently used algorithms will be broken before reaching their estimated death time. For instance, a quantum computer (still under development) is known to be thousands of times faster than a normal computer. This tremendous speed imposes a serious risk on modern cryptographic algorithms, especially the ones based on public key infrastructure (PKI) such as RSA and Elliptic Curve Cryptography (ECC). These two algorithms are still used by the Transport Layer Security (TLS) protocol, which is used to secure the majority of online applications such as web browsing, IM, e-mail, VoIP services, and so on. TLS achieves its secure work by encrypting the connection between the client and the server using a symmetrical key. However, it will use asymmetrical algorithms such as RSA to exchange the secret key first, which is generated automatically upon initiating each session. These protocols are still very secure by today's security standards and nearly impossible to break. However, an attacker could record the encrypted traffic and then wait until the technology advances (for example, until the quantum computer arrives) and then try to decrypt the traffic.

The DROWN Attack

DROWN stands for Decrypting RSA with Obsolete and Weakened eNcryption. This kind of attack affects servers that are still supporting SSLv2. Nearly all modern Internet applications do not use SSLv2. However, if there is a misconfigured server that still has SSLv2 enabled, this may impose a risk as it allows an attacker to decrypt the newer TLS connection between up-to-date clients and the servers by using the same private key used for the secure connection. Disabling SSLv2 is necessary to close such a vulnerability. You can find more information about this attack and the countermeasures at `https://drownattack.com`.

Man-in-the-Middle (MITM) Attack

This is another form of active attack that targets encrypted traffic flows online, and it is mostly applicable to the public key cryptography schema. In this type, an attacker intercepts the communication but still relays the message between the sender and the receiver as if the communication was not touched. Discovering such attacks is difficult because nothing appears to be unusual for the communicating parties. Here's an example:

1. If Nihad wants to communicate privately with Susan, he needs to request her public key first.

2. An attacker intercepts the communication and sends his public key instead to Susan. In this way, the attacker is able to decrypt anything Nihad sends to Susan.

3. Capturing one side is not enough; the attacker needs to maintain the connection, so he or she encrypts the data after reading it and resends it to Susan.

4. The attacker now sends his public key impersonating Nihad so that anything Susan sends is decrypted by the attacker.

Such attacks are difficult to conduct because they involve a real intrusion into the communication channel, but when it does happen, it results in a serious compromise.

Brute-Force Attack

In this type of attack, the attacker already has the encrypted data and knows the encryption algorithm. The attacker needs to know the decryption key or the password/passphrase. The attacker tries all possible combinations to find the correct key. If the key (password/passphrase) is long, cracking it can take a long time. There are many programs to automate such attacks, such as John the Ripper (`www.openwall.com/john/`) and RainbowCrack (`http://project-rainbowcrack.com`), which is used specifically for cracking password hashes.

A variant of brute-force attack is a dictionary attack, which uses words and phrases from different dictionaries in order to crack the password/key. A dictionary attack is faster than a brute-force attack as the attacker needs to try small combinations of possible words/phrases compared with a regular brute-force attack. However, this attack has its limitations because if the key/password does not exist in the dictionary, the attacker will never find it. Brute-force and dictionary attacks can be deterred by using complex, long passwords that have no specific meaning (follow our tips in Chapter 2 for creating secure passwords).

Bootkit

A bootkit is a kind of malware that installs on the master boot record (MBR) of your operating system. It usually stores its code in the unallocated disk space or host-protected area using its own file system. It runs before the operating system boots, giving it the ability to bypass full disk encryption because the MBR is not encrypted; this allows the OS to boot up and the encryption software to launch its login screen from within the MBR. This will effectively allow it to capture the decryption key/password once entered. A bootkit can get direct access to the Windows kernel, giving it wide abilities to do its dirty work and bypassing all security software already installed on the infected machine.

If you are curious about bootkit development, you can check out www.stoned-vienna.com, which gives information about and the source code of one type of bootkit named Stoned Bootkit. This kind of bootkit attacks all Windows versions from 2000 up to 7. It also has a demo version for Windows 8.

A bootkit is considered a type of rootkit (covered next). However, the main difference between them is that the bootkit launches early during the boot process.

Rootkit

A rootkit is a type of malicious software designed to gain low-level access to the target computer. A rootkit in itself is not malicious; however, if exploited by intruders, it can spy on a legitimate computer owner's usage and steal his or her decryption keys. Rootkits work stealthily in the background without leaving any traces in the infected machine. They do not have a process name, a registry entry, or an associated Windows service running. A rootkit has the ability to disable security solutions already installed on the infected machine. It can also make modifications to the OS (e.g., install itself as a software driver) to further conceal itself, install a keylogger, and install other malware in addition to maintaining administrative access to the target machine by the attacker.

Detecting a bootkit or a rootkit can be extremely difficult because normal antivirus programs cannot detect all types of them. However, there are many tools that have been designed specifically to detect and remove this kind of threat. You can find some in Table 5-1.

Table 5-1. *Anti-bootkit and Anti-rootkit Tools*

Name	URL
RootkitRevealer	https://technet.microsoft.com/en-us/sysinternals/bb897445
TDSSKiller	https://support.kaspersky.com/viruses/disinfection/5350#block1
GMER	www.gmer.net
Rootkit Detection Framework for UEFI (RDFU)	https://www.reversinglabs.com/open-source/rdfu-uefi.html
UnHackMe	http://greatis.com/unhackme
Sophos Anti-Rootkit	https://www.sophos.com/products/free-tools/sophos-anti-rootkit.aspx

Operating System Leak

Windows can leak sensitive information, even if you are implementing a full disk encryption scheme in your PC. For instance, decrypted files (or parts of them), passwords, encryption keys, cached files, and other secret information can reside in different places in Windows, such as in paging files, hibernation files, memory dumps, and system restore points (created by the Volume Shadow Copy Service). Many single-file encryption tools offer a feature to delete the original file upon encryption and leave the encrypted result only; this is a good security practice. However, the majority of such programs do not wipe the deleted file securely, making it recoverable later.

The previous attacks against encryption techniques are all based on software attacks. However, there are more attacks that require physical access to the target machine to work successfully. The following section covers the most popular one.

Evil Maid Attack

In this scenario, an attacker gains physical access to an unattended target PC that has full disk encryption enabled using programs like VeraCrypt, PGP whole disk encryption, or BitLocker. The attacker (like a maid in a hotel) boots the target PC using a CD/DVD or USB drive, or even through a network, and installs a bootkit (backdoor) into the system and then shuts off the PC.

When the legitimate PC owner returns, he or she powers up the PC as usual and enters the decryption key/password to decrypt the disk. The bootkit will record this information somewhere in the disk drive (e.g., in unallocated space or in a host-protected area); the attacker can return later to recover them and delete any traces left from the attack. Some kinds of bootkits can also send the user decryption key/password via the Internet when a connection is available.

Nearly all disk encryption systems are vulnerable to this attack unless some precautionary measures are followed (covered in a moment) that can make performing this attack extremely hard to achieve.

■ **Note** EvilAbigail (`https://github.com/GDSSecurity/EvilAbigail`) performs an automated Linux evil maid attack.

Cold Boot Attack

In this type of attack, an attacker gains physical access to the target machine immediately after it has been turned off (or the attacker can reboot a running machine using the power button; this called a *cold reboot*) and then tries to boot using a USB stick or CD/DVD. Using specialized software, the attacker captures an image of the RAM and stores it on the removable device. Finally, the attacker shuts down the PC as if nothing happened. In old desktop computers and some laptop models, an attacker can also remove the RAM module entirely from the target machine and install it on his or her own machine and then boot normally to extract its contents.

The captured image will get analyzed to recognize important artifacts stored within it using a variety of techniques. By using a specialized tool, there is a high probability that an attacker can find and extract the decryption key from the target machine.

This kind of attack is possible because of the volatile nature of RAM. Anything stored in RAM will disappear when it loses power. However, research conducted by Princeton University in 2008 found that information stored within RAM can last for seconds after it loses power. This period can extend into minutes or even hours if RAM is frozen using liquid nitrogen to cool the volatile memory modules to slow down the degradation of the contents.

The majority of encryption systems store their encryption key/password in RAM. This attack also proves its effectiveness against full disk encryption employed by BitLocker.

Direct Memory Access

Direct memory access (DMA) is a type of physical attack where an attacker gains direct access to the target machine's RAM by exploiting some types of ports (FireWire, Thunderbolt, PCI Express). This allows direct access to RAM without passing first through the target machine's CPU. By doing this, an attacker can access/capture the RAM contents directly and then by using specialized software can investigate it thoroughly to extract encryption keys and other sensitive information like passwords, chat messages, and decrypted files. In the same way, an attacker can bypass all the security solutions already deployed by the target OS and install a keylogger or rootkit to monitor everything done on the subject device.

Hardware Keyloggers

Keyloggers come in two forms, software and hardware. We already talked about some types of software bootkits and rootkits that have the ability to record user activities stealthily and send it later through the Internet or Wi-Fi signals to their operator. The same thing applies to hardware keyloggers, which are more sophisticated and have the ability to surpass all the security solutions already installed on the target machine. By installing a hardware keylogger, usually installed between the target computer and its keyboard or simply attached to the DVI, VGA, or HDMI port, an attacker will have the ability to capture everything the user types on the machine in addition to taking screen captures and then send this information through e-mail. Some modern types of hardware keyloggers have built-in Wi-Fi support, enabling them to use their own connection to deliver reports. A hardware keylogger looks similar to cabling used with a PC to connect different external devices, making it less suspicious for nonexperienced users. A hardware keylogger is more dangerous than its software counterpart as it can begin logging user activities once the computer starts. This gives it the ability to record BIOS passwords and full disk encryption passwords.

Hardware Backdoor

As more companies select to manufacture their IT products in Asian countries to reduce costs, you can expect to see more devices equipped with hardware backdoors. Backdoors allow cyber-criminals to gain remote access to target machines/networks without being discovered. Some types can also get embedded within memory modules (volatile memory) and wireless microchips (e.g., radio frequency identification [RFID]). Hardware backdoors are a real threat to IT operations, especially when they are embedded in security devices such as access control systems and network devices. An attacker can modify the hardware device upon manufacturing so he or she can bypass security measures and full disk encryption on the target machine/network. This kind of attack works below the OS level, making it able to bypass all security software solutions currently deployed. Hardware backdoors and firmware attacks that work by modifying the BIOS code to exploit the target machine are usually used by security services and big criminal organizations with adequate resources to monitor users/companies for intelligence. This threat is not only related to exploiting target systems; it can also be used by cyber-criminals to control affected systems remotely and as a botnet to launch further attacks (e.g., DDoS attacks).

Countermeasures Against Cryptography Attacks

Most attacks against cryptographic techniques can be mitigated if the user uses the proper device/OS and takes some precautionary steps. This section gives you some advice.

Mitigate Future Attacks Against Encrypted Data

We already covered the harvest-then-decrypt attack, which works by capturing current encrypted data and then waiting until the technology advances in order to be able to crack it. Countering such attacks is difficult because the majority of encrypted data travels online, and anyone with adequate tools can capture it for later analysis. The most practical advice against such future attacks is to use similar technology to counter for it. Currently, quantum computing is still in the development stage. Quantum cryptography (which depends on physics rather than mathematics to create its cryptosystem) is also gaining more attention to fight against future attack techniques. For instance, it is impossible to crack an encryption key encoded using quantum cryptography. This issue boosts confidence in deploying advanced techniques to exchange top-secret information online.

Another mitigation technique that can be used regardless of future attack and protection techniques is to stop sending any critical data online. Sensitive and high-grade information can be exchanged physically using encrypted storage devices offline, without exposing the contents online.

Mitigate Brute-Force Attack

Such an attack is not practical against the Windows OS sign-in authenticator or BitLocker (with a BitLocker password or recovery key) when the target machine is protected with a strong, complex password and the account lockout is activated (the user needs to wait a certain time after entering an invalid username/password three times). Windows devices with TPM microchips offer more protection against such attacks. To protect a VeraCrypt container and similar full disk encryption tools, it is highly advisable to use at least 20 characters in your password and follow our tips in Chapter 2.

OS Leak

Even if you are using full disk encryption to protect your data, you still need to decrypt this data to access it. Windows stores opened files and fragments of them in different locations on the hard drive. For example, when you want to read a Microsoft Word document stored inside a VeraCrypt-encrypted container, you need to decrypt the container first. Then after opening this document, Windows needs to upload it into the computer RAM to make it available for reading. In the same way, Windows will record opening such a file in different locations (recently opened files, Microsoft Word history files, among other places). In addition, Windows may need to store this file or parts of it in another location without the user's knowledge. To counter for such risks, you need to configure Windows properly to limit the cases that may leak your sensitive data without your knowledge.

- *Disable memory dumps*: A memory dump file can contain unencrypted data if Windows faces a problem and needs to restart. To disable this feature, go to Control Panel ➤ System, select "Advanced system settings," go to the Advanced tab, and click the Settings button in the Startup and Recovery section. In the "Write debugging information section," select "none" from the drop-down menu. Click OK and then OK and you are done.

- *Disable the Windows hibernation (Hiberfil.sys) feature*: This file is located in the same partition where Windows is installed (usually on the C:\ drive). As you may have guessed, opened files, encryption keys, passwords, key files, and anything that was running or open on a computer when it goes into hibernation mode may go into this file. If an attacker gains physical access or network access to this file, he or she can copy it to extract useful information from it. To disable hibernation mode in Windows, open a command prompt as the administrator, type **Powercfg -hibernate off**, and press the Enter key.

- *Disable virtual memory*: This feature allows Windows to copy part of the RAM contents into a special file on the hard drive (usually stored on the same drive where Windows is installed under the name Pagefile.sys) to compensate for RAM storage when it becomes full. A user can't determine which file or files will end in the paging file, so it is better to disable it. To disable the paging file on Windows, go to Control Panel ➤ System, select "Advanced system settings," and go to the Advanced tab. In the Performance pane, click Settings, and on the Advanced tab, click the Change button in the "Virtual memory" section. From this menu, you can select the drive where you want to disable the paging file by selecting "No paging file" and then clicking Set.

- *Disable Volume Shadow Copy Service*: This service allows Windows to take automatic backup copies of all files and folders and system settings on all system volumes where it is turned on (usually it is turned on by default on the system volume only). This imposes a great risk; for example, a user can delete a file and wipe its location securely, but Windows could save a previous version of this file in one of the system restore points, without the user's knowledge, to be easily retrieved later. To disable a system restore, go to Control Panel ➤ System, select "Advanced system settings," and go to the System Protection tab. Select the partition you want to stop generating a restore point for and click the Configure button. In the new window, select "Turn off system protection" (in Windows 10 this option is called "Disable system protection").

It is good practice to surf the Internet using a limited Windows account to avoid installing any rootkit inadvertently; you should also keep your antivirus solution up-to-date and install a dedicated program to fight against malware. Also, do not forget to set the Windows OS to update itself automatically.

Mitigation Strategies Against Physical Attacks

In this section, we provide you with advice on how to protect against both hardware/physical attacks and bootkits and rootkits. The last two types of attacks are indeed software oriented, but we decided to group them in this section because the majority of such attacks require physical access to the target machine in order to embed successfully. Nevertheless, some types of rootkit can infect machines throughout a network or by installing malware from the Internet inadvertently.

- Set a password for your BIOS. This will prevent attackers from booting using a CD/DVD or USB device and will make launching many physical attacks more difficult to conduct.

- Use a computer with a TPM module when encrypting disk drives using BitLocker so you can discover any tampering with OS files upon booting. If your computer does not have a TPM microchip, you should protect your drive using both a password and a USB token.

- Always use two-factor authentication, even if your computer has a TPM module. For example, use a PIN and a smart card or USB startup key to decrypt your drive. Do the same thing when using the VeraCrypt tool; use a password and a key file stored on a USB flash drive.

- Use a computer with Unified Extensible Firmware Interface (UEFI) support. UEFI is a new programmable interface intended to replace the old BIOS program; it defines a software interface between the computer's OS and the firmware. UEFI can help you to secure your machines against sophisticated malware like bootkits and rootkits by securing the boot process of the OS. For instance, EUFI will check each hardware piece's firmware digital signature in addition to its bootloader digital signature against a list of signatures available within it. If attackers modify the bootloader or insert malware in the firmware to capture the encryption keys/passwords, EUFI will detect this and prevent Windows from booting. Most modern Windows (8 and 10) devices support EUFI.

- Use modern Windows versions and stop using the discontinued editions. For instance, XP and Vista should never be used, as Microsoft no longer supports them. Modern Windows versions like 8 and 10 support many features for preventing bootkit and rootkit attacks.

  - Secure Boot is enabled by default on all devices that carry the Windows 8 or 10 logo; it checks whether the bootloader has been tampered with before loading it.

  - The trusted boot feature continues from where Secure Boot ends. It works by verifying the Windows kernel first. If successful, it will pass the check to the Windows kernel, which will in turn check all components used by Windows to start up. If an attacker has modified any startup file, Windows will refuse to load the modified file and will try to repair it by replacing it with another original one to continue the boot process normally.

  - The Early Launch Antimalware (ELAM) feature allows Windows to start the anti-malware solution before Windows loads all non-Microsoft drives to detect any tampering with third-party component files.

- A cold boot attack is practical against computers with old hardware. Modern computing devices have new versions of RAM (DDR3 and DDR4), which store remnants of information for a limited time after losing power. In addition, the RAM in many modern computing devices comes soldered with the mainboard. Thus, you cannot remove it and boot it in another machine. In all cases, it is a good practice to always shut down your computer gracefully and protect your computer BIOS with a password.

- To mitigate DMA attacks, you can use Windows InstantGo–certified devices that do not have any DMA ports. Another solution if your PC has such ports is to stop it from using firmware settings or to use Group Policy settings. Starting with Windows 8.1, DMA access by external devices was rejected until the user authorized the connection.

- To mitigate hardware backdoor threats, you should buy your computing devices (whether it is a computer, tablet, smartphone, or IoT device) from a trusted and reputable vendor. Always ask and investigate before buying sensitive devices such as access control systems and spy cameras, which are products manufactured in Asian countries.

Securing Data in Transit

Earlier in this chapter we covered how to secure your data while it is at rest. Data at rest is all the data that is stored in computers/laptops, tablets, storage servers, backup tapes, USB drives, and all storage units that hold data without moving it between locations using local or external networks. To cover all security angles, you also need to learn how to secure your data while in transit. This includes securing sensitive data when moving it from one location to another using a local network within an organization or sending it through the Internet (or uploading it to a cloud storage server). It is essential to protect data in both states (at rest and in transit) to cover all cyber-attack possibilities. You will learn about encryption and steganography and about how you can use these technologies to protect your private data in today's digital age.

In this section, we will demonstrate how to use different tools to assure the security and integrity of your data to protect against eavesdropping on network traffic by unauthorized users.

Cloud Storage Encryption

As the costs of storing data on a remote server online go down (many services offer it for free), more and more people are willing to use cloud storage services to back up and store their sensitive data (such as documents, personal pictures, contact lists, address books, and the like). The majority of smartphone users use cloud services in one way or another to store some type of personal data. Giant cloud providers such as Google Drive, Apple iCloud, and Microsoft OneDrive invest a considerable amount of resources to protect their users' data. However, no one can guarantee 100 percent protection when your data travels to the Internet. To protect your personal data from unauthorized access while storing it in the cloud, it is advisable to encrypt this data on your local machine before uploading it. This section will introduce some secure and open source tools to perform this easily.

■ **Warning**   Don't rely on the cloud service provider to secure your data. Always encrypt your data before uploading it to the cloud and make sure to have a backup copy stored somewhere else when dealing with sensitive data.

Duplicati

Duplicati (https://www.duplicati.com) is a free, open source program for backing up data to the cloud. It works with major cloud storage providers and with other protocols like FTP and SSH. It uses AES-256 or GPG to encrypt your data and incorporates an incremental backup feature to save space and limit the size of uploaded data to the cloud.

Cryptomator

Cryptomator (https://cryptomator.org) is free, open source client-side encryption software. It works by creating a virtual hard disk on your PC. Anything you put inside this disk will get encrypted transparently. Cryptomator uses AES-256 to encrypt your data and uses SCRYPT to protect against brute-force attacks. For example, when you want to use Dropbox to store your data in the cloud, create a virtual Cryptomator vault inside your local Dropbox folder. Now anything you put into this vault will get encrypted before uploading it to your Dropbox account in the cloud.

In this section, we covered only two programs that offer native support for cloud storage service. However, bear in mind that you can use the previous encryption tools we already talked about in this chapter to secure your data before uploading it to the cloud. For instance, 7zip, AES Crypt, VeraCrypt containers, and Gpg4win (with the file encryption feature) can be used to secure your data upon uploading it to your cloud account. This will effectively add another layer of protection to your personal information if your cloud account suffers some form of compromise.

Encrypt DNS Traffic

As we mentioned in Chapter 4, using a VPN with DNS leak protection is essential to prevent your ISP from recording your browsing history. However, not all VPN providers offer this kind of protection, and in some technical circumstances a VPN leak can occur despite using a VPN with a DNS leak protection feature. In addition, many modern attacks are launched against poorly configured DNS servers, not to mention the danger of man-in-the-middle attacks that work by hijacking DNS queries traveling between your device and the DNS server to facilitate launching phishing attacks or stealing your sensitive data.

To protect against such threats and to take steps to accommodate privacy online, it is advisable to add another layer of protection between your PC and the DNS server you are using to resolve the IP addresses into their corresponding domain names. This can be achieved by encrypting the DNS requests between your PC and the DNS server using the DNSCrypt protocol. This protocol works by establishing a secure connection between your device and the DNS server (which must support the DNSCrypt protocol) by using cryptographic signatures to verify that responses originate from the intended DNS and haven't been tampered with during transit. A list of supported DNSCrypt-enabled resolvers is available at `https://dnscrypt.org/dnscrypt-resolvers.html`.

There is a simple tool to implement this secure protocol to protect your privacy. It is called Simple DNSCrypt and can be found at `https://simplednscrypt.org`. Configuring it is quite easy and can be found on the same page where the download resides.

Encrypt E-mail Communications

Now, it's time to learn how to use Mozilla Thunderbird with the GnuPG encryption engine to send and receive signed encrypted messages.

Thunderbird is a free, open source e-mail client developed by Mozilla, the developer of Firefox. You can configure it to work with multiple e-mail accounts from different providers easily. As we already mentioned, it is highly advisable to use open source programs from reputable sources to handle your sensitive communications and data.

In a previous section, we demonstrated how to use Gpg4win to create, import, and export a key pair. The main advantage of Gpg4win is that it gives you the ability to manage your key pair and the public keys of the people you are corresponding with across many encryption programs. For instance, you can use Enigmail, which is an extension for Thunderbird to handle encryption and digital signatures using OpenPGP to create a key pair (public and private key). However, to make things more organized, you can opt to use Gpg4win to create the key pair, as you already did before, and to manage the public key of other users who you are going to correspond with. This allows you to keep everything organized instead of creating and managing key pairs across different programs.

For now, let's begin setting the stage for your work by downloading and installing the needed programs.

■ **Warning** This section assumes you have followed the steps and have already generated your key pair and installed Gpg4win. If not, please do so in the section "Create a Cryptographic Key Pair Using Gpg4win."

---

1. Download the Enigmail extension from `https://www.enigmail.net/index.php/en/home`; it has an `.xpi` extension.

2. Download Thunderbird from `https://www.mozilla.org/en-US/thunderbird` and add the e-mail account you want to use to send/receive encrypted e-mails. Setting up a new e-mail account is easy in Thunderbird because it can recognize your account settings once you enter the correct username and password of this account.

3. Now, you need to install Enigmail in Thunderbird. Go to the Thunderbird Tools menu, and select Add-ons. The add-ons tab displays; click the Tools button and then select Install Add-on From File (see Figure 5-42).

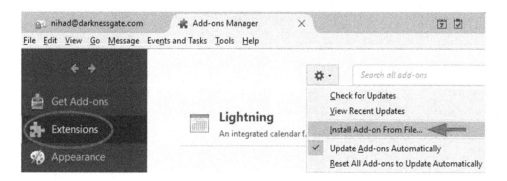

Figure 5-42. *Installing the Enigmail add-on in Thunderbird*

4. Navigate to where you saved the XPI file and select it to complete the installation. You need to restart Thunderbird to start using the Enigmail extension.

5. To confirm that Enigmail was successfully installed within Thunderbird and is fully integrated with GnuPG (installed as part of the Gpg4win installation), go to Enigmail (this menu item will appear after installing Enigmail). Then click Preferences and go to the Basic tab. In the Basic Settings section, in the Files and Directories pane, you should see the following statement: "GnuPG was found in C:\Program Files\GNU\GnuPG\pub\gpg2.exe" (see Figure 5-43). If instead you see the statement "Could not find GnuPG," then select the "Override with" box, click the Browse button to navigate to where the GnuPG program is installed (`gpg2.exe`), and select it.

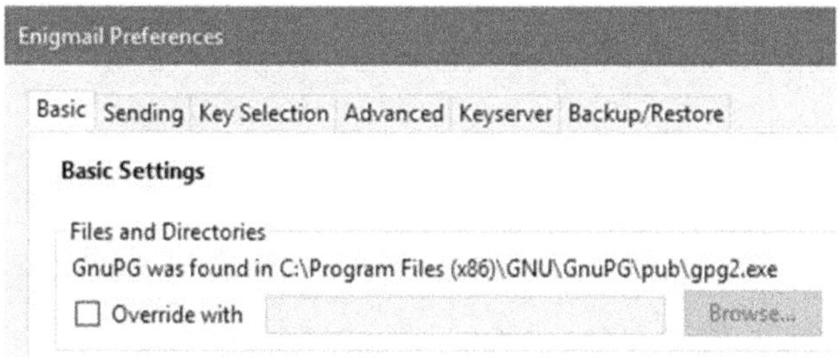

Enigmail Preferences

Basic Sending Key Selection Advanced Keyserver Backup/Restore

Basic Settings

Files and Directories
GnuPG was found in C:\Program Files (x86)\GNU\GnuPG\pub\gpg2.exe
☐ Override with [   ] Browse...

Figure 5-43. *Checking whether Enigmail is integrated successfully with GnuPG*

■ **Note** If the Thunderbird menu is hidden, right-click an empty section of the tab strip and select Menu Bar in the pop-up menu to make it appear. You can also press the F10 key to hide or show the menu bar.

6. You need to set up Enigmail to begin using it for e-mail encryption. Go to the Enigmail menu and select Setup Wizard. The Enigmail Setup Wizard is displayed. Select the option "I prefer a standard configuration (recommended for beginners)" and then click the Next button.

7. The next wizard window asks you to create a new key pair or to select yours from the lines listed. In your case, you already created your key pair using Gpg4win, so select "I want to select one of the keys below for signing and encrypting my e-mail." Select your key and click Next to continue (see Figure 5-44).

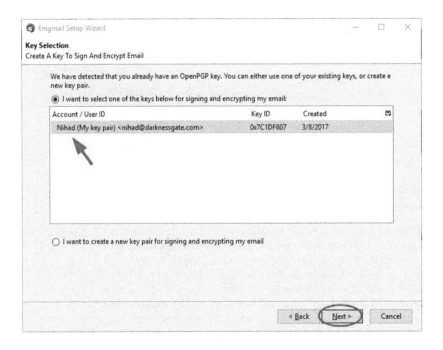

Figure 5-44. *Selecting the key you want to use to encrypt and sign e-mails*

8. The Enigmail Setup Wizard ends with a thank-you message. Click Finish to exit the wizard.

NOTE

The next time, if you want to generate more keys outside Gpg4win (the Kleopatra program) using Enigmail, you can do this by selecting Enigmail ➤ Key Management ➤ Generate ➤ New Key Pair. Select the e-mail account you want to create a key pair for and supply the passphrase to protect your private key. Finally, click the "Generate key" button (see Figure 5-45). You can also customize key size and key type by going to the Advanced tab.

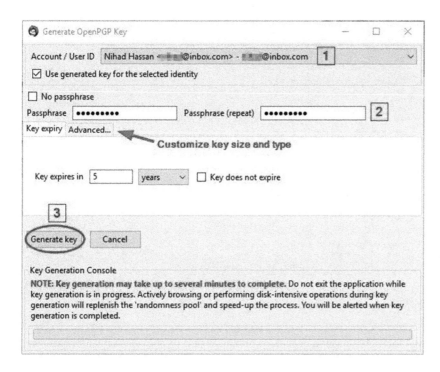

Figure 5-45. *Generating a new OpenPGP key pair using Enigmail*

The newly created key pair will appear in Gpg4win (Kleopatra) also. Usually each e-mail account should have one key pair associated with it to exchange encrypted e-mails.

Before beginning your work to encrypt/decrypt messages, let's make sure that everything is settled properly and your e-mail account is configured to use OpenPGP. Select Tools ➤ Account Settings. Select the e-mail account in the left pane. If you have more than one e-mail account, then click OpenPGP Security, and make sure the option "Enable OpenPGP support (Enigmail) for this identity" is selected (see Figure 5-46).

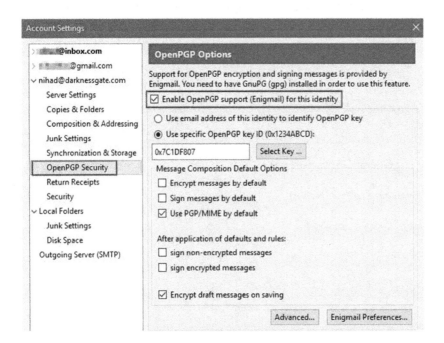

Figure 5-46. *Making sure that Enigmail is integrated with the selected e-mail account*

In a previous section, we thoroughly covered how to export and import public keys using Kleopatra, but to send and receive encrypted messages, you still need to do a final step, which is validating (trusting) the public key of the person you are going to communicate with. To do this, follow these steps (required for a one-time use only):

1. Open the Kleopatra program, go to the Other Certificates tab, right-click the certificate you want to validate, and select Certificate Details. Alternatively, you can simply double-click this certificate to open its details window.

2. Go to the Overview tab and click Trust Certifications Made by This Certificate (see Figure 5-47).

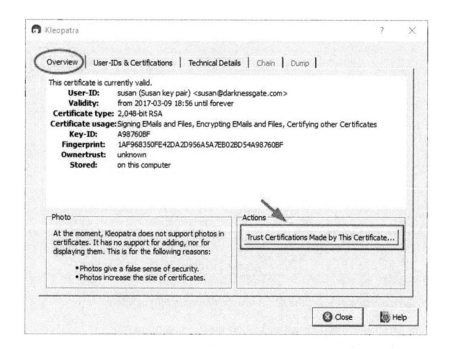

Figure 5-47. *Opening the receiver public key certificate details window to trust it*

3. In the new window, select "I believe checks are very accurate" and then click the OK button. A success window should appear.

4. Now the key needs to be certified to move it to the Trusted Certificates tab. While the certificate details window is still open, click the User-IDs & Certifications tab. Select the certificate you want to validate and then click the Certify button (see Figure 5-48).

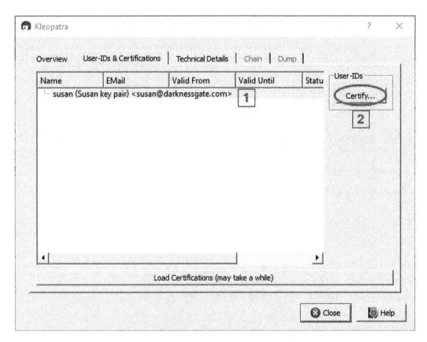

Figure 5-48. *Certifying the selected certificate using the Kleopatra Certificate details window*

    5.   A new window appears (called Reconfirmation). Select the username that you want to certify and then select "I have verified the fingerprint." Click the Next button to continue (see Figure 5-49).

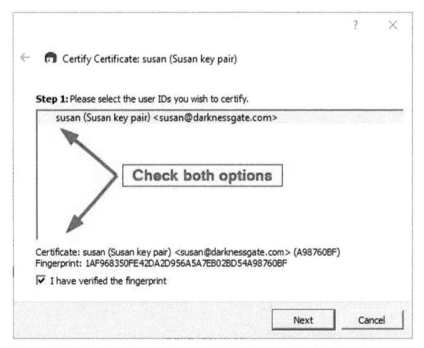

Figure 5-49. *Checking that you have verified the fingerprint of the intended user*

NOTE! HOW TO VERIFY THE CORRESPONDENT'S DIGITAL CERTIFICATE FINGERPRINT?

When you create your digital certificate in Gpg4win, it will have a digital fingerprint (40 characters). This is unique all over the world and is used to identify the certificate and its owner. To verify your correspondent's identity, you can request his or her certificate fingerprint by using the phone, secure instant messaging, or a face-to-face meeting. If the fingerprint supplied by your correspondent matches the certificate you already have, this means you have the right certificate.

You can find a certificate fingerprint by double-clicking the certificate in the Kleopatra program (see Figure 5-50).

Figure 5-50. *Viewing the certificate fingerprint in the Kleopatra program*

Some people prefer to print their digital certificate fingerprint on their business card to save the trouble of confirming their certificate.

---

6. In the next window, select your own OpenPGP certificate, which you will use to authenticate the certificate selected in the previous step. If you have more than one certificate, select the one you want to sign with, select the option "Certify only for myself," and finally click the Certify button (see Figure 5-51).

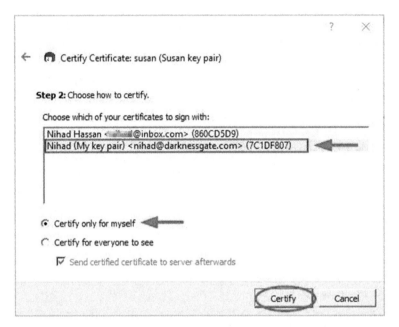

Figure 5-51. *Selecting your OpenPGP certificate to authenticate your correspondent public key*

7. Now, a pop-up window will appear asking you to enter your passphrase (private key password) to authenticate your selected correspondent certificate. Without supplying the correct passphrase, the process will not complete. Enter it and you are done.

8. The final window will inform you that the selected user has been certified successfully (see Figure 5-52).

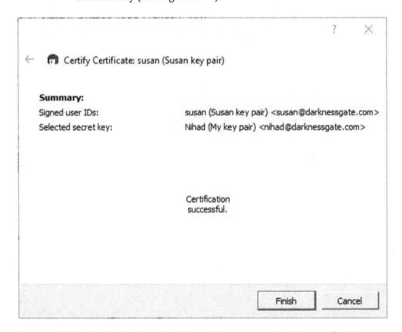

Figure 5-52. *The final wizard window informs you that the certification was successful*

Check your Kleopatra program. You will see that the selected user certificate has been moved to the Trusted Certificates tab.

The person you are corresponding with (here Susan) must also certify (confirm the fingerprint of) your digital certificate (Nihad) to be able to send you encrypted messages using the same steps. However, keep in mind that if your correspondent does not have your public key imported, they are still able to open and read the encrypted e-mail sent by you.

After validating the trust of the public key of the receiver, you are ready to send him or her your first encrypted message.

⬛ **Note**   Please note you should validate the trust of each user you are going to correspond with. This is required only one time.

Let's assume that Nihad wants to send an encrypted signed e-mail to Susan. The prerequisites are mainly two conditions.

- Nihad must have the public key of Susan.

- He should trust verify her digital certificate fingerprint.

Susan must also have the public key of Nihad, and she must also certify his certificate fingerprint (this is required only if Susan wants to send encrypted e-mail to Nihad; however, she will still be able to receive/decrypt his encrypted e-mail safely without adding him to her to the certification manager).

From Thunderbird, click the Write button and select "message" to create a new e-mail message. When you enter the e-mail address of the receiver, his or her e-mail should display in black if you already have his or her public key and it is already certified. Otherwise, the e-mail will display in red. Make sure that the Padlock icon (which indicates the e-mail will get encrypted) and the Pencil icon (if you want to sign this e-mail) should light up after entering the recipient's e-mail address (see Figure 5-53). Enigmail will automatically encrypt all new e-mails to the people whom you already have public keys for. After finishing writing your message, click the Send button. If you select to sign your e-mail, as we did, you need to enter your private key passphrase in the pop-up window before sending your e-mail.

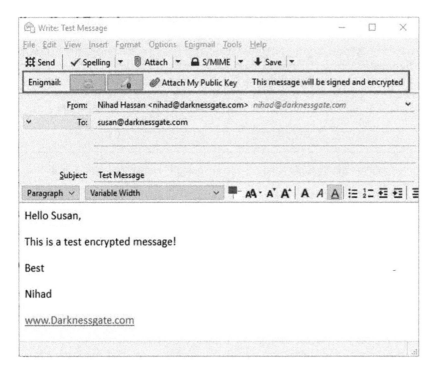

Figure 5-53. An e-mail that is signed and encrypted. The receiver e-mail displays in black because it is a trusted person.

When Susan receives this e-mail, she needs to enter her passphrase (private key password) to decrypt the e-mail. Enigmail will show a message on the e-mail stating that the message was successfully decrypted and the signature is authenticated (see Figure 5-54).

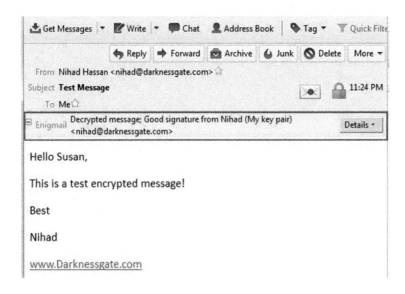

Figure 5-54. Message decrypted successfully on the receiving end

■ **Warning** Bear in mind that GnuPG only encrypts the content and attachments of your e-mail. The following information will not get encrypted: e-mail subject line, sender's e-mail address, and recipient's e-mail address. The default Enigmail settings (PGP/MIME) encrypt all attachment file names unless you change the settings to use inline PGP. This setting can be changed regardless of the default settings for each new e-mail from the Enigmail menu within this e-mail.

It is advisable to practice encrypting all your personal and sensitive work e-mails to teach the people you are corresponding with how to use e-mail encryption (you can send them this guide!). However, if you opt not to encrypt all your e-mails, you should at least sign them all (you can sign unencrypted e-mails as well). In this way, your correspondent will know that your e-mail originated from you and has not been tampered with during transit. Signing e-mail is also a great practice that will encourage others to begin using GnuPG to secure their online communications.

■ **Note** You can direct your Thunderbird e-mails through the Tor network by using an extension for Mozilla Thunderbird called TorBirdy. According to its creators (it belongs to the Tor project), TorBirdy is still in beta release and should not be used to secure communications in extremely hostile environments. You can find information on how to install and use this extension at `https://trac.torproject.org/projects/tor/wiki/torbirdy`.

So far, we have covered the main steps to send and receive signed, encrypted e-mails using Thunderbird, the Enigmail extension, and the Gpg4win encryption program. For advanced users who want more in-depth coverage about all the security features offered by these tools, they can find more details in the Gpg4win documentation (also called the Gpg4win Compendium) at `https://www.gpg4win.org/documentation.html` and in the Enigmail documentation at at`https://www.enigmail.net/index.php/en/documentation/user-manual`.

There is a browser extension available for both Firefox and Google Chrome called Mailvelope that can be used with most web e-mail services. It allows its users to exchange encrypted e-mails using the OpenPGP encryption schema. You can either generate your key pair or import existing one, for example, from Kleopatra using this extension without the need to install any tools except the extension on your browser. The extension is open source, and it is available at `https://www.mailvelope.com/en/`. However, we do not recommend encrypting messages within web browsers because this will make them more vulnerable to cyber-attacks that regularly hit browsers.

Encrypt Files/Folders Using Gpg4win

Gpg4win is not only used to encrypt and sign e-mails but also to sign and encrypt individual files and folders. The same steps apply.

1. You use your private key to encrypt the file.

2. Then you use your correspondent public key to encrypt the result.

GpgEX, which is a plug-in for Microsoft Explorer, is installed as part of the Gpg4win program and allows you to encrypt/decrypt a file or folder directly by right-clicking it. From the Windows Explorer context menu, select More GpgEX options ➤ Encrypt (or you can select "Sign and encrypt" from the same submenu if you want to send the encrypted data to your correspondent). A new dialog appears with more options (see Figure 5-55).

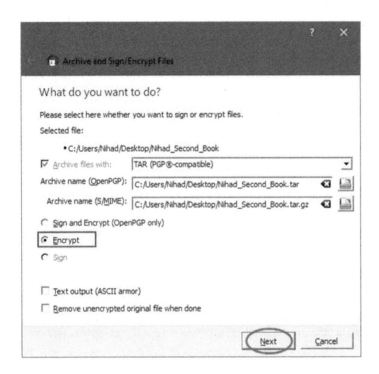

Figure 5-55. *Selecting file/folder encryption settings*

In this experiment, you will not sign and encrypt your data to send it to an outside user like you did in the previous section. Instead, you will use Gpg4win to secure your data like you might do using any regular encryption program.

Select Encrypt. You can also activate the option "Remove unencrypted original file when done" to delete the selected file/folder after encrypting it. (However, this practice is not fully secure as an attacker can recover deleted files easily if gaining access to your hard drive. You should make sure to overwrite deleted file/folder area on the hard drive after deletion to avoid recovery, as you did in Chapter 3.) When done, click the Next button. Here you should select to whom you want to encrypt the data. In this case, you are encrypting the data for yourself, so you should select your key pair to encrypt it. Then click the Add button to activate your selection. Finally, click Next and you are done (see Figure 5-56).

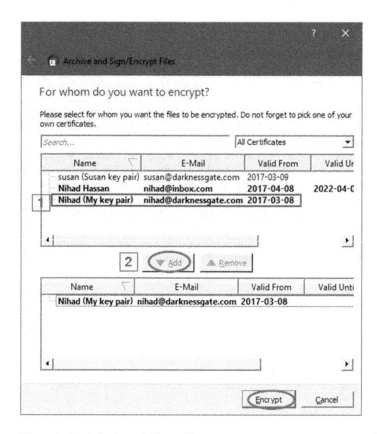

Figure 5-56. *Selecting which certificate you want to use to encrypt your data*

The final wizard will show the encrypted result. If the encryption was successful, a new file with the same original name but with the tar.gpg extension will appear in the same folder/directory. Click Finish to exit the wizard. To decrypt the file gain, right-click it (the file with the .gpg extension) and select "Decrypt and verify." A new dialog appears; click Decrypt/Verify. Then enter your private key passphrase to decrypt the file; the decrypted result appears in the same folder/directory.

Secure Webmail Providers

Most Internet users have free e-mail accounts. Yahoo, Gmail, and Microsoft Live offer free e-mail service with excellent features in relation to inbox size and yearly downtime. However, no one can guarantee that such giant companies are not reading your e-mails or simply handling them to a third party. Many new revelations show that the security services in different countries have always requested access, sometimes bulk access, to users' data for different purposes.

In this section we will give you some free web e-mail providers that offer extended privacy features to their users by using encryption and other features to make surveillance on your e-mail activities more difficult.

ProtonMail

ProtonMail (`https://protonmail.com`) is different from other regular e-mail providers in many ways. For instance, it is based in Switzerland and follows that jurisdiction, which is considered the best in the world in protecting user rights to privacy. ProtonMail uses two passwords to protect your e-mail account. The first one authenticates your account credentials on the server, and the second decrypts your inbox within your web browser or app, meaning that it never goes online to the ProtonMail server. ProtonMail uses open source cryptography based on a secure implementation of AES, RSA, and OpenPGP to build its system and all messages are stored encrypted on the server. In addition, your e-mails are end-to-end encrypted (when both the sender and the receiver use the ProtonMail service). Finally, this service doesn't record metadata about your connection to its server such as your IP address or any tracking information. For security-concerned people, the main downside of this service is that users' cryptographic keys are stored within the ProtonMail keyserver. This means ProtonMail can technically find a way to decrypt messages stored on its servers as it is the authority that distributes these keys in the first place.

ProtonMail is still considered the best free, end-to-end secure e-mail service available today. The basic free account has 500MB storage space. If you are not dealing with sensitive or high-grade information, it is highly advisable to use this service because of the enhanced security features offered.

Disposable Temporary E-mail Address

Sometimes you may want to register with a free online service or receive an offer. For example, you download a free e-book and need to supply your e-mail address. You should not use your work or private e-mail address to receive such offers. Reputable web sites do not sell your data to other third parties. However, no one can guarantee anything in today's digital age where cyber-attacks come from everywhere. Thus, if you want to supply your e-mail address to receive such offers, it is advisable to use a temporary e-mail address.

Hidester (`https://hidester.com//temporary-email/`) offers free disposable e-mail addresses that last for one day (or it can last forever if you want). You can send and receive e-mails as you do with any other service. The reply will appear on the service web site. Finally, you can delete it when you want and you are done!

Guerrilla Mail (`https://www.guerrillamail.com`) offers a similar service.

Secure IM and Video Calls

Many proprietary services offer free IM, voiceover IP, and videoconference services. Many of these services, like Skype, WhatsApp, Viber, and Google Allo, are popular among Internet users globally. Viber and WhatsApp are now offering end-to-end encryption, allowing user devices to establish a secure channel directly between communicating parties. This will effectively make eavesdropping on your communications almost impossible.

We cannot discuss the security features of each available application in this book. However, we will focus on the security feature that makes one application more secure than the rest. For instance, most VoIP and chatting applications work the same way. They encrypt the messages exchanged between the people involved in the conversation, but they do not encrypt the message metadata.

Message metadata includes all the technical information related to each message sent during a conversation, such as the following: people involved in the conversation and their phone numbers (the entire user phone contact list will be stored on the app server, although this action is optional, but the majority of users allow unrestricted access to their phone address book by the messaging app), message time sent, message length, last time user connect to server, message read status, and anything technically related to each conversation. All this data is stored unencrypted and may be handed to a third party, for example, security service or advertisement company if necessary. Another security concern related to these applications is the backup process; they usually offer a method to back up user data, including private messages, to free cloud storage providers like Google Drive for Android or iCloud for iPhone. The uploaded data is not encrypted and relies only on the cloud storage provider security (which can be breached like with iCloud in 2014). Finally, all proprietary programs are not open source, making them vulnerable to backdoor and other security flaws.

The best secure VoIP/IM application is one that has the following technical characteristics: it should be open source so its code can be audited by independent security experts, it should not offer/show ads or any type of commercial advertisements, the provider and hence the app should not store the decryption key on its server so no one can request the key to decrypt user data, it should not store any metadata about the user connection, and the user contact list should not be stored on the app server and if necessary it should be saved encrypted. It should offer clear options to choose what you want to back up before sending it to the cloud provider.

Many messaging applications offer strong security features; the main disadvantage is the limited user base, which requires its users to convince their correspondents to use it. The following are some popular secure and well-supported messaging apps.

Tor Messenger

Although Tor Messenger (`https://trac.torproject.org/projects/tor/wiki/doc/TorMessenger`) still is in beta version, it is considered one of the most secure IM apps available. It was developed by the creator of the Tor project. Tor Messenger works on different platforms and offers great encryption features by using off-the-record (OTR) messaging automatically. All its traffic is directed through the Tor network by default, making it secure and anonymous at the same time. People who are involved in mission-critical tasks are not encouraged to use it because it still in beta (although this can change to stable anytime).

Cryptocat

Cryptocat (`https://crypto.cat/security.html`) is a free open source program for IM chatting and sharing files. It uses AES-256 and SHA-256 to secure its connection and to encrypt shared files. The main disadvantage of this program is that your buddy list and linked devices are stored unencrypted and can be accessed by the app service provider.

Signal

Signal (`https://whispersystems.org`) is a free open source secure messaging and VoIP app; it is easy to use and offers similar functions as WhatsApp and Viber Apps. This app runs on Android and iPhone devices only. It is recommended by internationally renowned security technologists like Bruce Schneier and privacy advocates like Edward Snowden to have secure online conversations. Signal offers the strongest security measures among all similar apps; it covers all the recommend security criteria for VoIP/IM applications already mentioned.

Ghost Call

Ghost Call (`https://ghostcall.io`) is a free service that offers an end-to-end encrypted calling service; it uses ZRTP media encryption to encrypt the connection, and Linphone, which is a popular open source VoIP program for making audio calls. This service is 100 percent free. Upon signing up (you do not need any personal information and it allows you to register using the Tor Browser), you will receive a virtual phone number (ten-digit number) that can be used to contact other Ghost Call numbers only.

Gruveo

Gruveo (`https://www.gruveo.com`) is a free, anonymous video-calling service. You do not need to supply any personal information to use it; just enter a username and the site will give you a code that you need to give to your correspondents to join the conversation.

> ■ **Note**   It is worth mentioning a free, open source service called SecureDrop (`https://securedrop.org`). It is intended to be used by whistle-blowers around the world as a submission system for sending documents and other leaks to media organizations. This service is managed by Freedom of the Press Foundation, and it offers strict security features for its users.

Another IM program that works only on iOS is ChatSecure (`https://chatsecure.org`). This is an open source program configured to use OTR over XMPP.

Steganography

In the previous sections, we demonstrated how you can protect your information using different encryption techniques. Encrypting data is still the most secure method to protect your confidential files, but what if you are living in a country where encryption is banned by law?

For example, in China, downloading encryption software is considered a crime and can lead to different legal consequences. In addition, VPN services are considered illegal and are barred technically by the Great Firewall of China (this is a kind of framework that regulates Internet usage in China legally and technically).[8] Restrictions on encryption are not limited to China; many countries, even some western democratic countries, consider using encryption to be a suspicious action. For instance, trying to encrypt your data will make you a target of security agencies in many countries, as the encrypted data looks different from normal data when passing through automated monitoring machines deployed by many nations to monitor their citizens' Internet traffic.

In China, people use steganography techniques to conceal their messages in images, audio files, and video files so that their sensitive conversation will not get intercepted by their government. This is an effective method to counter technical and legal restrictions against using encryption to secure transmitted data.

Steganography is the science of concealing a secret message within an ordinary file, thus maintaining its secrecy during transit. This science is very old; its roots go back to Cypress, which has the first record of using such techniques 2,000 years ago.

In this section, we will teach you how you can use different steganography techniques to conceal your secret message inside an ordinary file. If you are fond of steganography and you want to learn more, we recommend *Data Hiding Techniques in Windows OS: A Practical Approach to Investigation and Defense* (Syngress, 2016). It covers the sophisticated techniques used to conceal secret data and other malicious code in digital files.

What Is Digital Steganography?

In *digital steganography*, the carrier used to conceal the secret message within it can be of any type. In reality, nearly any digital file type can be used to conceal data. See Figure 5-57.

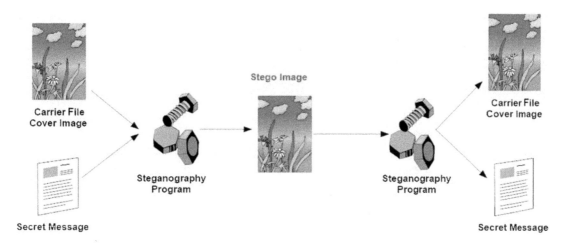

***Figure 5-57.** How digital steganography works*

Steganographic techniques have been used since the dawn of history. Ancient civilization used physical mediums like paper, eggs, invisible ink, and even human skin to conceal secret messages. However, with the advance of computers and the Internet, modern techniques were developed to conceal data in digital files without affecting its visual appearance/quality.

In this section, we will cover digital steganography only and describe how you can use it to conceal your secret messages from an outside observer using different digital file types such as text, image, audio, and video files. Digital steganography does not alter the structure of the secret message but hides it in an overt file so that it cannot be seen.

Secret data may also be hidden inside the Windows file system (NTFS file system). Indeed, there are many techniques you might use to exploit the NTFS Windows file system to conceal secret data or an executable malware program. However, to remain within the book's scope, we will limit our discussion to using steganography to conceal users' private data only.

Differences Between Steganography and Encryption

Both steganography and cryptography (we mean encryption here) share the same goal of securing transmitted messages. However, they differ in the methods used to achieve this goal. The term *cryptography* describes all the techniques used to obscure data, whether it is scrambled and hence encrypted or concealed using steganography techniques. However, digital steganography has evolved a lot in recent years as a result of the huge advancement of computing and networking technology. Table 5-2 differentiates between the two techniques.

Table 5-2. *Steganography vs. Cryptography Comparison*

Context	Steganography	Encryption
Hidden message status	The message does not appear (hidden).	The message appears scrambled.
Outside party	Communication is hidden from outside parties.	Third parties know that a communication has occurred, but they cannot read the contents.
Level of development	Still undergoing development.	Matured technology.
Cipher text status	The structure of the message remains the same.	Encryption modifies the message structure through a cryptographic algorithm.
Carrier file	Image, audio, video, text, Internet protocols, OS files.	Mostly text files.
Types of secret files	Image, audio, text, almost all kind of digital files.	Mostly text files.
Output result	Stego file.	Ciphertext.

The majority of steganography applications combine both encryption and steganography to achieve their goal of secrecy and security. Obviously, combining both techniques boosts IT/cyber-security and gives strong protection for sensitive data, whether it is at rest or in transit.

Digital Steganography Techniques

To conceal your secret message inside digital files, you need to use one of the following techniques.

Injunction

Here you insert your secret message in a nonreadable location in the overt file, thus concealing it without affecting the look or functionality of the overt file. A good example of this technique is hiding secret data after the end-of-file (EOF) marker. For example, if you have a JPEG file that you want to conceal data inside, you can insert this data after the EOF marker and any image-viewing program (for example, Window Photo Viewer) will read the image source to open it and will stop when reaching the EOF. Anything after the EOF will remain hidden without affecting the overt file quality or appearance.

Substitution

In this technique, you are replacing insignificant bits from the overt file with those bits that belong to the secret message. The most famous practical example to achieve this technique is by substituting the least significant bit (LSB) of the overt file with the bits of the secret message. Substitution is more secure than the insertion technique because it does not increase the overt file size since there is no additional data inserted into the overt file source. Nevertheless, there is still a finite capacity to store hidden messages because this technique is limited to the number of insignificant bits available in the overt file.

Generation

This is the most secure technique to achieve digital steganography. With this type you are producing a new overt file that contains your secret message. A site that demonstrates this technique is at www.spammimic. com. This web site allows you to enter a secret message and conceal it inside a spam message that can be transmitted securely in plain sight to the intended recipient.

Digital Steganography Types

There are different ways to categorize steganography techniques. To keep things simple, we will categorize them according to the type of overt file used to conceal the secret message.

Text Steganography

This is a type of steganography that uses text files to conceal secret data within them. Historically, written letters were the main medium used to conceal secret messages. However, with the advance of computing, digital text files replaced the physical paper messages. This type of steganography is considered impractical in today's digital world, as it can conceal only small amounts of data compared with other digital file types. Some examples include inserting spaces between words and/or inserting one or two spaces at the end of each line to store hidden bits. Microsoft Word text documents offer many places to conceal data using different formatting features such as the following:

- Using the hidden text feature

- Making text white on a white background

- Reducing the text size to 1 pixel

- Hiding data within document attributes (metadata)

Using the RTF File Type to Conceal Secret Data

Rich Text Format (RTF), which is a proprietary document file format developed by Microsoft, can be easily used to conceal data within it. You can create RTF documents by using WordPad or Microsoft Office Word and saving the file in RTF format. To conceal your secret data, right-click the RTF file and select "Open with" from the Windows context menu; then select Notepad to view the raw source file of the RTF file. You will notice that the source code contains tags similar to HTML files that do not appear when viewing it using the regular Microsoft Word processor. Anything enclosed within the tag {\} will not display in a regular viewer; in addition, anything written after the closing bracket, }, will get ignored (see Figure 5-58).

Figure 5-58. *Concealing a secret message after the EOF within an RTF document*

Change of Spelling

A secret message can be concealed within ordinary text by changing the spelling of some words or even the entire overt message's words. This technique is also effective to fool surveillance software used by governments to monitor inbound and outbound traffic. Surveillance systems and many firewall solutions used by giant enterprises are mainly dependent on finding interesting keywords while scanning the network traffic; by changing the spelling of important words, you can safely avoid being captured by such machines. http://txtn.us is a web site that provides free tools for transforming Unicode text into another string that looks visually similar to the original text; however, it is read differently by automated monitoring machines. See Table 5-3 for illustration.

Table 5-3. *Changing Spelling to Fool Surveillance Systems*

Original Text	Misspelled Text Variations		
Syria	Sʏrͺa	Sʏria	Syrla
Plane	Plɑɯe	Plaɲe	Pɩɑпe
Attack	Aттɑcκ	Aттacκ	Attacχ

■ **Note**   You can conceal secret messages within Twitter tweets in plain sight. http://holloway.co.nz/steg/ is a web site that offers such a service.

Image Steganography

This is the most commonly used file type to conceal secret data. What makes this type popular is the huge number of images exchanged daily online. People tend to post a large volume of images to social networking web sites or cloud-based photo storage. In addition, exchanging images in e-mails does not raise suspicions about the possibility of the existence of hidden data. Image steganography works by embedding a secret message inside the overt file (hence the image) using a predefined steganographic algorithm; this produces what is known as a *stego-image*. This stego-image is then sent to the recipient, who will use the same algorithm to extract the hidden message from the overt file.

Concealing Messages After the End-of-File Marker

Experiments show that secret data text files can be embedded within images without leaving any visual effects on overt files. You can achieve this by inserting the text file that contains your hidden data after the end-of-file marker. To demonstrate how to do this trick, prepare a JPEG image and a text file that contains your secret data. Launch a command prompt elevated as the administrator, change to the working directory where the image and text file reside, and type the command shown in Figure 5-59.

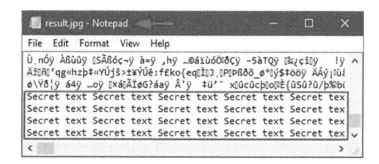

Figure 5-59. *Concealing a secret text file within a JPEG image*

Here you have combined your secret file named `secret.txt` within `image.jpg` and output the result, which contains the secret file, as `result.jpg`. To view the secret message, you can simply open the stego image `result.jpg` using Windows Notepad to view its source (see Figure 5-60). The secret message will appear after the end of raw code.

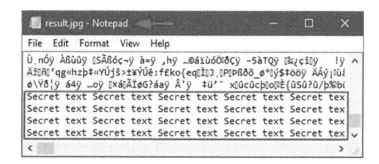

Figure 5-60. *Using Windows Notepad to view concealed data within a JPEG image after the end-of-file marker*

After concealing something using this method, the image quality or appearance will not change. However, you should make sure to avoid inserting a large amount of secret text within the overt image, as its size will increase, which may be suspicious if investigated. Data concealed in this way has some limitations. If you update the image (resize it, change the format, edit it, or crop it), the secret message will get destroyed.

The previous method can conceal text files only. However, if you want to conceal other file types (binary files or Microsoft Office documents, for example), you can do the same steps, but instead of storing your secret data within a text file, use the zip format and then insert your secret like you did in your last experiment.

Concealing Within Image Metadata

This was already covered in Chapter 2 from a different viewpoint. For instance, a large amount of secret information can be concealed within digital image metadata easily and even without using any third-party tools. The following programs can be used to edit image metadata and to insert new metadata without affecting the image's visual appearance:

- Exif Editor (www.colorpilot.com/exif.html)

- Metadata++ (www.logipole.com)

- PhotoME (www.photome.de)

- XnView (www.xnview.com/en)

Digital Steganography Tools

You can use many steganography programs to conceal secret information within images and other digital file types. The main advantages of such programs, in addition to being easy to use, are that they offer an encryption feature for the concealed data. As you already saw, secret information can be concealed easily in digital files and in plain sight without encryption. However, if an outside observer expects a hidden message in an overt file, he or she can detect and read the hidden message easily. As a result, it is advisable to encrypt your secret message before concealing it in a digital medium, so if an observer were successful in detecting the secret message, he or she could not read it.

We will not demonstrate how to use steganography tools because they are straightforward. Table 5-4 lists the most popular tools.

Table 5-4. *Popular Digital Steganography Tools*

Program	Supported Overt Files	Support Encryption	URL
Crypture	BMP	Yes	http://sourceforge.net/projects/crypture/
OpenStego	Different media files	Yes	www.openstego.com/
Gifshuffle	GIF	Yes	www.darkside.com.au/gifshuffle/
wbStego4open	Bmp, text files, HTML, PDF	Yes	http://home.tele2.at/wbailer/wbstego/fs_home.html
Our Secret	Image, audio, and video files	Yes	www.securekit.net/oursecret.htm
SilentEye	JPEG, BMP, WAVE	Yes	www.silenteye.org/
Steghide UI	Different media files	Yes	http://sourceforge.net/projects/steghideui/
Camouflage	Different media files	Yes	http://camouflage.unfiction.com/
DeepSound	Audio files	Yes	http://download.cnet.com/DeepSound/3000-2092_4-75758214.html

■ **Warning**   If you are living in or planning to visit a country where encryption is banned by law, do not encrypt your message before concealing it in another digital file because surveillance systems can detect encrypted data.

Audio-Video Steganography

Audio steganography takes advantages of the physical characteristics of the human ear to conceal secret data. Scientists discovered that the human ear can detect noise in the audible frequency range from 20Hz to 20KHz. To conceal a secret message, an audio steganographic algorithm embeds secret data in a low-tone frequency signal; the human ear will not notice this modification because it is not able to detect such a low tone in the presence of a higher frequency. This also called *frequency masking*. Video files are composed of a series of images and audio files. Video files have a higher capacity to store secret data than other digital files because of their large size; this allows the concealment of a considerable amount of secret data without affecting the quality of the original file (overt file). Most steganographic techniques implemented on digital images and audio files can also work with video files.

The most popular audio steganography tool is MP3stego, which conceals secret data in the most used audio file format, MP3. You can find it at `www.petitcolas.net/steganography/mp3stego`.

Network Steganography

In this type of steganography, you are concealing your secret message using networking protocols by exploiting their design features. There are two main ways to achieve this.

- Masking secret messages as the honest traffic of other protocols

- Exploiting empty areas within networking protocol segments to conceal secret message bits

Streaming protocols used to transmit multimedia content are undergoing continual development. The use of such protocols is expected to grow to stay in line with future computing and networking development, opening up more possibilities for places to conceal data.

A good example program to conceal data within networking protocols (TCP/IP header) is called covert_tcp; you can find it at `http://firstmonday.org/ojs/index.php/fm/article/view/528/449`.

Summary

In this chapter, we covered how to protect your privacy using cryptography. Cryptography is an old science that deals with all techniques used to assure the security of your communications when communicating in an untrusted environment. There are two main types of cryptography.

- Encryption techniques that secure private data by making it scrambled

- Steganography techniques that protect data by hiding it in plain sight

As computing technology advances, knowing how to use cryptographic systems in real-world programs becomes an indispensable tool to protect your data.

We began this chapter by discussing a fundamental concept of encryption, the public and private key pair. This knowledge is essential to understand how current encryption techniques work. We demonstrated practically how to use an open source program (Gpg4win) to create your first cryptographic key pair and showed you how you can import/export your keys (and your correspondents' keys) into the Gpg4win program to facilitate secure communications.

In the second part of this chapter, we demonstrated how to use encryption to secure your data at rest. Data at rest includes all the data stored in computers, servers, tablets, USB flash memory, external HDs, SD cards, and any device that can store digital data for later usage. You experimented using the VeraCrypt program to create encrypted containers and BitLocker to encrypt Windows partitions, and you learned about many other tools to secure individual files, especially when uploading them to the cloud. Full disk encryption is important to protect your data from unauthorized physical access. Also, a detailed discussion of the best selection criteria of cryptographic algorithms was covered in addition to cryptography attacks and countermeasures.

In addition, we covered how to use encryption to secure your communications in transit (when sending e-mails and exchanging confidential files) using Thunderbird and the Enigmail extension; then we talked about alternative free webmail providers, secure IM applications, anonymous calling services, and video-calling services.

We concluded this chapter by talking briefly about steganography, which is an ancient science that deals with concealing data in overt objects (in other words, in digital files) without making any visual modifications to the overt file. This science is important to protect your confidential data in situations where encryption cannot be used.

This was a rich chapter. If you went through it in detail, your digital assets are now much more secure and your ability to defend against cyber-criminals has increased greatly.

Notes

1. Russell Brandom, "Google just cracked one of the building blocks of web encryption." The Verge, February 23, 2017. `www.theverge.com/2017/2/23/14712118/google-sha1-collision-broken-web-encryption-shattered`.

2. Russell Brandom, "NSA paid $10 million to put its backdoor in RSA encryption, according to Reuters report." The Verge, December 20, 2013. `www.theverge.com/2013/12/20/5231006/nsa-paid-10-million-for-a-back-door-into-rsa-encryption-according-to`.

3. Paul Ducklin, "Anatomy of a change – Google announces it will double its SSL key sizes." Naked Security. `https://nakedsecurity.sophos.com/2013/05/27/anatomy-of-a-change-google-announces-it-will-double-its-ssl-key-sizes/`.

4. Bruce Schneier, "Twofish." Schneier on Security. `https://www.schneier.com/academic/twofish/`.

5. Paulo S. L. M. Barreto, "The WHIRLPOOL Hash Function." `www.larc.usp.br/~pbarreto/WhirlpoolPage.html`.

6. Open Crypto Audit Project. `https://opencryptoaudit.org/`.

7. Andreas Junestam, Nicolas Guigo, "Open Crypto Audit Project TrueCrypt." iSECpartners, February 14, 2014. `https://opencryptoaudit.org/reports/iSec_Final_Open_Crypto_Audit_Project_TrueCrypt_Security_Assessment.pdf`.

8. Jean-Baptiste Bédrune, Marion Videau, "Security Assessment of VeraCrypt: fixes and evolutions from TrueCrypt." Quarkslab's Blog, October 17, 2016. `http://blog.quarkslab.com/security-assessment-of-veracrypt-fixes-and-evolutions-from-truecrypt.html`.

CHAPTER 6

▨ ▨ ▨

What's Next?

The Future and Its Impact on Your Privacy

No one can predict the future, especially when it comes to computing technology. It is still the fastest-growing field among all industries, with radical changes continually shifting future trends in different directions.

In 1965, Intel cofounder Gordon Moore made a prediction that is still considered the rule of thumb for measuring advances in computer processing speed. Moore's law says that computer processing speed will double every year in the foreseeable future; he revisited his prediction in 1975 to say it will double every two years (Intel's predication was that chip performance would double every 18 months). Many experts say that Moore's law will be in effect until 2020, when it will be impossible for integrated processor circuits to get any smaller.

The impact of Moore's law seems obvious in our daily lives. The smartphone that fits into your pocket is faster than the supercomputer that filled an entire room in 1982. This rapid development of computing technology makes computing devices more affordable for all end users, and it drives explosive growth for industries that use computing devices to increase productivity and improve client service. In the future, a large portion of computing devices will be Internet of Things (IoT) devices as such devices become more widely used by both individuals and companies. Gartner forecasts that 20.4 billion connected computing devices will be in use worldwide in 2020.

The ultimate purpose of any computing device is to process data and act upon it. Obviously, each of these devices will eventually process and store some sort of data related to its owner. Personal identifying information (PII) and non-PII will need to be transferred across insecure networks such as the Internet and be stored somewhere on an Internet-connected resource. The transferred data will contain different types of information about users, who are being profiled by third parties such as governments, Internet service providers, hackers, and identity thieves. With all this information available and with the advancement of artificial intelligence systems that can process vast volumes of data daily, it will be easy to categorize people according to a set of criteria settled by the entities conducting information gathering online. In short, this is how the digital age we live in is having a radical impact on both our security and our privacy.

This is the last chapter of this book, and obviously a book about digital privacy cannot end without talking about future trends in computing technology and how they will impact our digital lives. In these pages, we will try to foresee the future and explain how emerging technologies will impact the future of security and privacy.

© Nihad A. Hassan and Rami Hijazi 2017
N. A. Hassan and R. Hijazi, *Digital Privacy and Security Using Windows*, DOI 10.1007/978-1-4842-2799-2_6

The Future of Computing Technology

Traditional forms of computing devices and stand-alone devices are vanishing slowly; we are moving toward a more cloud-centralized scheme. In this scheme, a user can use a computer with low hardware specifications to remotely access another cloud computer with premium hardware specifications to run programs that require intensive computing resources such as games and digital editing tools.

Originally, the main model of a cloud service was for users to store data on a remote server somewhere on the Internet (cloud storage). However, more models were developed to exploit the benefits of cloud services, mainly by adopting it to reduce IT hardware costs in organizations. For instance, more and more companies are using different cloud service models to reduce IT infrastructure costs and management efforts.

- *Infrastructure as a service (IaaS)*: In this model, a company uses remote computing resources to perform local work without needing to purchase costly hardware or to worry about backups or the physical/logical security of data.

- *Platform as a service (PaaS)*: In this model, users access a remote computer where they can find everything to develop applications or to perform their regular IT work. The cloud provider sets the stage for the development by installing the appropriate operating system (OS), programming language, web server, and anything needed to perform the required tasks. Good examples are Windows Azure, Google App Engine, and Apache Stratos.

- *Software as a service (SaaS)*: In this model, a user will get access to a specific application he or she needs to run in the cloud. For example, a user can have access to the Microsoft Office suite hosted remotely on the cloud to create and edit Office files without needing to install anything locally. Good examples are Google Apps and Microsoft Office 365.

■ **Note**   The previous three cloud service models belong to what is called *cloud computing*.

Many individuals already use cloud storage to back up and store private smartphone data (Android users uses Google Drive, and iPhone users use iCloud), and as Internet speed becomes faster, we can expect to see more users opting to use cloud computing services. Currently, there are many companies that offer paid monthly subscriptions for their users to play games that require intensive computing resources. For example, a gaming laptop with 4GB and a dedicated graphics card and compatible hardware costs at least $1,500, while players can pay $30 a month to use a gaming cloud service and play games on a remote server, with 8GB of a dedicated graphics card. We are seeing more companies shifting their products to the cloud by offering a lightweight interface to their programs to run on end-user machines, while transferring the heavy tasks that require intensive computing resources to run on a remote server; the companies charge users a monthly subscription fee.

The use of cloud services is expected to grow explosively for both end users and companies in the next five years. Gartner forecasts that more than $1 trillion in IT spending will be directly or indirectly affected by a shift to the cloud in the next five years.[1] This widespread adoption will increase the security risks associated with moving sensitive data across the Internet and will raise legal issues about which jurisdiction has the right to request access to this data if your account becomes part of a law enforcement investigation.

We already covered the Internet of Things in Chapter 2. In the future, more computing devices are moving into the fabrics in our clothing and body. In addition, healthcare providers are moving steadily to digitize all their services, so we can expect a tremendous growth in health- and fitness-oriented wearable devices. These devices can collect biometric data about their users, such as heart rate, body temperature, perspiration, oxygen, and even alcohol levels in the bloodstream. Sensitive health data will need to be sent across the Internet using your smartphone or device's direct connection to a healthcare provider. During the transmission, this data will be susceptible to all types of online threats.

The danger of wearable devices is not limited only to user-specific personal data. For instance, many wearable devices can be configured to connect to other home appliances such as lighting, cooling, and security access control systems to adjust/control it automatically according to a predefined user preference set on the wearable device. If a security breach occurs to such a connected system (usually called an *intelligent house*), a lot of confidential information could be exposed.

■ **Note** Healthcare cybersecurity spending is expected to exceed $65 billion from 2017 to 2021.[2]

The Future of Cryptographic Algorithms

Cyber-attacks are continually evolving and using more sophisticated techniques to crack the most secure systems. In the previous chapter, we discussed popular attacks against classical cryptographic systems. We called them "classical" because they depend on math to achieve their encryption work. As you already know, the main concern when using cryptography systems is to protect the decryption key that is used to decrypt the data to its original state.

There are different countermeasures used to prevent the compromise of the decryption key. However, one particular style of attack you cannot do anything to stop is the harvest-then-decrypt attack. In this type of attack, an attacker will capture encrypted data and then wait until technology advances in the future to decrypt it.

To deter such future attacks, you need to use future cryptography techniques. Quantum cryptography offers a confidential method to exchange secret data between parties communicating through public networks like the Internet. Quantum cryptography is considered the answer to mitigating all attacks against data in transit.

Quantum cryptography uses photons (light particles) to transmit secret data (such as cryptography keys) using suitable medium channels like fiber-optic cables over long distances. The process of exchanging cryptographic keys between communicating entities using this method is called *quantum key distribution* (QKD). If an eavesdropper tries to intercept the transmitted information, both the sender and the receiver will detect this action and thus stop using the compromised key to encrypt/decrypt data. In addition, the attacker cannot copy the traffic and save it for later analysis. This effectively makes QKD able to mitigate both risks: detecting any attempt to tap the wire to capture secret information and preventing attackers from capturing transmitted data for future analysis.

Currently, the adoption of QKD technology is still in its early stages. It is used on a limited basis in Europe (especially Switzerland) and the United States. However, once matured, it is expected to be the main method used to secure the transmission of high-value data.

In this section, we covered the quantum cryptographic technique as a primer in the field, but it is worth mentioning another encryption technique that is based on math that can bring additional security to current cryptographic systems. *Honey encryption* is a type of encryption in which the cryptographic algorithm produces fake data to mislead attackers. For instance, when attackers capture sensitive data, they usually use brute-force software to guess the decryption key or password used to protect the data, so whenever an incorrect key is tried, fake data will be presented to them instead of showing no data or any other indicators that the entered key was wrong. This will effectively mislead attackers by presenting plausible-looking plaintext data.

Innovations continue to create more secure techniques that can offer unhackable data security. Until then, QKD is considered the most secure technique to protect high-value data.

Legal Issues

As you saw, cloud-based solutions are expected to form a large percentage of IT operations in the coming years. Many giant cloud service providers store users' data in different data centers around the globe. This spread of personal and business data outside a user's national borders will have a deep impact on user security and privacy.

The main question when you have a cloud account is, whose laws will apply? For example, if a German company is using a cloud computing service based in the United Kingdom, what rules govern the access to this data? Do the UK authorities have the right to access the German company's data because it is in the United Kingdom? Does the German law protect this company's data because it is registered in Germany and contains data belonging to German users?

The same question applies to individual users; for example, if a user has a cloud storage account (or e-mail account) with a Swiss company, can the U.S. authorities request his or her data from the Swiss provider?

Another concern when using cloud services is the management of private data. Cloud providers may replicate users' data on different servers (sometimes for backup and disaster recovery), and some of them offer fault tolerance so that your data is always available in case one server goes down. The problem here ensuring that your data is getting deleted from all those locations. Can you ensure that your cloud provider uses the proper secure data destruction techniques to erase your data when it is no longer needed?

Legal boundaries are vanishing because technical boundaries are vanishing. Data stored and transferred to the cloud can fall under different national regulations. As you already saw in Chapter 1, the Data Protection Directive in the European Union and the regulations issued by the Federal Trade Commission (FTC) in the United States govern how private consumer data will be handled. A cloud service falls under these regulations, and these regulations are continually being updated to keep up with the technical advancements in the computing technology, especially the storage of personal information outside national borders.

Developed countries are working to harmonize their data protection regulations so each country can better secure its citizens' digital data by making cooperation agreements with foreign countries that regulate access of such data when it is stored outside a user's own country.

■ **Note** Encrypting data locally before uploading it to the cloud is still a great countermeasure against all cloud threats.

Social Networking Sites and Users' Privacy

Giant tech companies such as Facebook, Google, Microsoft, and Apple are expected to continue to grow in coming years. Nowadays, it is unlikely to find an Internet user who doesn't use a service from one of these providers.

Social networking sites in particular collect vast volumes of information about their users to simplify bombarding them with targeted ads; they also get other commercial value from their users' personal information and browsing habits. Unfortunately, there is no indication that this action will stop soon. Moreover, the continual revelations of mass surveillance programs boost the debates among the public about the importance of protecting users' civil rights of privacy. Giant tech providers should consider updating their privacy terms to stop recording users' online habits and then linking the data to each user's real identity. This practice will remain the greatest danger to user privacy in the foreseeing future. We think social sites can do more to protect user privacy. For example, anonymous data should be gathered wisely and maintained for a limited period. Social sites should declare clearly what data they are collecting and how they are going to use it. It is preferable to give the user an option to opt out from offering additional information that is not related to the service being used. Letting users handle their data in a trusted way will make them more willing to use social sites that most respect their rights of privacy.

Regardless of what companies do, people should get educated about both security and privacy. Children should understand that posting personal information and photos online is a bad habit and can pose real risks for them and their families. Social sites should also consider monitoring users' posts and deleting inappropriate content instantly, possibly using artificial intelligence techniques, to avoid becoming exploited to promote criminal acts.

We are still at the beginning of the information technology age; people soon will be more IT literate. They will thus be more willing to pressure their governments to legislate the act of harvesting public digital data on a large scale for surveillance purposes. IT equipment vendors can play a crucial role in developing IT infrastructure that promotes privacy by design. On the political side, U.S. tech companies such as Facebook, Google, Microsoft, Apple, and Twitter will continue to dominate the global market share. To increase this share, more services will be offered and tailored specifically to each user's needs. This will result in acquiring more sensitive data about each user to customize these services.

Policymakers are a long way from understanding future IT trends and their overall impact on society. They will continue to focus on the short-term and on exploiting IT services to acquire more intelligence.

It is unlikely that the United States voluntarily will give up its control of the main Internet backbone (do not forget that most mass surveillance programs deployed globally are operated by the United States). In other words, the fight to maintain Internet users' security and privacy on a global level is still far from a real implementation despite all the new U.S. and international regulations.

The War on Terror

We live in an unstable world. Today many countries are vanishing slowly (Syria is an example), and the destabilization in many Middle Eastern countries is leading to a vast uncontrolled area that can be exploited to conduct all kinds of criminal activities on a global level. Terrorist organizations are using the Internet to acquire resources (detonations), coordinate attacks, recruit fighters, communicate efficiently with each other, and promote/broadcast their propaganda to the entire world.

Terrorist web sites are also used as a virtual training field, offering tutorials to manufacture bombs, use guns, learn attack tactics, and draw virtual maps of the places they are aiming to attack.

In the future people will find it difficult to balance the trade-off between security needs and personal privacy. Security services will continue to intensify their surveillance activities to harvest more online data to protect national security. Users tend to blame IT companies (such as social sites and other e-mail providers) when they hand over a user's sensitive data upon request to security services. However, regular folks do not know the hidden battle taking place underground to counter terrorism and protect the prosperity of society.

Terrorist attacks generate increased anxiety among the public. For instance, many surveys conducted after certain terror attacks in the United States and Europe demonstrate that people think the government's anti-terror policies are not enough to stop such attacks. Public attitudes in relation to privacy and societal security are largely dependent on current context in terms of current threats and attacks. Governments will use this public fear to increase their surveillance activities on both local and foreign citizens.

Summary

A lot of ideas were covered in this book, and the topics of security and privacy are strongly interconnected. In today's world, the transformation of business from traditional models to a digital one is still in its beginnings. Gartner estimates that by 2018 digitizing business processes will require 50 fewer workers[3] as businesses move steadily to using computerized systems to do their work.

The rapid development of mobile technologies (primarily smartphones and wearable devices) will drive people's behavior in the future. More people will use mobile computing to access Internet resources, make purchases, and use social networking web sites. Acquiring a suitable education and hands-on training of digital skills is of extreme importance for people and organizations to better utilize technological developments and to mitigate different threats raised by them.

We began this book by talking about government mass surveillance programs. No one is happy to find out that his or her personal information and behaviors have been revealed. However, this should not make you forget the benefits of surveillance in today's digital age. There is a legitimate reason to conduct surveillance activities. No society can live and prosper without protecting its people and public safety from criminal and terrorist activities. The problem arises when surveillance activities are exploited in the wrong direction. For example, some countries with less freedom like China monitor people's online activities for political reasons. This kind of surveillance is against basic human rights and cannot be done in developed countries involved in global mass surveillance. In developed countries, the greatest danger to user privacy is from giant companies trying to acquire personal and nonpersonal data of their users to sell for commercial pursuits. It is highly unlikely that government security services will sell, for example, users' browsing history to advertising companies. Government surveillance is conducted in secret. Without the recent revelations about government mass surveillance programs, few people would be concerned about it at all. As we already said, government surveillance will continue to intensify in the future, and legalizing these activities is still the best countermeasure to avoid taking surveillance in the wrong direction.

From the start, you've seen the folly and dangers of cyber-attacks against computing systems. This book provided you with a way to stay private in today's digital age. We covered a range of techniques and demonstrated how to use reputable tools to enhance your security and privacy and protect your data at rest and in transit. Armed with this knowledge, you should feel confident when going online.

In the ever-changing online world, no one can predict the future. In this book, you learned about common security misconceptions and discovered methods that attackers use to steal your private data. We tried to present this information in plain English so users with varying IT skills can benefit from this book. We showed you who is collecting your personal data and for what reasons, and then we covered everything you need to know to stop this invasion into your privacy. This book offered a practical approach to understanding and mitigating current and future cyber-security threats. No writer can assume that his or her book is the best in the field, but the book in your hands is unique considering all books published about the digital privacy topic to date.

Notes

1. Gartner, Inc., "Gartner Says by 2020 'Cloud Shift' Will Affect More Than $1 Trillion in IT Spending." July 20, 2016. `https://www.gartner.com/newsroom/id/3384720`.

2. Maciej Heyman, "Healthcare cybersecurity spending $65 billion, 2017 to 2021." Cybersecurity Ventures, May 4, 2017. `www.military-technologies.net/2017/05/04/healthcare-cybersecurity-spending-65-billion-2017-to-2021/`.

3. Gartner, Inc., "Gartner Reveals Top Predictions for IT Organizations and Users for 2015 and Beyond." October 7, 2014. `https://www.gartner.com/newsroom/id/2866617`.

Index

Get the eBook for only $5!

Why limit yourself?

With most of our titles available in both PDF and ePUB format, you can access your content wherever and however you wish—on your PC, phone, tablet, or reader.

Since you've purchased this print book, we are happy to offer you the eBook for just $5.

To learn more, go to http://www.apress.com/companion or contact support@apress.com.

Apress®

All Apress eBooks are subject to copyright. All rights are reserved by the Publisher, whether the whole or part of the material is concerned, specifically the rights of translation, reprinting, reuse of illustrations, recitation, broadcasting, reproduction on microfilms or in any other physical way, and transmission or information storage and retrieval, electronic adaptation, computer software, or by similar or dissimilar methodology now known or hereafter developed. Exempted from this legal reservation are brief excerpts in connection with reviews or scholarly analysis or material supplied specifically for the purpose of being entered and executed on a computer system, for exclusive use by the purchaser of the work. Duplication of this publication or parts thereof is permitted only under the provisions of the Copyright Law of the Publisher's location, in its current version, and permission for use must always be obtained from Springer. Permissions for use may be obtained through RightsLink at the Copyright Clearance Center. Violations are liable to prosecution under the respective Copyright Law.

CPSIA information can be obtained
at www.ICGtesting.com
Printed in the USA
LVHW01s2012200817

33164300227217   /P
September 2017